W9-CUF-976

FACING ALI

FACING

STEPHEN BRUNT

THE OPPOSITION WEIGHS IN

ALFRED A. KNOPF CANADA

PUBLISHED BY ALFRED A. KNOPF CANADA

 Published in 2002 by Alfred A. Knopf Canada, a division of Random House of Canada Limited, Toronto. Distributed by Random House of Canada Limited, Toronto.

National Library of Canada Cataloguing in Publication Data

Brunt, Stephen

Facing Ali : the opposition weighs in / Stephen Brunt.

ISBN 0-676-97350-7

1. Ali, Muhammad, 1942–. 2. Ali, Muhammad, 1942– — Adversaries. 3. Boxers (Sports)—United States—Biography. I. Title.

GV1132.A44B78 2002 796.83'092 C2002-902093-X

Page 301 constitutes a continuation of the copyright page.

First Edition

www.randomhouse.ca

TEXT DESIGN: CS RICHARDSON

Printed and bound in the United States of America

2 4 6 8 9 7 5 3 1

For Andy MacFarlane,
mentor, friend and father-in-law

CONTENTS

SECONDS OUT: **INTRODUCTION**

SEVERAL YEARS BACK, A former champion of the world began his comeback in humble surroundings. He certainly wasn't a great fighter—more a creation of promotional and managerial smarts than anything else—but still, he'd known better places than Lulu's, once, in an earlier life, a discount department store. Now it was billed as the world's biggest nightclub, an enormous place containing several different bars and featuring musical acts from the fringes of the nostalgic imagination. The mystery of whatever happened to so-and-so, a one-hit wonder from the mid-1960s, was often solved when his name appeared on the marquee.

But staging a fight at Lulu's was more of a risk than bringing in Mitch Ryder or Gary Lewis and the Playboys, and so even with a big name on the bill, the crowd was limited to a few hundred zealots, huddled together in one corner of the vast floor space. Those who were hip to the ways of boxing understood that a classic probably wasn't in the cards. Though the glamour boy's name was still worth money in the pugilistic economy, he needed a confidence builder. So his opponent would be chosen purely for his unthreatening nature, a career loser, a tomato can, an afterthought. His list of credits mattered not at all, since his role was entirely supporting. He would show up, act like a boxer, ideally put up a bit of a struggle and then be knocked out and forgotten—on his way out of town before the star had even begun discussing his bright future with the attending sportswriters.

The opponent came from one of those places that seem to spawn them—West Virginia, or Ohio, or Kentucky—and he played his role to perfection. The ex-champion looked terrific, landing all his punches at will, while the man standing opposite him would get credit for bravery, and perhaps for masochism, until finally he surrendered. Then, just as the boys in the ringside-press section were wrapping up that neat, familiar little story, the man who had been working the opponent's corner, a friend from way back where, walked out and confronted them. "You're going to say he's a bum, aren't you? You're going to write that he's a stiff." The friend went on to tell the fighter's story, how he was a tough guy from a tough town, where he had grown up without advantages, who had fought because he had to, and always gave an honest effort, never taking an out-and-out dive. Before coming here, his wife had left him. Still, he got in the car for the long, long drive and the minuscule pay, all in the interests of the man standing opposite him in the ring, who had made the kind of money an "opponent" could only dream of.

"Just wanted you to know that," the friend, a true friend, said before he walked away.

This exchange drives home an important point that I have never forgotten. In boxing, in everything else, only one side of the story tends to be told. Occasionally two great fighters collide, each bringing with them some grist for the mill. But far more often, the script calls for a meeting of a star and a secondary character, the latter disposable unless he somehow achieves the impossible, unless he breaks out of his assigned role and makes a real fight out of it—unless, by some miracle, he wins.

Without question, there has been no greater star in the history of the sport than Muhammad Ali. Even before he won the heavyweight championship of the world with an unthinkable upset of Sonny Liston in Miami Beach in 1964, he had shown that he had the makings of a very different kind of athletic celebrity, his act drawn in equal parts from Sugar Ray Robinson and the professional wrestler Gorgeous George. Once Ali proved that he could back up the talk, back up the boasts, with a unique and overwhelming talent, he stepped immediately to the forefront of boxing. Once he became a political figure, both by design and by accident, his fame outstripped that not just of any other fighter, but of any other athlete. Ali's celebrity stretched far beyond the boundaries of his game. He was for the better part of his career, and for some years after, the most famous human being on the planet, period.

Anyone who lived through even a portion of Ali's twenty years in the spotlight couldn't help but be entertained or enraged, insulted or inspired. The delineations, by and large, were generational. My father was born when Jess Willard (the man who beat Jack Johnson and would lose to Jack Dempsey) was the heavyweight champion of the world, and as a fight aficionado, idolized two of the greatest of all time: Joe Louis and Sugar Ray Robinson. Each, in his own way, was every bit as revolutionary as Ali. Louis became the first African-American athlete to be regarded as a purely heroic figure by fans black and white. He achieved that status through his boxing skill and through a convergence of sporting and world events that culminated in his knockout victory over Max Schmeling, the symbol of Nazi Germany, in 1938. Louis joined the army, where he fought for benefits for the armed forces (and ironically, because of the taxes unpaid from those benefits, was driven to financial ruin by the same United States government that he'd served so well). When Ali arrived on the scene, at another moment when sports and world events would come together, many—including my father—couldn't help but compare him unfavourably with the man who had done his duty to his country, and who had said, "God is on our side."

Robinson was admired both because of his remarkable skills, and because of his style, his flamboyance, his panache. He travelled with an entourage, retired from boxing for a time to become a professional tap dancer, and owned businesses that filled an entire block in Harlem. There couldn't have been a Muhammad Ali if there hadn't been a Sugar Ray. But while he was a different, more modern breed of professional athlete, nothing about him shook the larger status quo. Those who lived for the Friday night fights could worship him without reservation.

Ali, though, even when he was Cassius Clay, even before his act turned political, rubbed those of my father's generation the wrong way. They felt that the sport they loved was already in inexorable decline by the time he came along (though Liston has become a bit of a cult figure in death, not many loved or admired him then), and his ascendance became a sure sign that the ancient game was going to hell in a handbasket. Then came the name change, the Muslims and the draft. In my family, as in so many North American families, the folks at the head of the table certainly weren't cheering Ali on.

Born at the back end of the baby boom, I remember the early years only fleetingly: My first memory of boxing is of sitting with my father watching Ali fight brave Henry Cooper on television, of course in black and white. I was eight years old when Ali was stripped of his title. During the early days of my romance with the sport, reading *Ring Magazine* and watching Howard Cosell on "Wide World of Sports," Joe Frazier became my favourite heavyweight. In March of 1971, I was certainly happy that he won the Fight of the Century. Three years later, the giant George Foreman captured the crown and seemed unbeatable. Here was a new breed of heavyweight champion. I was convinced (as were so many others) that he would end Ali's career, that the Rumble in the Jungle would punctuate a true changing of the guard. (It wasn't the last prediction I got wrong.)

My real appreciation of Ali came late, during those sometimes desperate fights towards the end of his career where he relied on guile and experience and courage to slip by opponents who wouldn't have been able to carry his gym bag in the old days. As a teenager, I began to understand the nature of his personal sacrifice. I rediscovered the old fights on film, watching the three-round demolition of Cleveland Williams in 1966 (the absolute peak, in terms of pure skill) over and over again. And I found myself cheering for Ali as I never really had before, even as much of the crowd had begun to watch his fights, in anticipation that, finally, he might lose. A bunch of us watched his first fight with Leon Spinks in a university dorm. I'll never forget the thrill of the upset, the joy that came with watching the unlikely champion announced as winner, and the deep sadness that immediately followed, understanding that it was over now, that the athletic figure who had dominated my entire conscious life was finished.

During my first years as a sportswriter, I would see Ali at the big fights, where his introduction at ringside would inevitably spur the loudest ovation of the night. No one in his wake (with the exception of the young, untarnished Mike Tyson) came close to filling the void he'd left, even if politics and culture were put aside. Michael Jordan might have become a universal commercial icon with nearly the same global reach, but compared to Ali, he always seemed merely a hollow, Nike-made shell.

A few years ago, a friend, Davis Miller, told me that one could visit Ali. Just show up at the gate of his farm, ring the bell, and hope for the best. My two oldest children were very young then, so their memories of that trip now need to be prodded along. What they saw, what my wife and I saw, was a near-silent, gentle man who wasn't much interested in yet another fan/worshipper coming to pay homage, but who revelled in the chance to perform his magic tricks for a new audience and to chase a toddler around the driveway, brandishing a plastic sword in mock anger.

Yet his aura was undeniable. Though older, though unwell, though scarcely able to express himself verbally, Ali was a *presence*.

Consider the lot of his opponents. Consider how it must have been when he was young, and vital, and dangerous, and as big as all the world.

Those who shared the ring with him were illuminated by the intense wattage of his public persona, and tended to disappear in its glare. With the exception of Ali's two bouts with Liston, his three with Joe Frazier, and his one with George Foreman, they hardly even merited billing in what were, promotionally and in the public imagination, Ali Fights. Whether or not the opponent was a legitimate contender (like Ken Norton, who beat him once, and probably deserved to beat him twice), or a rising young champion in his own right like Larry Holmes, or a historical lightweight like Jurgen Blin, or Jean-Pierre Coopman, or Chuck Wepner, they were to one degree or another lost in the Ali shuffle. What did Ron Lyle, for instance, think about facing off against the political and social icon? "Nobody ever asked me," he said, before answering the question. Nobody ever asked most of them how it felt, what it meant, how it changed their lives, and what they really thought about Muhammad Ali.

This book brings together a few of their stories. They aren't intended to be definitive biographies of this assortment of fifteen men who faced Ali in the ring as professionals. The most famous of them—Foreman, Frazier, Norton, Holmes—have published their own life histories. Rather, these are portraits fixed in a particular place and time, with a particular set of subjects in mind: who they were before they came to fight Muhammad Ali; how those fights altered the course of their careers and their personal lives; what they knew of the man, then and now; how they felt about him, and his politics, and his legacy; how their lives have proceeded since; and how they might have been different were it not for the great, often unexpected opportunity of meeting the giant face to face. (The great regret here is that the man whose two encounters with Ali would have inspired the most mysterious, complex, compelling story never really told his tale. A penny for the true thoughts of Sonny Liston, who was found dead of a suspicious drug overdose in 1971.)

There are common elements in these stories. Boxing, obviously, is a sport limited to the very brave, which tends to lay a fighter's character bare, to strip away pretence, to force upon them a brutal honesty. And fame. Each of these men became better known, and had their lives drastically altered, simply by coming into contact with the force that was Muhammad Ali.

Not surprisingly, each of them sees Ali a little differently, a trick of time and place and personality. Some view him now with a kind of good-hearted nostalgia, in part because of Ali's current physical frailty; some believe that they were blessed, financially and otherwise, when he happened to pass through their lives;

some have come to understand the high price of being suddenly famous, only to plunge back into obscurity; and some view Ali with a lingering bitterness, or suggest that they know a darker side of the man lost in the current wave of hagiography, which began in earnest when he lit the cauldron at the 1996 Olympics in Atlanta.

For biographers, even the very best of them, Ali has proved in some essential way unknowable, inexplicable. It remains an open question whether Ali's stature is simply too great to process at this short remove from his career or, as Mark Kram strongly suggests in *Ghosts of Manila,* that there was in fact far less depth to chart than the prevailing myth would suggest. His image has been shaped and reshaped according to what the times have required, from the innocent, simple clown (in contrast to Liston's menace), to the dangerous racial separatist and subversive, to the shining anti-war symbol for the young and the progressive—and further still to the fighter who proved in Zaire that maybe a generation wasn't aging quite as fast as those passing birthdays suggested. Ali has been loved and hated in equal measure; he has been sentimentalized and made the object of pathos. He has been used as a cautionary example of what happens when an athlete holds on too long, what happens when they don't look after their money. He has been characterized as the cruel man who tortured opponents, who directed racist taunts at a great black champion, and he has become the benign symbol of tolerance and reconciliation, the subject of a hugely flattering documentary and feature film, now living somehow beyond the boundaries of black and white, or Muslim and Christian.

Every one of us, in some way, feels that we know Muhammad Ali. But only a select few understand him as these men do. Each stood alone, stripped to the waist, revealed in a lighted square in a darkened room or arena or stadium. They faced Ali, they felt the sting of his jab, the power of his right cross, they felt his flesh give as they struck him in return. A couple know how it felt to stand over Ali as he lay on the canvas. A handful had their hands raised in victory.

All of their lives were changed as a result of the experience, for the better mostly, and for the worse. Some have told their stories many times, as a way of extending their own celebrity. And some, until now, have been waiting for the chance.

TUNNEY **HUNSAKER**

Fayetteville, West Virginia

AT THE FRONT DOOR OF HIS home, a big, ramshackle Victorian house on a quiet street—though, the fact is, there isn't really any other kind of street here in this sleepy little town—Tunney Hunsaker greets a visitor with a great, open smile and a firm handshake. He looks hale and hearty for a man seventy-two years old, not far off his fighting weight, and when his grip locks on, he laughs at the reaction of discomfort from his guest. Hunsaker's hands are still strong, and so huge that they swallow up the mitt of an average-sized man.

"Tell him what your mother always said to you when you ate your dinner," his wife, Pat, prompts him.

"'Get them elephant feet off of my table,'" he hollers.

Everyone laughs at what's obviously an ancient family joke. Soon afterwards, though, sitting in Hunsaker's well-lived-in front room, it becomes clear that there won't be many more jokes this afternoon—or at least Hunsaker won't be the one offering the punchlines. Dementia has robbed him of so many memories, and jumbled most of the rest. He is genial but confused, and when he does answer a question, his wife almost always has to jump in with a correction, or a clarification. No one can say definitively that boxing played a part in his condition, though the list of old fighters with one form of memory loss or another is undeniably a long one.

"I've seen signs, since about 1996," Pat says, as Tunney sits across the room in an easy chair, by all signs oblivious to the subject of the conversation. "I've seen small things. Then in the last year or two, you could really see it. Of course he had a sister who died of Alzheimer's disease, so you can't say for sure that it's from boxing. But I know Tunney wouldn't change a thing. It's like Ali saying he doesn't regret anything; Tunney doesn't regret anything. He's had a good life. As healthy as he is, he'd be really healthy if he had not had that. Of course you don't know what life is going to bring. But at the same time he has enjoyed it so much, and loved the boxing. He wouldn't change a thing."

Still, it means that now, when occasional fan letters come in, when the autograph seekers find him here, deep in what used to be West Virginia's coal-mining heartland, when the occasional reporter or boxing nut comes to the door, it's up to Pat Hunsaker to fill in the details. She has become the historian, the custodian of the story of the first man to fight Cassius Clay as a professional.

IT'S A FAMILIAR TALE in so many ways. Hunsaker was born into a working-class family in Princeton, Kentucky, in tobacco-farming country not far from Paducah, and named after the great heavyweight champion Gene Tunney. He was a big strong kid who first laced on boxing gloves at the county fair, where boys were pitted against one another in an informal tournament. Hunsaker won the first time he entered, then won again the next year, though it's never been suggested that anyone considered him gifted enough to have a future in the sport.

Instead, he went into the United States Air Force and was stationed at Lakeland, Texas, where he met his first wife, Phyllis. Hunsaker picked up fighting again while in the service, and had his first pro fight in 1953. In 1954, when he was discharged, his mother-in-law, who was from Okea, West Virginia, told him about a position opening up for a police officer in Fayetteville. Hunsaker applied and was hired, and he settled into the job that would be his for the next thirty-eight years. "He was made the chief right off," Pat says. "Maybe for a week, he was just an officer. But then, they had only one person on the force."

Those who remember Andy Griffith's ancient television series will recognize this, accurately, as Mayberry. "Not only was Tunney important to this town because he was impressive, because he fought Ali, but also because he was a police officer," Pat Hunsaker says. "And he cared more about the people. He knew everyone by name. He wore his shoes out. I was constantly buying him shoes because he walked the beat so much. He didn't care about getting in that car and arresting people. But he would see little old ladies who were going to walk to the store and he'd wait for them and take them home. All of the kids, all of the little ones, were so eager to go to school so Tunney could take them across the intersection going to the grade school. He would be there for the buses in the evening. He was so much for the town. When Tunney retired, they lost that. You don't know the officers now. You don't know the policemen. They like to be in their cars." Hunsaker led every parade, and was famous for the flamboyant way in which he directed traffic at what was, for years, the town's only major intersection. A couple of generations of kids in Fayetteville, when asked what they wanted to be when they grew up, didn't say "a policeman"; they said, "a Tunney."

Once, a new mayor decided that Hunsaker, late in his career, had just a little too much power and influence, and decided to try and put him in his place. "He took on the mayor and was suspended," Pat says. "You've never seen such an outpouring of support. When they had an election, Tunney helped defeat the mayor because he wouldn't give Tunney any say in running the town. Tunney campaigned for the man who won. Then of course the new mayor reinstated Tunney. This town wanted to lynch that other mayor."

All the while, Hunsaker continued to fight occasionally, travelling as far as Chicago, and once appearing on an undercard at Madison Square Garden. He was really a light heavyweight, at most a very small heavyweight, and not just a straight-ahead brawler. "I stayed on my feet," Hunsaker says. "I was a boxer and a puncher." In October 1960, his manager called and asked if he'd be willing to travel to Louisville and take on a young kid making his professional debut, the light heavyweight gold medallist from the just-completed Olympics in Rome. "I told him that if he was willing to fight me, we would all get together and make it happen," Hunsaker says.

Clay's management was looking for a seasoned professional, but one who wouldn't present much of a risk, a durable fighter who would take their debutante a few rounds and then deliver that first win on his record. "I don't know that Tunney knew that much about him at the time," Pat says. "But Tunney was fearless. He just would take them all on. He was quite a fighter. He's got quite a reputation. All of the people in town had a tremendous respect for him."

The fight, held on October 29, 1960, is memorable only as a historical footnote. "He kept me away from him," Hunsaker says. "But I nailed him." He did, in fact, connect a few times, but Clay's speed made the difference. Still, Hunsaker went the six-round distance and, without knowing it at the time, fixed his place in posterity as the answer to a trivia question. As Ali's stature grew, that first fight, a minor event at the time, took on more and more significance. For the people of Fayetteville, their beloved town cop gradually became someone the whole world seemed to know about.

Fame brought with it a few fringe benefits. Once, he and Pat went to New York, where Hunsaker stumped the panel on "To Tell The Truth." (They still have the hotel receipt from their room at the Waldorf Astoria, in one of their old scrapbooks.) And once they drove all the way to Ottawa to appear on a similar television guessing game, called "Claim To Fame," where the actress Lois Maxwell was one of the resident celebrities. They gave the contestants a list of accomplishments from which to choose Hunsaker's rightful claim to fame: he was either Priscilla Presley's bodyguard, Loretta Lynn's brother, the referee of the Ali–Liston bout, or the first man to fight Cassius Clay as a pro.

Nobody got it right.

WHAT IS LESS WELL remembered now is the fact that Hunsaker made global headlines not for the Clay fight, but for the one that came after, what turned out to be the last bout of his career. He probably shouldn't have accepted it. He'd been out of the ring for nearly two years; he was rusty and he wasn't in the best of shape. But the match was being held just down the road in Beckley, and though he didn't know much about his opponent, a guy named Joe "Shotgun" Sheldon from Cleveland, Ohio, Hunsaker had always been willing to take on all comers. Immediately before the fight, there was some confusion about which gloves the boxer would wear. Hunsaker protested, but eventually gave in.

For the spectators that night, it must have been fabulous entertainment, an old-style ring war. Both men were knocked down. Both men got up and kept right on fighting. And then at the end of a vicious round, Hunsaker walked back to his corner and collapsed. He fell into a coma, from which he would not emerge for ten days.

Sadly, those types of things occasionally happen in boxing. But the timing of Hunsaker's accident proved to be especially dramatic. Just a few days before, in a nationally televised fight, Benny "Kid" Paret had suffered fatal brain injuries in a brutal match against Emile Griffith. The entire world seemed to be rallying to ban the sport. And here was more evidence, another ring death apparently imminent. The newspaper clippings from the time always link the two fights together.

"We are walking a tightrope," Hunsaker's doctor is quoted as saying. "He has a 50-50 chance."

His Wife Says: I Wanted Him To Quit, reads one headline. (In fact, Phyllis divorced Hunsaker soon after he suffered the injury.)

Hunsaker was taken to the Bluefield Sanatorium, where daily news bulletins were released on his condition, and where his recuperation, though slow, was celebrated by the staff.

In their front room, Pat Hunsaker walks over to the chair where Tunney is sitting and points to a small mark near his right temple. "That dent you see in his head is from that," she says, referring to the almost-fatal blow. "As he's gotten older, the doctors think that has caused some of this memory loss and the dementia.

"He did remarkably well coming out of the coma and going ahead and earning a living. For awhile he had problems with his right side. He wouldn't pick up anything with right hand, and he was always yawning. But he got through all of that. He was robust and healthy. He was the picture of health for many a year. He still is healthy. He doesn't take any medication. But it's affected his memory."

The town of Fayetteville rallied behind Hunsaker after his injury. The country-music star Roy Acuff even came to town to play a benefit concert on his behalf. And just as soon as Hunsaker was able to return to work, they gave him his old job back.

"For a long time, I wanted to contact Sheldon, and find out about his fight with Tunney," Pat Hunsaker says. "A fellow who interviewed Tunney told me that he had gotten in touch with him. But the interviewer told me . . . he warned me about it. He said, 'You be the judge if you want to listen to him.' Sheldon called on the answering service, and his conversation . . . he was radical, he was angry. It didn't sound like someone that we wanted to invite into our home or have a relationship with. I thought, I'd better not go ahead with this. I didn't want to pursue it."

LIKE JUST ABOUT everyone else in these parts, Tunney Hunsaker wasn't awfully impressed when Cassius Clay announced that he was Muhammad Ali, that he didn't have anything against the Viet Cong, that he wasn't going to be drafted into Uncle Sam's army. "We don't approve of his religion because we think that that's a false religion," Pat Hunsaker says. "But we have to respect him because of the stand that he took. Tunney was very upset that Ali took the stand that he did because he had served his country himself. He told me, 'He wouldn't have had to fight. He could have just been a recruiter.' The kind of man that he was, if he had gone into the service, he wouldn't have had to have done anything like that.

"At first he was very upset with Ali. But then he realized that the man really did pay a price for what he believed. He finally said, 'You have to respect Ali. He stood for his principles.' Tunney finally had to give him that."

Though linked by six rounds of shared history, the two men had no contact for seventeen years. Tunney and Pat finally married after ten years of courting, but they rarely left Fayetteville, and there certainly wasn't any reason for Ali to venture to their part of the world.

Then in 1987, there was an attempt to revive the Golden Gloves amateur boxing program in the Charleston, West Virginia, area. As a promotional hook, someone had the bright idea to bring Ali in and reunite him with his first professional opponent, who by then had become a local legend. "We were ushered into his hotel room there across from the Civic Center and got to meet him," Pat says. "He remembered Tunney. He remembered everything about him. He shadowboxed constantly. We even have video of it.

He remembered Tunney so well and he was making up his poetry and everything else. We rode over to the Civic Center that night in a limousine and they signed autographs together.

"Later they were doing an interview with local stations. They were trying to get Ali to say something about Tunney. And he could have. And what made him even greater to me was the fact that he did not build himself up by tearing Tunney down. He was so good. He said, 'Tunney's in the books like I am. He was a scientific fighter with a good punch.' Really, for the hometown crowd, he was doing Tunney proud. That was so nice of him."

For a little while, it became almost a regular act. The next year, they added Larry Holmes to the program. The year after that, it was James "Buster" Douglas. But always the centrepiece was Ali and Tunney, together again, signing autographs at a local car dealership. In 1992, the year Hunsaker finally retired as a policeman, Ali happened to be in the area. "He was at an autograph signing, and we were anticipating that he was going to be at a dinner and Tunney was going to be at that dinner, maybe in the Beckley area," Pat says. "But then Ali told them, 'No, I want to go to Tunney's hometown.' Ali—I mean, he just took charge. So . . . wow. I mean, we had to get together. We had to call that evening for a place where we could invite all of the people in the town that we wanted to invite. All the townspeople, all of the officials. We were all going to meet Ali.

"Now with Ali you really don't know. We've been with him in Charleston where you were supposed to be with him that night and he took off that morning. He never showed up. So here we had this group waiting here that morning. We were sitting over at the freeway exit in Beckley waiting for Ali to come through so we could guide him into town. And knowing we've got all of these people waiting—you talk about some tall praying; we're doing some tall praying. Seeing his car, that was the most gorgeous sight in the world. He was on time and drove right into Fayetteville. All of the TV stations were there. And he had the greatest time in Fayetteville.

"We took him across the New River Gorge Bridge [the largest span of its kind in the world] and stopped so he could look down. No one stops on that bridge, unless of course Tunney could stop the traffic. And Ali went into the local merchant stores. The beautiful thing about Ali—he's really a nice guy. Even at the autograph sessions, he would always make sure that the person who was with him would bring the people in wheelchairs and on crutches to the front of the line. He wouldn't make them wait. He would bring them to the front and take care of them. When we were in one of the shops, this bus came by with disabled children going to a special school. He happened to spot this bus and these kids. So he came out of the shop and Tunney stopped traffic there and he boarded that bus and talked with those children. He always tried to sign every autograph. He could have just rubber-stamped his picture. He tried to sign for everyone that wanted an autograph. It was hard for him because he does have the Parkinson's. But he just enjoyed his day immensely. He didn't want to leave.

And of course people around here are still talking about it.

"They were having a time getting Ali out of Fayetteville. The fellow that was with him at the time said, 'Ali would just love to come back and visit with you all.' He asked if I would cook dinner for him. Well, I'm a pretty good cook. He said, 'Yes, he'd love to have dinner with you.' But we never did. It just seemed like he mushroomed into such popularity."

That was the last time the two old foes saw each other. "We were supposed to go to a black-tie dinner for Ali in Chicago," Pat says. "I'd never been to a black-tie affair. His daughter called us. This was a couple of years ago. Well that never did materialize. They called us again. He was in Europe. He was on the West Coast. He was here or there or the other and that never did materialize."

THERE IS VERY LITTLE in Tunney Hunsaker's house that even suggests he once had a career as a boxer. Pat has put most of the old newspaper clippings into scrapbooks, though a few are framed and hanging on the wall from the terrible days after the Shotgun Sheldon fight. His old black leather boxing shoes sit in one corner. And there's an autographed photo of Ali. Dated February 17, 1987, it reads, "You gave me my first fight as a professional. Thank you and may God always bless you. Muhammad Ali."

The rest of the memorabilia comes from Hunsaker's other life. There's a parking meter from Fayetteville's main street, and a collection of brass knuckles and other weapons taken from bad guys over the years. There are plaques celebrating the fact that three times he was named Sunday School Teacher of the Year by the Church of the Nazarene. Down at the old jail, now transformed into a museum, they have a mannequin set up, dressed in Hunsaker's uniform.

Pat and Tunney almost never venture afar, and though there have been suggestions of a visit to the Boxing Hall of Fame, that doesn't seem likely now. "We'd never leave Fayetteville, if it was up to me," Pat says. Life is comfortable and good. There's a brand new deck and hot tub in the backyard. And Tunney certainly seems content.

"Nice to meet you," he says. "Thanks for coming."

He extends his hand, sets a grip with his great paw and tells the elephant-foot joke once again.

HENRY COOPER

Kent, England

ON A CLEAR DAY, FROM the crest of a hill, you can see the top of one of the skyscraper towers at Canary Wharf, but otherwise London seems a million miles away. Here in the verdant rolling countryside, commuters can have it both ways, living a village life on city wages. And if they're exceptionally well off, they can get in a few rounds of golf on a course so exclusive, so expensive to join, that on a perfect weekday summer morning, the links are virtually deserted, and the magnificent clubhouse is as quiet as a church.

"I'll tell Mr. Cooper that you're here," says one of the hired help, offering a seat on the mezzanine level above the entrance hall. A few minutes later, the familiar figure arrives, a little bent with age but otherwise looking fine and fit. Properly, he is Sir Henry, or perhaps Sir 'Enry, his knighthood one of the most popular ever bestowed by the current monarch. He is a member here at the club, though one suspects that is part of a larger business relationship, that having Henry Cooper around to play a few rounds and swap a few stories with the big spenders is as attractive an asset as a well-manicured green. Though anything but to the manor born, he seems comfortable in the posh surroundings, and exudes an easy, unpretentious charm. That voice, the cockney accent that became so familiar to British fight fans during his days as a broadcaster with the BBC, immediately makes me feel like a friend.

"I still do bits and pieces," Cooper says, settling down with a cup of coffee. "I'm involved in the after-dinner circuit. I do a lot of corporate golf days, where I get well paid—play the biggest load of rubbish and still get well paid. You do the prize presentation, you do the after-dinner thing, and you get paid. Shake a few hands and give a few autographs. It's marvellous. It's not a bad old life."

And it still might have been like that if Cooper had simply been the British and Empire heavyweight champion, if he'd only won the European title, if he had been merely the best of a single generation of English heavyweights including Jack Bodell, Joe Erskine, Richard Dunn and Brian London.

But what separated him entirely from that pack, what lifted him to a level of sports celebrity shared by only a handful of footballers, was a single left hook delivered with perfect leverage and timing and aim to the jaw of Cassius Clay in June 1963. Not just one fight, but one punch, elevated Henry Cooper into a permanent state of grace. In the end, what he proved that day doesn't have anything to do with the joy of victory, which is why it was entirely beside the point that Clay got up and won, and won again the second time they fought. Instead, it was a lesson about the nobility of having your finest moment—giving your best effort—when it absolutely matters most.

HIS NOT-BAD-OLD-LIFE began in a very different place than this, in working-class Southeast London, where the Cooper family long struggled to eke out a bare-bones existence. "My grandad George Cooper was half-Irish," he says. "He came from the Elephant and Castle, which was a pretty tough area in them days. In them days, they had some railway arches, where the old railway was built. Underneath them they had a horse repository, where all the farmers used to come up and buy and sell horses. My grandfather was an expert on horses. He could run his hands over a horse and look at the teeth and tell the guy, 'Well, don't touch it.'

"Naturally in a place like that, it was easy to get into fights. You'd just get into fights by looking at anyone. And my grandfather used to love it. He used to fight twenty-round bare-knuckle fights up on Blackheath. He met the same guy there for three months. They fought every other Sunday. They had stand-up twenty-round fights. And they used to put a hat down and then the public just threw in whatever they thought they were worth. They used to call [the donations] nobbins in them days."

He tells another story of his grandfather's fighting exploits, from the days when he was living in the Peabody Buildings, housing for the poor. "He comes home from work. When he got on his landing, there was his next-door neighbour knocking the life out of his wife. Givin' his wife a real belting—they used to do that more in them days than they do now. Grandfather, who was interested in any sort of fight, he watched him for two or three minutes, and then when the old girl was getting a belt, he said, 'Leave her alone, you've given her enough, leave her alone.' The guy said, 'Shut your mouth or I'll give you some of the same.' Grandad just piled into him. Well, the wives in them days were very loyal. A few minutes before she'd been getting a belting from her husband. Now, she pulled out a seven-inch-long hatpin and pinned the cheeks of his arse together.

"Grandad pulled it out—and being a horseman, he treated himself. But it all went wrong. It turned septic. For the next three weeks he had to have every meal standing up, and when he went to bed he had to lie on his stomach." From that painful experience came a lesson passed on from one generation of Coopers to the next: "You never interfere between a man and his wife."

Aside from his bare-knuckle bouts, the closest George Cooper came to the big time was when he was summoned to London's famed National Sporting Club to guard the door one night. "Jack Johnson was threatening to come over after being slung out of America because he took a white bird across the state line. So he came to Europe, and he threatened he was coming to the National Sporting Club. They'd got my grandad on the door to stop him. Thank god Johnson never turned up."

Henry Cooper never met his grandfather—but his grandmother, who lived to be ninety-two, and his father, Harry, regaled him and his twin brother, George, with stories of George Sr.'s exploits. When Harry Cooper wasn't in the army (he served in both World Wars, and did a four-year stint in India and Burma), he worked in the building trades as a plasterer. That would become Henry Cooper's work as well, until boxing finally lured him away. "We started when we was kids. Coming from a working-class family in southeast London, the only thing you could do in them days was kick a football, or box. You couldn't play tennis, you couldn't play squash, you couldn't play golf because they all cost money. They were rich men's games. So George and I joined a boxing club when we were about nine and half years old. We had a great old trainer, a guy named Matt Wells, who used to be British lightweight champion. He had two of the best cauliflower ears you've ever seen. Two lumps of gristle and little pinholes. People used to look at him and say, 'Look at the belting he must have had.' I said, 'Belting?' He never took a belting. Only clever fighters got cauliflower ears. They were slipping punches, and the laces on the inside kept rubbing their ear. I mean if you've got lumps and bumps and a flat nose, that's when you're a mug."

Wells schooled the Coopers in the manly art of self-defence, while the clever manager Jim Wicks would later deftly guide their professional careers. Both were tall and lean, both were skilled boxers, but while a hand injury during his amateur days robbed George of much of his power, Henry had the Hammer, a quick, thudding left hook, which would become his trademark punch. "I think it was always there," he says. "I'm naturally left-handed, but I never fought as a southpaw. My dad, he got on his knees and gave us a little bit of tuition, me and George, and we always stood orthodox. And when I was plastering, the left was my trowel hand. We were pushing a lot of heavy stuff in them days, sand and cement. You did that all day, you developed muscles. That's why I had a good left hook. That was a natural punch for me." It wasn't just the punch, but the delivery: "I had that sneak left hook. I perfected a technique which the board of control eventually took away. They took away one of my greatest weapons. When I first turned pro in '54, the referee used to speak to you, and the last thing he ever said to you was, 'Shake hands and defend yourself at all times.' Now, I perfected a technique where I could, in a clinch, just drop my shoulder and the guy might think I was going to break. But as he relaxed momentarily, I'd throw a left hook on the break. That was my biggest weapon. But then they changed the rules. They said you've got to have a clean break."

Cooper won the British amateur title in 1952, fought in the Olympics that year, and then, following a two-year stint in the army, turned professional in 1954, eventually winning what was then called the British and Empire title from Brian London in 1959. That victory made him England's undisputed heavyweight king and its most popular fighter.

But it was a bout four years later that made him something else again.

When he arrived in London in 1963, his first boxing foray outside the United States since the Rome Olympics, Cassius Clay was fresh from the toughest test of his professional career, the disputed-decision win over Doug Jones at Madison Square Garden. But that close call hadn't robbed him of any of his confidence, any of his bluster. He marked his crossing of the pond by wearing a gold crown decorated with fake jewels and a royal blue–velvet robe with "Cassius the Greatest" stencilled across the back. He predicted that he would stop Cooper in the fifth round.

Culturally, that kind of public display clashed more with English sensibilities than it did with those of Americans, which made the humble, unassuming Cooper even more popular among the hometown crowd. "No one had seen that kind of act before," Cooper says. "In them days, the public over here didn't like him. I used to be on the road training at quarter to four in the morning. And I used to meet old girls, old ladies and office cleaners going to work. I'd be running, and they'd be saying, 'Button that loudmouth's lip!' People asked me if I was upset. I said, 'Tell him to carry on. I'm on percentage. He's earning me money. Don't stop him.'"

Cooper certainly understood what he was watching. By the time they stepped into the ring at Wembley Stadium, more than forty thousand fans were there to watch Our 'Enry give the loud, brash Yank a beating.

Strangely enough, it was those same English fans who were among the first to fully embrace Muhammad Ali, to accept him for what he was, to acknowledge his political stand—though on the latter point, Cooper himself is a dissenter with what would eventually become the prevailing sentiments. "After our first fight, it all changed," Cooper says. "We loved him over here more than they liked him in America. Because in America, there are still people who think he was a draft dodger. He didn't help his cause there. When they called him up in the army, if he'd have gone in the army, he'd have done no army service. He would have boxed exhibitions, going around encouraging the troops. But what he did, he fought it. If he'd gone into the army, he'd have been a hero. Like Joe Louis. Louis was in the army. He could have done the same. Can you imagine? It's just like me being British, saying in 1940, 'I've got no axe to grind against the Nazis.' Britain would have turned against me. Can you imagine him saying, 'I've got no grudge against the Viet Cong'—when there's people's sons and fathers being killed. And he's come out and said, 'I've got nothing against the Viet Cong.' Naturally they all turned on him, and a lot of people still think of him as a draft dodger.

"But over here, it changed completely. They all loved him. After he fought me, they all loved him. They said here, 'This is all a blooming act. He's just trying to whip up interest.' Ali was the first one to do eyeball-to-eyeball. But he always had a twinkle in his eye. He always had a slight little smile on his face. The public realized it over here: This is all a gimmick; this is clever; this is funny. And they laughed with him."

Behind the act, Cooper understood, was an exceptionally talented young fighter, with a style no one had really seen before—certainly not among the heavyweights. He also understood the kind of calculations made in these circumstances: Clay was an undefeated American gold medallist with a bright, lucrative future ahead of him; Cooper was a nine-year pro who had probably reached his level, good enough to take on the best Europeans, not quite good enough to beat the best Americans (which put him in the same bracket as every other English heavyweight between Bob Fitzsimmons and, arguably, Frank Bruno or, less arguably, Lennox Lewis). Clay's backers wanted their man to absorb the experience of fighting far from home, and to face a fighter with a distinctive style. It would all be a learning experience. But they certainly weren't bringing him to London to lose. The risk had been carefully measured.

Still, Cooper worked harder than he ever had before, sparring with an American journeyman named Alonzo Johnson, imported solely for this one fight. And he thought that he saw a weakness in Clay that could be exploited. "We'd heard of him coming up. We'd seen him. And I was confident because I knew I had the style to upset him. If you looked at Ali's career, Ali always looked good against the big guys. You look at Ernie Terrell, six-foot-five. Cleveland Williams. Ken Norton. Now, I always remember that he fought a guy in America, Doug Jones. Little guys who were nearly as fast as Ali always gave him problems. So I knew I had the style to upset him.

"He was fast. The two fighters who had the fastest hands were him and Floyd Patterson—I still think Patterson had slightly faster hands than Ali did. Ali didn't punch as hard. Patterson was a better one-puncher than Ali was, with his left hook. [Patterson stopped Cooper in four rounds in 1966.] The big thing with Ali though was that he was six-foot-three and a half. His measurement across here [his reach] was something like ninety inches. So he knew when he was that much out of reach of an opponent. He was unorthodox. Ali was totally unorthodox. He was so tall and so fast and had such great reflexes. He was the original. And he got away with it. All that Ali shuffling. No heavyweight in the past could move as fast as he did on his feet—or is ever likely to in the future. He was the best moving heavyweight of all time. That's why I couldn't stand off him. I knew the way to beat him was basically to pressure him all the time."

THAT WAS THE PLAN. Though history, and the film record, suggests that Cooper couldn't really cope with Clay's speed from the opening bell—nor could any other heavyweight, for that matter—he remembers a slightly different fight. "I had his nose bleeding in the first round. He kept on appealing to the referee. Basically in those days he was very novice at inside fighting. When you got into a clinch with him, he just held you and waited until the referee said 'Break.' So in there I was roughing him up, I was giving him upper cuts and I had his nose bleeding. And he kept on pleading to the referee."

In the third round, though, by anyone's estimation, the tide turned decisively when Clay opened a deep, ugly gash over Cooper's left eye. Though Henry was prone to bleeding, and bleeding theatrically, the sheer volume of blood cascading down his face was still shocking. "Ali was the type of guy that would cut you and damage you, because he was a flicker—he flicked his punches. He wasn't a sort of short, sharp puncher. He always dragged your flesh. And then when he saw punches coming, he went to knock the punches down, and he chopped down on my eye twice with the heel of his glove. I thought he nutted me at one time. I thought it was his head that done it, but it wasn't. The Ali fights were the two worst cuts that I ever had in boxing.

"I got back to the corner after the third round and Jim Wicks said, 'Look, this cut's bad.' I said, 'Jim, for Chrissake, work on it. Get Danny,'—because Danny Earl was my cutman—'Let him work on it. I'll catch him in the next round.' In the time we were arguing, the bell went for the fourth round. So thank god I got out for the fourth round. When Jim Wicks said to me, 'We've got to stop it [the fight],' I knew it was a bad cut, and I knew that the referee now was going to stop it, or if not Jim Wicks would stop it in the next round. So I had to do something."

Clay had never been knocked out in his young career, and he'd only been dropped once—a flash knockdown in the first round against Sonny Banks a year earlier. Now, with his opponent moving at full speed, circling away from him, flicking the jab, all but impossible to hit, Henry Cooper understood that he had three minutes left to hunt Clay down and knock him cold. For the first two minutes and fifty-five seconds, that quest proved futile. "I didn't follow him," he says. "I went across him. You had to try to anticipate. You had to stop his mobility. You had to try and trap him in the corners. Get him on the ropes. If he's on the ropes, then he can't move, and that's the only chance you have to catch him with a punch. So that's what I had to do. You had to cut his entrances and his exits out. And that's when I caught him, when he was on the ropes. He'd gone back to the ropes, one, two, three, and he couldn't get back any further, I slung the left hook. That's when I hit him."

It's a beautiful thing to look at, as British fight fans have over and over again, for the past forty years. When Clay backs into the ropes, Cooper launches his left, lunging forward as he throws it. Clay's hands are down, and the punch catches him square on the side of the jaw.

During the course of his long career, especially in the later years, he would be hit very hard by some of the biggest punchers in the history of the sport: Joe Frazier, George Foreman, Earnie Shavers. But it's near certain that no single shot ever hurt Ali more. "He always said that in the fifteenth round of the Frazier fight, he went down more from exhaustion," Cooper says, "but 'the punch Cooper hit me with, he didn't just shake me. He shook my relations back in Africa.'"

For the man who delivered the punch, it felt like a dream come true.

"It just felt solid all up my arm," Cooper says. "When you sling a lot of punches and you hit them with the top part, or there [gesturing to the side of his hand], perhaps it hurts you. But when you hit 'em solid, it's just that lovely feeling. And the eyes tell you everything in boxing. When he went down he was in trouble. He had gone. He had gone. I said to myself, I've got him. And then the bleedin' bell went."

In fact, it wasn't just the bell that saved Clay, but also the ropes. They helped break his fall. "The ropes let him down gentle," Cooper remembers. "You went from the top, to the middle, to the bottom rope. Now, if that had been in the middle of the ring, and he'd gone down on his head, that would have shook him up. But unfortunately he was on the ropes. If that had just been off them bloody ropes."

The round ended as Clay rose to his feet, wobbling forward as if about to fall, only to be caught by his trainer Angelo Dundee and led to his stool. (In those days, unlike now, a fighter could be given a reprieve if the bell rang before he was counted out.) What followed was either a bit of blessed good luck, or one of the great bits of chicanery in the long history of the sport. In any case, it would become one of the key moments in the career of Muhammad Ali. What if he'd still been desperately hurt at the start of the fifth round? What if he'd lost the fight to Cooper and hadn't been given a shot at Sonny Liston's title eight months later? What if all of his many doubters had suddenly been able to say, 'We told you so'?

Instead, as the huge Wembley crowd was screaming with shock and joy, ready to celebrate Cooper's stunning victory, there was confusion in Clay's corner. Dundee summoned referee Tommy Little over, and showed him one of Ali's gloves. A seam had split near the thumb, revealing some of the horsehair stuffing—which, in theory, could have injured the eyes of his opponent. It would later be suggested that Dundee caused the rip, that he actually cut it open with a pair of scissors to buy his man some time. The true story, it seems, is a little less startling, though the effect is the same. "I've had dinner with Dundee a couple of times," Cooper says. "He told me, 'I had less than fifty seconds to recover him, and I knew I couldn't do it. So I had to cause a commotion. I noticed the stitching on the glove had stretched a bit. So I just pulled it and ripped it and called the referee over.' Now, the referee had to go to the steward in charge, who was sitting outside. The steward in charge had to send a guy back to the dressing room where all the gloves were. Now, the dressing room at Wembley Stadium is 150, 200 yards away. He had to go there, bring them up. They had a confab and decided to change the glove the next round. But he'd had a two-and-a-half-minute interval. I mean, to a fit guy, that's all you need. That's why they only give you ten seconds to recover from a knockdown."

Sitting in his corner, Cooper was aware of the delay. "I knew something was going on. Because what you've got to realize is that as a fighter, I could judge three minutes to a second, and I could judge a minute to a second. What am I sitting in the corner for? I'm not retiring? Jimmy said, 'Don't talk.' Something was going on and we never knew what it was. What it was, it was all this confab—see, that's all part of boxing."

In the end, the added delay was just about a minute and a half. New gloves would be ready for the fifth round. But in the end, that wouldn't prove necessary.

"You've got the guy but now he's recovering," Cooper says. "He came out refreshed. And then he knew he had to start going to town on me—which he did. He came out and threw more left hands. He hit me on the eye, and the eye was then pumping blood, and the referee had to stop it. He had to because the cut was in the worst part of the eye and it was two inches long." The end came two minutes and fifteen seconds into the fifth round, with Cooper's face a bloody mask.

Clay had risen to the challenge, had done what he had to do, but for the first time in his professional career, had looked vulnerable. This wasn't Doug Jones catching him on a bad night and nearly finessing his way to a decision. A very good puncher, with otherwise limited skills, had nearly knocked Clay out. The handlers of an even better puncher, the man who held the heavyweight championship of the world, who had demolished Floyd Patterson in the first round twice in a row, saw an easy payday on the horizon. Sonny Liston would surely track him down and he'd finish him, and that would be the end of the Louisville Lip. It would be a piece of cake.

While Clay's reputation was diminished in victory, Cooper's was enhanced in defeat. Only bad luck, a little sleight of hand by Dundee, and his own, tender skin, had denied him his moment of glory. And of course everyone at home loved him to begin with. Three years before the great victory in the 1966 World Cup final, the British sports fan had no bigger athletic star.

For his part, Cooper long ago stopped getting drawn into a game of what-ifs. "Everyone remembers that punch," he says. "But to me, it's still a losing fight. I like to remember my winning fights. I fought a lot of good Americans and beat 'em all. . . . You're inclined to remember your good fights. But everyone remembers that punch, which is great. What I should be doing is getting, like, a fee every time the BBC shows it. And they still show it. Marvellous. I'm not knocking it."

Of course, they met again, three years later, this time for Muhammad Ali's heavyweight title. Having been forced to fight outside of the United States because of the threat of boycotts after he refused induction into the army, Ali returned to England, this time to Highbury, where an even bigger crowd gathered for the rematch. "There were forty-four thousand people there," Cooper remembers. "In the dressing room I could hear them. 'He-ne-ry, He-ne-ry.' Christ, I mean that lifts you up. It was a marvellous time. Christ, a crowd like that—now they don't get crowds like that. They get twelve thousand or fourteen thousand bodies and they think they've got big crowds. In them days it was bloody marvellous.

"I still had the style that could upset him. But I must say that he's a quick learner, Ali. The second fight he learned. He would stand no nonsense. I could not mess around inside. I've never been held so bleedin' tight in my life. In the second fight, I think that's all I can remember. Ali was twenty-two pounds heavier than me. People don't realize I was very light for a heavyweight. I was twelve-stone-twelve. And he was fourteen-eleven. Whenever I got close to him, he held me. It was just like being in a vice. He held me, and when the referee said 'Break,' he made sure he pushed me back, and he took a right step back. He'd learned well from the first experience."

The second Ali–Cooper fight was like the most one-sided moments of the first, without the dramatics of Cooper's career-defining punch, but with just as much carnage. Cooper suffered a terrible cut over his left eye and bled profusely, until the fight was finally stopped in the sixth round. "That fight was stopped with the same eye, the same cut. But to me, the first two or three rounds I'd been falling short with my left hand, because he was ready for it. Just in the fifth round and the sixth round, I was beginning to get my range, I was starting to catch him when the bloody eye cut again. I was choked at that, because I was just beginning to get to him when the eye let me down again."

Over the years, when Ali came to England, or when Cooper broadcast big fights from America, the two of them occasionally got together to relive those moments.

"In fact, I was with him and his doctor about eighteen months ago," Cooper says. "And when Ali went out of the room, I said to his doctor, 'Boxing hasn't done that to him. You look at Ali's face—he hasn't got a flat nose.' The doctor said, 'Oh yes it has, Mr. Cooper. What you've got to realize is that Ali, being the clever fighter, he used to turn his head, and he got hit on the back of the neck. He got thumped on the back of the neck so often some brain cells at the base of his brain, because they've been thumped, they've been killed off.'"

The second Ali fight would be Cooper's last crack at the big time, but hardly the end of his boxing career. In England, he carried on, knocking off a succession of young challengers, known as the Golden Boys, for his British title. It wasn't until 1971, at age thirty-seven, that he finally called it a day after losing a decision to the rising young contender Joe Bugner, a decision that Cooper still disputes.

By the time he retired as a boxer, heeding Wicks' advice, Cooper had already begun easing into a new career. "Jim was a great old man, bless his heart. He always used to say, 'Save your money. Boxing's not for all your life. You'll still be a young man when you have to retire. Be careful. Invest your money.'"

NOW FOR THE IRONY of ironies. Boxing is a sport in which vast amounts of cash seem to disappear in a heartbeat, in which fighters who earn what are reported to be enormous purses routinely wind up broke. Taxes aren't paid, mysterious percentages are deducted and exploiters are everywhere. And those who have never had money in their lives—which would be the demographic that produces nearly all professional prizefighters—don't necessarily deal with newfound wealth wisely. Garages fill with luxury cars, great palaces are constructed, children are fathered hither and yon, and then, with one big loss, the cash flow stops, the bills are due, the piper must be paid. It's not like boxing prepares anyone for anything else, never mind a nine-to-five, forty-hour-week office job with a decent dental plan.

Henry Cooper, though, was always extremely careful with a buck. He was managed by an honest man and kept close track of his ring earnings. Once he retired from boxing, he made an almost seamless transition into the life of a broadcaster and a professional celebrity. "If you've got a distinctive voice, people want to use you," he says, "and it's lovely." When he did build up a tidy little nest egg, he chose to invest it with a company whose very name suggested stability: Lloyd's of London, the people who would insure anything, who would underwrite any risk, or provide security for any famous body part for a price.

And despite all of that, eight years ago the world witnessed the sad spectacle of Cooper auctioning off his three Lonsdale Belts, each representative of three successful defences of the British heavyweight title, which he held longer than anyone in history. He looked, at that moment, like just another crestfallen ex-fighter down on his luck, selling his most valued possessions—though the story was, in fact, a bit more complicated, and less dire, than that.

Cooper was one of those investors (along with several other high-profile British athletes) given the chance to become one of Lloyd's "names." "In them days," he says, "you had to show you had assets of

150,000 quid. You had to put, I think, ten thousand pounds in them days in shares or whatever, which I did. For the first year it was all right, and then it all went wrong." If the company went south, the "names" were left with unlimited liability; of course, given Lloyd's sterling reputation, none ever dreamt that might be a possibility.

"The great tragedy in the Lloyd's thing is that, in this country, for a working-class boy to even be invited to become a 'name' at Lloyd's was something special. . . . I still think there was skullduggery done. A lot of sporting stars—you take Virginia Wade; Virginia Wade lost a fortune. Tony Jacklin lost two million quid in there. I never lost nowhere near that. You're talking, with me, fifty or sixty thousand quid. Some of them lost millions. They put thirty suicides down to the collapse of Lloyd's."

There was a cash call, and Cooper's options were limited. "I had my old house, and I didn't want to sell my house. I had three Lonsdale belts, gold belts, sitting in a bank doing nothing. So I said, all right, as much as I don't like it, I'm not going to sell my house. They had to go first. So I put them up for auction. I done wrong, really, because they put the auction in Kent, where they should have done it in London. We would have got a lot more. That paid off the debt I owed to Lloyd's." (The 1993 auction brought in a total of £48,300, far less than the pre-sale estimate of £70,000.)

Cooper is careful to point out that he's hardly indigent. "I still had my Lloyd's deposit, and all them years in Lloyd's, that had all gained value. I had very good shares. Once I sold all them shares, I made money. And I've got a pension. Don't feel sorry for me. I came out recouping all that I lost, with a nice bit of interest.

"It's just a shame about them gold belts. I know who's got them, but now they've gained such value, I couldn't go to the guy and say, 'Here's your money, what you paid for them, give them back.' He'd want two hundred grand, and I haven't got that money to spend. If ever I win the lottery, they'd be the first things I'd go out and get."

That disappointment aside, judging by the surroundings at the golf club, Cooper's life certainly seems comfortable now. And his knighthood, which was bestowed on Cooper by Queen Elizabeth in 2000, went some way towards erasing the pain and humiliation of that very public financial fiasco.

"I can remember Mum used to take us just after the war to Buckingham Palace," Cooper says. "In them days, the guards were outside. Me and George used to walk along with them. We always wanted to be guards. I used to look at Buckingham Palace and, cor, I never dreamt, never in my wildest dreams, that I'd ever walk through them gates.

"I've been to Buckingham Palace now on twenty different occasions. I've had dinner with the Royal Family, just me and two other commoners, with the Queen, Prince Philip, Prince Charles and Princess Anne. I've had breakfast there at half past one in the morning, been to a big ball, danced in the ballroom. I got my OBE [Order of the British Empire] there. I've been to garden parties.

"Them things you don't expect. I look back and think my mum, my dad—bless their hearts, they're dead now—I think they'd be proud as punch. Dear old Jim Wicks, he'd be over the moon. Cor bloody hell. Unbelievable. It's just brilliant. Brilliant."

GEORGE CHUVALO

Toronto, Canada

George Chuvalo has always enjoyed being a little famous, enjoyed strolling into restaurants in his hometown and being treated like a king, enjoyed being stopped on the street, enjoyed the perks that go with celebrity. Nothing about his face betrays the fact that he fought ninety times as a professional and faced all of the top heavyweights of his era. (Though, thanks to Joe Frazier's left hook, there is that little piece of plastic inside his face that holds one of his eyes in place.) Chuvalo is erudite and charming and, these days, fit as a fiddle.

In other places, if they remember him at all, it's as a catcher, an absorber of punches, as a fighter good enough to hang in with the best, but not good enough to beat them, as a bit of a boxing masochist, a guy who would take any manner of punishment and simply refuse to go down. Once, while watching a half-talented Canadian fighter take a beating, one of the Americans in press row automatically turned back towards his Canadian confreres and hollered a single word: "Chuvalo." Everyone understood the reference.

But in his home country, where sports icons have almost invariably come from the hockey rink, it's different, and as a fighter, Chuvalo stands alone, his name instantly recognizable, at least to those of a certain age: Chuvalo the courageous; Chuvalo the hard rock; Chuvalo the toughest man in Canada. Chuvalo, who in 1966 stood up to the great Muhammad Ali for fifteen rounds and never took a backwards step, defining a national stereotype: the plucky underdog; the gritty competitor, unfazed by long odds or the overwhelming Goliath to the south, undefeated even if, technically, truthfully, that fight in '66 was a loss. Forget all of his other fights, forget the twenty-year career, forget even the second time he met Ali, under very different circumstances, in 1972. Forget that he was a far more skilled fighter than his one-note reputation would suggest. That night in Toronto at Maple Leaf Gardens in 1966 is, for Canadians, a cultural point of demarcation. The only sporting moments that compare are the country's hockey victories over the Russians in 1972, over the Americans in 2002, and the twin 100-metre gold medals won by Donovan Bailey and the later-disgraced Ben Johnson—moments when, for an instant, the country stood tall.

But what a double-edged sword to have most of your finest moments forgotten, while being remembered for a night when you were clearly, definitively second best. And what a thing, later in life, to become famous all over again, for enduring unimaginable personal tragedy, for watching three sons and a wife all die by their own hand. "In my own mind, I was, like, special. In my own mind, I always said to myself that I couldn't be hurt. I felt, a crazy part of me felt, indestructible," Chuvalo says. "If somebody else said they were indestructible, I'd start laughing. But in my own mind, I had to play to my own sense of ego, my sense of who I was. And I was supposed to be a pretty tough guy." He never wanted to have to prove he was quite so tough, though. Taking on Goliath was one thing; he sure never wanted to play Job.

CANADA HAS NEVER BEEN much of a boxing country, which, all told, is not such a bad thing. All of its greatest fighters were produced in the late nineteenth century and the first half of the twentieth, foremost among them Sam Langford, the heavyweight from Nova Scotia who might have been champion but for the colour of his skin, and Jimmy McLarnin, the brilliant welterweight champ, who was born in Belfast but grew up in Vancouver. There is a scattering of others who held titles, but just one heavyweight king—Tommy Burns, notable as the smallest man to ever hold the title, and for losing to the first African-American who was given the chance to challenge for the belt, Jack Johnson. Lennox Lewis might be considered his successor, except that Lewis was born in England, and though he was raised in Canada and won a gold medal for the country at the 1988 Olympics in Seoul, was eager to reclaim his British heritage because of the commercial possibilities it offered.

There are various cultural reasons why Canada failed to produce more fighters, the most obvious that it is a small country, in terms of population, and a relatively prosperous place, that it has long enjoyed a social safety net, that there simply weren't as many who fit the demographic that has perpetually produced the sport's best raw material: the poor and the desperate. That plus the fact that any boy with athletic potential immediately gravitates towards the hockey rink, eager to follow in the footsteps of those heroes who had gone before.

George Chuvalo grew up with different dreams. His parents were part of one of the great post-war immigrant waves to Canada, arriving from Bosnia-Herzegovina, setting up house in a working-class neighbourhood near Toronto's stockyards. His father, Steve, worked on the killing floor. He so feared that he might lose his job, lose his footing in the new world, that he spent his two weeks of annual vacation sitting outside the plant, watching the man who replaced him. His mother, Kata, plucked chickens in a poultry plant. At lunch hour, she'd run to the schoolyard, hand her boy—a momma's boy, he'd acknowledge—a bag of potato chips or a pomegranate, and kiss him through the fence. Chuvalo was big for his age, and he sometimes fought on the street, but he was secure and comfortable and would no doubt have lived out the same immigrant dream that his parents had realized. But then one day he picked up a copy of *Ring Magazine* at Morgan's Cigar Store, and all at once saw his future.

He trained diligently, developed a bodybuilder's physique and (counter to his father's low expectations) didn't quit the first time he suffered a bloody nose. He left school at the age of fifteen and worked with his father at the meat factory. In 1955, at seventeen, he was the amateur heavyweight champion of Canada. (Many, many years later, his sons Steven and George Jr. would take that medal and sell it to buy heroin.) The title qualified him to represent his country at the 1956 Olympics in Melbourne. "You know what I knew about the Olympics?" he says. "What I read about in the history books. I didn't have a television. I was picked on May 7, 1955, to go. [Chuvalo has an impeccable memory for dates.] The Olympics were in November 1956. I couldn't wait that long to turn pro. I was starving."

Chuvalo became a professional heavyweight on April 23, 1956, entering a "Jack Dempsey Tournament" at Maple Leaf Gardens. Originally, the competitions for novice heavyweights were designed to produce white hopes, but by the time Chuvalo entered, they were integrated. He knocked out four opponents in a total of twelve minutes and thirty-six seconds, earned five hundred dollars and had his hand raised by the great Manassa Mauler himself. Already, some of the locals were comparing Chuvalo to Rocky Marciano.

By the time he fought Ali the first time, Chuvalo would have already completed what for most boxers would be an entire professional career. He was pushed too fast by managers who didn't entirely know what they were doing. He wasn't given the chance to fully develop his talents. He was beaten before he should have been. He won the Canadian title, and then lost it. He was in and out of the *Ring Magazine* top ten. For a while, he stayed away from the sport entirely. And then, just when it seemed that he'd played out his hand as a local hero, Chuvalo reached another level. Late in 1963, Ernie Terrell was scheduled to meet Mike DeJohn in a televised fight from Louisville, and whoever won the match would take on a young up-and-comer called Cassius Clay. Then Terrell pulled out, and Chuvalo was summoned as a last-minute substitute. "That's when I remember seeing Ali for the first time," Chuvalo says. "And I remember thinking that he dressed more like a preppie white guy than a black guy. Very straight pants and a three-button suit. I remember posing for photos with Ali. I felt his left bicep. And I remember thinking to myself, 'This guy's got pretty small biceps.' For a heavyweight, he didn't look that imposing. So I made a little joke. I said, 'Hey Popeye, what's happening?' He says, 'Why are you calling me Popeye?' I say, 'Hey Popeye, you must have pretty big forearms, because you've got awfully small biceps.'"

Chuvalo won the DeJohn fight spectacularly, creating a lingering image: his opponent stretched over the top rope, helpless, and Chuvalo just pounding away. It's from seeing that, Chuvalo figures, that

Ali came up with the nickname "the washerwoman"—his arms pumping up and down like someone using a scrub board. "George Chuvalo fights rough and tough like a washerwoman," Ali announced. "I ain't going to fight him. He fights too much like a washerwoman."

And why take that risk, given that he'd already signed to challenge Sonny Liston for the title in Miami Beach in February 1964?

AFTER THAT, CHUVALO HAD his chances, but the fates weren't with him. If Liston had beaten Ali in their rematch in Lewiston, Maine, the Canadian would have been Liston's first title defence. Then came the phantom punch, the suspicious blow with which Clay knocked out Liston. If Chuvalo had beaten Floyd Patterson in 1965, he would have been in line for a shot at Ali's title. He fought the fight of his life that night at Madison Square Garden, and a lot of people thought he won, but he didn't get the decision. If Chuvalo had beaten Ernie Terrell right at home in Toronto later that year, he could have claimed at least the World Boxing Association portion of the title, which had been stripped from Ali. "Well the bell rang at the end of fifteen rounds," he remembers. "I go back to my corner, and everybody was in my corner. Photographers, reporters, friends, taking pictures and talking. Everybody's excited. In my book, photographers are going to go to the winner's corner. Reporters are going to jump in the winner's corner. They're not going to jump in the loser's corner." Then the decision was announced: Terrell was the victor. "There's a mass exodus over to the other side of the ring. But those people knew I won the fight. Why would they want to take a picture of me? Why would they want to take a picture of the loser first?"

In terms of the big picture, the championship picture, it seemed he was out for good. Then circumstances, for a change, began to break Chuvalo's way. Ali was scheduled to meet Terrell in Chicago. But by that point, his decision not to enter the draft was setting off huge political repercussions. Illinois wouldn't host the fight. Neither would any other American state. Montreal was briefly considered, but when the American Legion threatened to boycott the World's Fair there, Expo 67, the mayor got cold feet. Finally, Harold Ballard, the owner of Maple Leaf Gardens, offered to host the bout. But Terrell pulled out seventeen days before it was scheduled to take place, and so the call went out for a substitute, any substitute, so that the promotion could be saved.

Chuvalo was sitting in his manager's office when the promoter called. They listened on the speakerphone.

"I gotta call my wife first," Chuvalo joked, "to see what I'm doing on the twenty-ninth."

Then, after a theatrical pause: "It's okay. I'm free."

"The immediate horizon didn't look good for me," he says. "It was going to be awhile before I got another crack. I knew that. So when the opportunity arose, I had to go for it. Seventeen days or whatever. I had to go for it. . . . It was like a rush job. Like getting ready for a date—in five minutes you've got a date with a beautiful woman. You've got to get cleaned up and shaved and showered, brush your teeth, comb your hair. Everything real quick. And you don't get a chance, really, to prepare the way you're supposed to prepare."

It seemed to Chuvalo like he'd been pursuing Ali forever. Several times, in a lame effort to embarrass him in public and shame him into a fight, he'd actually dressed up as a washerwoman and crashed Ali press conferences. Chuvalo admired Ali's showmanship. "He was really doing a takeoff on Gorgeous George . . . that's where he got his act from. It was cute to watch. The poems, everything else. It was refreshing." As for his politics, at the time they seemed entirely beside the point, especially to a Canadian. "The cat's got his troubles, I've got mine," Chuvalo thought.

But when Ali arrived in Toronto for the fight—a different Ali, less boastful, more restrained, more sombre—Chuvalo's plight took on a sudden gravity. "The whole thing was quiet. I remember the press conference. It was quiet. He felt the sting of being a social pariah in so many ways. Today the man's an icon. Today the man's revered. Today the man's the most recognizable face on earth. And they love him—but he wasn't loved then. Far from it. People hated him. A lot of them. I remember people talking to me, saying 'My kid's in the war, my kid's in Vietnam. What the hell is he doing, what the hell is he doing refusing to go?' I heard people talk like that. They were angry. War veterans were angry.

"That must be a hell of a thing, when they don't want you in your own country. And they didn't want him. The general populace didn't want him. They were angry with him. And I remember thinking, this must be a pretty strong guy, facing the wrath of the U.S. government, facing possible imprisonment, facing possible exile from the fight game itself, and he's standing up to a lot of people, a lot of powerful people. And for what, for what gain? As far as the black Muslims were concerned, he was a hero. He was a hero to a lot of people. He made a lot of people feel proud of being black, a lot of people who were previously downtrodden. It was like giving them a new face. He made them feel good about themselves. And it was very easy to root for somebody like Ali if you're black—very easy to root for him."

ROMANCE ASIDE, NATIONAL pride aside, the fight itself was brutally one-sided. Chuvalo won a round or two, but only because Ali stopped punching for the heck of it. He let his opponent pound his body (which is why, afterwards, he suffered bleeding in his kidneys) because he was too skilled, too fast, too everything for a fighter whose greatest weapon was his sheer doggedness, his unwillingness to be discouraged. The combinations rattled off Chuvalo's head, rapid fire, but still he kept coming forward. And in that unwillingness to surrender, in that courage in the face of impossible odds, he was defined as he'd never been when he was winning. Simply hanging in against the greatest fighter in the world—at that moment, in 1966, perhaps the greatest heavyweight of all time—was all that Canadians asked of him. They didn't expect to beat the United States, in the ring or anywhere else. But after fifteen rounds, everyone would understand that it had been a fight. Though the pundits had called the matchup a disgrace, had urged fans to boycott, afterwards they gave Chuvalo credit for courage, for honest effort, and a few even wrote that it was the kind of night that could save a sport apparently rotting from mob influence and corruption.

"To me it's kind of negative," Chuvalo says. "I lost the fight. So people see me and they say, 'Oh George, you went the distance with Muhammad Ali.' I say, 'No, he went the distance with me.' When people say to me, 'You must be so proud of the fight,' I say, 'Proud of what? I lost the fight.' But in a crazy kind of way it made Canadians feel good. When I see people and they talk about the fight, I hear them say it made them feel good. Kind of proud. I made my fellow Canadians feel proud about being Canadian. And that part makes me feel good, made me feel nice. I can feel proud of that part. I can feel happy about it.

"That's what people remember me by. So that fight kind of will live forever. How many times do people come up and say, 'Hey, my dad saw that fight, my uncle saw that fight, I saw that fight. I was still a kid.' No matter where I go it's always the same. 'What a great fight. You fought Muhammad Ali.'"

THERE'S THAT, AND THEN there's other, terrible reasons why so many Canadians know George Chuvalo's name.

He met Lynne Sheppard in 1957, when she was thirteen years old. They began dating when she was fourteen, and were married when she was fifteen. "Lynne did not look fifteen," he says. "She had the body of a woman. Lynne was very mature. Not only mature physically. She was a lot smarter than girls I went out with who were more my age. I felt like Jerry Lee Lewis. I used to kid her—I told her I raised her, and did a lousy job. She was tough. A smart girl. She was street-smart. You couldn't fool her. She would spot you. She would read you in two seconds."

Lynne was always, at the very least, ambivalent about her husband's chosen profession. "She never liked the fight business. She never liked too many people in the fight business. She always viewed them as nothing more than pimps. Really, that's the way she would talk about it. . . . 'They don't love you,' she would tell me. 'They don't love you. They just want you to be there for the glory. They want to be there for the money.' That's what she would say."

By the time she was twenty, four of their five children had been born, all boys: Mitch, Steven, George Lee and Jesse (a daughter, Vanessa, would follow three years later). Mitch is old enough to remember his father's glory days as a boxer, to know the rhythm of training camps and fights. His brothers, though, really came of age after Chuvalo was past his prime, as he hung on in the game far too long, embarrassing himself in the end, failing to find another line of work that offered the same instant payoff. He wandered from one get-rich-quick scheme to another, never settling down, always on the move. (However, even fading celebrity had its benefits: Chuvalo hosted a television show in Canada called "Famous Knockouts" and had a few small roles in movies, including a memorable scene arm-wrestling Jeff Goldblum in the remake of *The Fly*.) Though the family, as far as the outside world knew, lived a comfortable suburban life, there were tensions on the home front. "In a lot of ways my father's lifestyle was at odds with what was happening in the family," says Mitch, who became a high-school teacher, and a very successful football coach. "When I was six or seven, we moved out to the suburbs. What are you supposed to do in the suburbs? You're supposed to settle down and do the nine-to-five shtick. You're supposed to cut your lawn. George couldn't do that. On the other hand, my mother wanted the suburban dream. She thought my dad was going to take some corporate job, make *x* number of dollars, and that would have been it. But he just can't live like that. He can't do that square crap. He just can't. I know him almost like I know myself. He couldn't do that. It would stifle his soul."

When he was eighteen months old, Jesse bit through an electrical cord, suffering burns that disfigured his face. He was constantly taunted by other children. And the Chuvalo boys, in general, found themselves targets, simply by being the offspring of the Toughest Man in Canada. "Growing up a Chuvalo is an object lesson in macho ethics," Mitch says. "I still get it today. 'Mitch Chuvalo . . . so you think you're tough.' You can see their minds clicking. Everybody becomes an icon of their own insecurities. Their chests puff up. They shake your hand with tremendous vigour. Everybody becomes a cartoon character. And I think my brothers really suffered because of that. My dad is such a mythopoeic structure: People who would never think of approaching him would, in a very sick way, project onto my brothers."

No one seems to know for sure why Jesse first started using heroin: He had a knee injury that left him in great pain; he met some people at a party; he was the victim of bad influences around the boxing gym where his father hung out. "I used to see the kids in the gym, and I used to say, 'Get the goddamned kids away from those people,' and George would really be offended by me saying something," Chuvalo's long-time manager Irving Ungerman says. "One time I did say, 'I wish those kids were like Mitch. I wish to hell you'd train your kids to be like Mitchell.' He didn't like that." Everyone agrees that it was Jesse, a strong personality, who led his brothers, Steven and George Lee, to the drug. They became addicts, junkies, shooting up right in the basement of the Chuvalo's suburban home, and George, it seemed, was the last one to know what was going on.

"I knew something was wrong," he says. "But when you've got five kids, you're running around trying to make a living. You get a little bit screwed up yourself. You have other priorities. If I knew what was happening to Jesse, that would have been my number-one priority. But I wasn't aware of it. Even when I found out he was using, I somehow thought he'd quit. You'll be all right. You're a tough kid. I thought my kid was a little more exceptional than somebody else."

The one who did know was their older brother, who was somehow fundamentally different. "I'm haunted by it in a lot of ways," Mitch Chuvalo says. "Sometimes it submits to some kind of logic. Then again, I had to deal with the same things in a lot of ways. But I don't have an addictive personality. Does it have anything to do with my dad fighting when I was growing up, in my formative years, and being in semi-retirement afterwards? Maybe that's it. I know I was a very goal-oriented kid.

"I know that you've probably heard tons of stories about my brothers. But my brothers were sensitive kids who would have people hold them down and spit on them. Who had cops burn cigars into their foreheads. Whenever my brothers responded violently, which eventually they had to do, they were demonized as Chuvalo's kids. How was my brother Jesse going to forge his own identity? He was going to become the tough guy that people are forcing him to become."

Mitch does think he understands why his brothers continued to use heroin, why even when it seemed like they'd beaten their habit, they inevitably went back to the needle. "I think it goes back to depression," he says. "I think it goes back to desperation. The pain gives you a reason, but fundamentally you don't do it for pain. You do it because you want to drop out. I think they wanted to travel inward. Society at large, the way they were treated by most people, the way they were expected to be—they couldn't take it. I often asked them what heroin was like. My brother Steve described it to me. He said it's like the delicious moment when you're falling asleep. Except it's intensified a thousand times and it lasts for hours. It's just a wonderful free fall. Except you wake up an addict."

Hearing that, knowing that, he long suspected it would end badly.

"I knew they were either going to kick it cold turkey," Mitch says, "or someone was going to die. I got a very cold rush."

ONE NIGHT IN FEBRUARY 1985, nine months after Jesse Chuvalo first experimented with heroin, the rest of his family went out for dinner, leaving him home alone. When they returned, his brother George Lee was the first one into the house and found Jesse lying dead or dying from a self-inflicted shotgun wound. "The shock of seeing that, you can't describe it," George says. "You're frozen. You see it, but you don't believe it. It's hard to believe, hard to swallow." It was after Jesse's death that Lynne proposed a suicide pact to her husband: If anything happened to another one of their children, she said, they should both kill themselves.

Life was never easy after that. Steven married, and fathered two children, but he and his brother George Lee were always in and out of trouble, in and out of jail, with drugs always at the root of their problems. They were, in the truest sense, pathetic. Once, the two of them robbed a pharmacy, stole narcotics, swallowed them during the getaway and passed out on the sidewalk, one on top of the other. During one two-month period, Steven overdosed fifteen times.

"After my brothers started getting into trouble, there was always the sense that my father could never commit to any kind of upwardly linear pattern in his life," Mitch says. "He was sacrificing a lot of time and mental energy—both of my parents sacrificed a lot of time and energy—to straightening their lives out."

George found Steven passed out in a snowbank, on a night when he might have frozen to death. He found him after he'd escaped from a drug treatment facility and was running across the city in the middle of winter, trying to find his way home. "I figured he was being kept alive for some greater purpose," he says. "Something is going to happen to this kid. He's going to be a success story."

On Halloween night in 1993, George Lee Chuvalo checked into a flophouse hotel known as a haven for drug addicts. "He was up there with a girl and a guy, some shit from the street," George says. "They woke him up from an overdose. He told the ambulance drivers to fuck off. The hotel phoned him the next morning at 11:30 to get out of there. By quarter to twelve he was dead." They found him with the needle still sticking out of his arm.

His mother had long been at odds with George Lee, who in some ways was a rougher, harder-to-manage character than his brothers. She took his death exceptionally hard.

"You've got to remember that when that happens, it's not like I'm walking around in a sober mind," George says. "You can't stand looking at your spouse. It just brings to mind what's happening, every second of every minute of every hour of every day. You hear about couples who lose their kid and then split up. I understand that."

Four days after George Lee's death, Lynne retreated to Jesse's old room. "She took the Bible," George says. "She took his cremated remains. She wrote a letter and left it on the kitchen table. She wrote it on the back of a grocery list. My wife wrote, 'Couldn't find love, couldn't even find proper paper. . . .' Some people were supposed to connect with her and they didn't. She was very let down.

"I was out. I came back, went to my room, and heard her fiddling around in the chest, a trunk. Apparently there were some pills there. I remember I didn't say anything to her and she didn't say anything to me. I'm up at eight o'clock in the morning and gone out of the house. She was lying in an orange tracksuit, her back to me. I said, Lynnie, I'll see you later doll. Let's talk. I came back at 1:47—I saw the clock. She was lying in the same position. That's how I knew she was dead, without even looking at her. That's too still."

Steven survived until August 17, 1996, but probably only because while in jail, he'd been forced to temporarily kick his habit. After being released for the last time, he was clean, as far as anyone could tell. Healthy. Ready to take one more crack at a normal life. He planned to stay with his sister, Vanessa, at least for a little while.

On a Saturday, Vanessa made plans to spend the night away. She left Steven with a hundred dollars and seventeen cigarettes in a pack. When she returned the next afternoon, the door was bolted shut from the inside. Steven was sitting slumped over a desk. The indentation in his neck from the furniture's edge made it look almost like his throat had been cut. He was wearing only underwear, and there was an unlit cigarette in his hand, and ten still in the pack. Obviously it hadn't taken him long to score, and the heroin had hit so fast that he didn't even have time to light up.

Three sons dead. A wife dead. Chuvalo might have imagined himself invincible, but never thought he'd have to put himself through such an unimaginable test.

IT'S BECOME A CLICHÉ IN Canada to talk about how George Chuvalo is still standing, about how, in life as in his boxing career, he's absorbed devastating amounts of punishment, yet never went down. But the fact is, he has managed to come back from the brink. There have been some tough financial times, to the point where fundraisers were held for his benefit, including one in Rochester, New York, at which both Ali and Joe Frazier shared the head table. And there have been some embarrassing moments—most notably, a front-page newspaper story in 1993 that reported how Chuvalo and one of his pals had been hired to "encourage" the tenants of a Toronto apartment building to move out so that the property could be converted into condominiums by its owner.

These days, though, Chuvalo seems to have found personal stability. He is remarried, to a woman named Joanne O'Hara. He is a devoted grandfather to Steven's kids. He spends much of his time speaking to students and community groups and anyone else who'll hire him about the evils of drug use, and about what it did to his family.

And he's been rediscovered by a new generation, not old enough to remember, but curious about Ali, and about the one Canadian who faced him down.

"I'm sixty-three years old now," he says. "That fight's over thirty-five years ago. But that's how people still remember me. It may even be young people who weren't alive at the time. They ask me about a part of history before they were even born. I kibitz with them. They say, 'You lost the fight,' and I say, 'Guess who went to the hospital after the fight? And guess who went dancing with his wife?' So that fight will kind of live forever. No matter where I go, and I go all over this country, and people come up to me and say, 'I remember that fight.' I like that."

BRIAN LONDON

Blackpool, England

IT IS A SUMMER DAY IN the northern English seaside resort of Blackpool, which means the water is grey-brown and angry, the sky is grey-brown and angry, an icy wind howls off the sea, the spray stings, and any stroll along the main promenade, past the famous tower, past the bingo halls and video arcades, requires both a tough hide and, for the vacationer, a suspension of disbelief.

Brian London's nightclub, the 007, used to be just up the street. The building is still there, under another name, leased to a series of owners who never quite recaptured the magic of the early days. His home is some distance away, in a relatively posh part of town, near the hospital, abutting a golf course and park. There is obvious pride in the place, from its name—Be Lucky—to the careful arrangement of beautiful things inside, to the discreet corner in the back where London keeps a modest collection of memorabilia from his boxing career. There are also the heavy and speed bags out front in the carport, which he pounds on every morning ("It gets the venom out," the sixty-seven-year-old explains), immediately after doing his four and a half miles of roadwork at dawn. One look at his physique and he looks like a man who could fight. One look at his face proves it.

"I got a broken nose, but I didn't get any cauliflower ears," he says. "Because when I was a kid, my father had the worst cauliflower ears you've ever seen. Me father said to me, 'Whatever you do, just keep your hands up like that.' Look at my bloody nose. I missed the ears didn't I? Not a mark on the ears." His ears, indeed, look pristine, while his nose is unnaturally flattened.

"I don't play much anymore," London says when asked about the golf course, as his wife, Veronica, offers tea in the formal sitting room, served in delicate china cups. "Not really my game, I think."

"Now remember what happened, Brian," Veronica says, filling in the blanks as she sometimes does.

"Oh, er, yeah, yeah."

"Remember that they said you couldn't come back."

"Broke a club. Guess I have a temper."

So now, Brian London doesn't golf. He does live comfortably as one of Blackpool's most famous citizens, happy in his second marriage, financially secure thanks more to the nightclub business than boxing. His three kids are grown and gone.

"What do they do?" I ask.

"They're all poofters," he says.

"Brian, they're not," Veronica gently scolds. Apparently, they're not: Brian Jr. runs a café; Jack has a carpet-fitting business; Melanie is married to a gym owner and ex-boxer.

LONDON WAS BORN Brian Harper, in the town of West Hartlepool, the son of a fighter of great national renown who had taken the nom de boxe Jack London, and won the British and Empire championship. His dad was a hard man, and a hard-drinking man, known for his toughness in and out of the ring. "My father was more of a boxer than a fighter," he says. "He fought Freddie Mills and Bruce Woodcock and all them lot. He had a very, very good record, me father. A good fighter, a nice fellow. The one thing wrong with me dad was his drinking. He was a bastard when he was drinking. And I used to watch him drink. I never drank. I've never drank in me life." The pictures of Jack London show a heavy-set, prematurely bald man. London the younger, it should be noted, still has a magnificent head of hair.

"Me father came to Blackpool and he liked it so much that he brought us to live over here. So I came over here when I left school at about sixteen years of age. Came to Blackpool, and started going downtown and having one or two fights in the streets and that. In my time, it was compulsory to go into the service. You had to go in for two years. So I went into the RAF [Royal Air Force]. The guy that was running the camp—my father had been there. He said, 'So you're Jack London's son.' He said, 'You'll be on the boxing team then, won't ya.' They gave you a lot of concessions for being on the team—better food, time off. I decided to start boxing. I think a lot of them thought that I was better than I was because I was Jack London's son." He says that he never really liked the sport, never really had a taste for battle, but still he showed some promise. "I won a lot of my first fights. I think I only lost two as an amateur. I was the British and Empire champion." He won that title in 1954, in Vancouver, and soon afterwards turned professional. "There was no point in me waiting two years to go into the Olympics. You couldn't wait—because I wanted the money. It was good money at the time."

While his father may have been a boxing stylist, Brian (who naturally became Brian London in the ring, though he still uses Harper in his private and business life) was a straight-on brawler. He was known for his punching power, for his courage, for the fact that he backed down from no opponent, and gave as good as he got. "I'd just sort of go in and try to knock them out as quick as I could. I wasn't a very good boxer. But I was mostly a fighter. I did quite well."

Did he have a real taste for boxing, he's asked?

"I had a taste for the money. What could I do then? I didn't have no degrees or nothing like that. What was I going to do? So I turned pro.

"The first guy I ever fought was called Dennis Lofton. He'd fought me brother—my brother was a pro, and he was a light heavyweight. My brother fought this guy and he'd beat him on points. I fought him, and I thought, I've got to do better than my brother. I knocked him out in about fifty-eight seconds. The same guy, Dennis Lofton, is now on the British Boxing Board of Control. . . . I think I won the first thirteen and knocked most of them spark out, and it was fantastic. Then they started putting me in with the big boys, didn't they? So then it was a little bit harder, then." The first of those big boys was Henry Cooper, who knocked London out in the first round the first time they fought.

RIDING THROUGH THE Blackpool gloom one afternoon, a taxi driver tells a story that, it later becomes clear, every long-time resident of the city knows. In one of his rare local appearances, London was to fight an opponent named Howard King. "It was outdoors," the cabbie says. "They set up a ring at the fairgrounds."

London picks up the story, once again revealing his bottom-line motivation. "It was a brilliant day. And I was on shares of the gate. Ah, fantastic. I wake up in the morning. Brilliant. I was fit as a fiddle. Fighting a guy I knew I could beat and the money was going to be brilliant. It comes to five o'clock and the bloody clouds start coming over. And then it got worse and worse. It never rained. It *never* rained. And then they started to take me to the corner for the fight, and the rain comes down. I get in the ring, and—it's a swear word, we call it pissing down—it's really coming down. It saturated us. We boxed and were sliding around. So we took our shoes off." They kept on punching in bare feet.

"They went at it 'ammer and tong," the cabbie says, giggling at the memory. London won the fight.

THE LATE 1950S AND EARLY 1960S were a relative golden age for British heavyweight boxing. It mattered little that no English fighter had held the world heavyweight champion since Bob Fitzsimmons, a freckled Cornishman who actually spent most of his early life in Australia and most of his boxing life in the United States, beat Gentleman Jim Corbett for the title in 1897, and then lost the crown to Jim Jeffries in 1899. On the world level, at least when pitted against the best Americans, British heavyweights were lightly regarded. But still, the European title was considered a great and significant prize, the British Empire title (later the Commonwealth title) likewise, and holding the British heavyweight championship could make a man a national hero.

Henry Cooper is still widely regarded as such, the great sentimental favourite of British boxing fans, in part because of his easy-going cockney charm, in larger part because he had Cassius Clay down and almost out before losing on cuts the first time they fought in 1963. London's career, to a significant degree, was played out in Cooper's shadow. He was rough around the edges, tended to say whatever was on his mind, and when given his shot against the man who was by then known as Muhammad Ali, didn't exactly distinguish himself. Still, though Cooper certainly had his number (they fought three fights, and Cooper won them all, two by knockout), London isn't willing to concede anything to his southern rival.

"They always say over this side that Cooper was the best of us all," he says. "I don't agree with that. He beat me three times. But he never ever fought any of the top fighters. You look at his record. He never fought [Eddie] Machen. He never fought any of the top Americans. He never fought [Jerry] Quarry. He never fought [Thad] Spencer. And the big fighters he did fight—Floyd Patterson knocked him out and Cassius Clay stopped him. So I don't agree with him being the best of our era. . . . He did have a fantastic manager in Jim Wicks and I didn't. I had nothing. I had no sparring partners. I was damned near minding myself. So what could I do? I was living in Blackpool, married with three kids, and he was up there with top sparring partners, all the best up there. He picks his fights, and I'll fight any of them. I could have been a lot better fighter if I'd had a proper manager. I just said, 'Yes, okay, how much.' It wasn't whom I was fighting. It was how much I was getting." Proudly, London says that he fought twenty-six Americans in his career, many of them in the United States—and beat sixteen of them. "That's more than any other British fighter."

(It should be noted that London did beat one Cooper—Henry's fighting brother, George, though

Henry disputes that result. "George knocked Brian London out in the first round," Henry says. "The referee talked to him, wiped his gloves. He must have had an eighteen count. And afterwards, two or three rounds later, he split George's eye and George had to retire. He suffered from cut eyes worse than I did.")

London's ambitious career path explains how a fighter who finished with a relatively unimpressive record—37-20-1—still wound up getting two shots at the world heavyweight championship. London was always willing, as long as there was a decent paycheque attached. His first crack at the title came in 1959, over the objections of the British Boxing Board of Control, which fined him £1,100 because he hadn't received its permission to challenge Floyd Patterson for the title. He paid the fine, pocketed the remaining $22,000, travelled to Indianapolis and was stopped in the eleventh round. "I would say that I would never have beaten Patterson, but I most certainly could have gone the distance with him," he says. "No doubt in my mind. But they didn't give me any sparring partners in America. Floyd Patterson was a thirteen-stone man—small—fast hands. They just give me a big fat guy, seventeen and a half stones, to spar with. I couldn't believe it."

That same road-warrior mentality took him to Gothenburg, Sweden, in 1963, where he met the former world champion Ingemar Johansson for the European championship. In the final round, London had Ingo down and out, only to watch him be saved by the bell and granted the victory by the judges. (It would be Johansson's final fight.) "It was a hell of a fight. It was a good fight, but I can't say that I thought I was in front. Anyway, the last round comes up and I hit him on the chin and I knock him spark out. They just rung the bell and that was it. He was out. And they cut the bell short. Two minutes. I couldn't defend meself because I had no manager. That's what you want a manager for."

"I met [Johansson] again in Majorca about two years ago," London continues. "And he was massive. A big, fat, ugly bastard. He wouldn't even speak to me. Never spoke to me. He just sat there. Big fat guy. I think he looked at me and thought how fit I looked. Gross. One lucky punch, knocked out [Patterson] and that was it."

Veronica enters the room with more tea and picks up the thread of the conversation. "We met Ingemar Johansson in Majorca," she says.

"He wouldn't speak to me, would he?" Brian says.

"Yes, but he phoned you up."

"Did he?"

"Yes. He phoned you at Norman's. He said he wanted to meet you. So we went and had a drink with him in Wellie's."

"Oh yes, I remember that."

"At the yacht place."

"Yeah, I remember that now."

"And he was very nice."

"Oh."

SEVEN YEARS AFTER THE Patterson fight, London was nearing the end of the line when the opportunity came to fight Ali. The champion was in the middle of a not entirely voluntary world tour, having been forced to defend his title outside of the United States because of protests that greeted his stance against the military draft for Vietnam. In May of 1966, Ali had beaten Cooper for the second time, to that point the biggest fight ever staged in England, and one of the biggest sporting events the country had ever seen. (Once again, Cooper had been forced to surrender because of cuts.) It made absolute promotional sense to bring Ali back against another local hero, and London, still considered a fringe contender, fit the bill perfectly. The fight was set for Earl's Court, on August 6. By the opening bell, nine thousand fans had gathered to watch, and another thirteen million listeners had tuned in through the BBC. London had seen Ali, of course, had watched him up close as he tore Cooper to shreds. He understood his own limited talents, and that he was at a late stage in his career in any case, while Ali was near his absolute peak. (The Cleveland Williams fight three months later is generally regarded by Ali aficionados to be the finest performance of the first phase of his career.)

It is standard practice for fighters in those circumstances to claim that they went into the ring expecting to win, that they figured they had a chance, that they were robbed by a quick stoppage or a bad decision, that they actually did better than the historical record indicates. Brian London suffers from none of those delusions. "I got a good hiding," he says.

London stepped into the ring wearing an ordinary white bathrobe, understanding that he had no chance at all. As Donald Saunders described it in *The*

Daily Telegraph: "This was the perfect example of how to be a good British loser. For most of this humiliatingly one-sided affair, London presented Ali with what must be the slowest moving, easiest-to-hit target the champion has been lucky enough to encounter." The actor Richard Burton, sitting at ringside, jokingly stood up and shouted, "Stop the fight!" the moment London and Ali first touched gloves. The fact is, he wasn't far off.

"I shouldn't say these things," London says. "I shouldn't ever tell. But I didn't really try. I decided that he was too good for me. Not going in. I gave me best for two or three rounds. But then I realized that I was going to get one hell of a hiding. The way I fought, I was going to keep coming to him and throw punches and invariably I may catch him. But he was so fast. He was faster than I was, he was faster than most heavyweights in the world. Ever. I don't know of any faster heavyweight even now." And so, for all intents and purposes, London surrendered before the fight was stopped, one minute and forty seconds into the third round—at which point he had absorbed seventeen straight punches without throwing one in return.

If Cooper became the embodiment of the good try, of the noble loss, and retained a little bit of the Ali magic, London was diminished by the experience of sharing a ring with the champion. He suffered in every point of comparison; he seemed entirely out of his element. And by tacitly acknowledging that, acknowledging the hopelessness of his own situation even before the fight was done, he became an easy target, especially for those who already considered him a charmless bully from an unromantic part of the country. Because of his non-effort, London became a laughingstock, an easy punchline. "If I'd stood there for fifteen rounds and got sliced to bits, they'd all have been saying what a great guy I was. But I didn't, and they crucified me for it."

"You are a great champion," London told Ali afterwards. "I would like a return fight." (Later, he amended that, saying that he'd fight Ali again only if the champ came into the ring with "two fifty-six-pound weights strapped to his legs.") "Now I must get off home," he concluded, "because I have three children to think of."

Back he went to Blackpool, where, legend has it, he was greeted at the railway station by a single fourteen-year-old fan standing on the platform, clutching his autograph book.

AND NOW, THE PART about who laughs last. London's last four fights featured three world-class opponents, finishing with back-to-back losses against Jerry Quarry and the new British hope, Joe Bugner. That was in 1969, the year London finally decided to call it quits. Meeting some of his father's old boxing pals as a boy and seeing the damage done, he was scared of what might happen to him if he hung around too long. "I didn't want to finish up punch drunk," he says. "And the fact that I didn't want the cauliflower ears. I got away without the cauliflower ears and I got away, I think, without being punch drunk. And I had had a lot of fights. And good money. Not brilliant money—good money, a good living. I thought, I've had enough, with all of these fights. Then I retired and I got a nightclub and I did fantastic."

London was always tight with a buck. It was reported that he travelled to London for the Ali fight on a second-class rail ticket. After that bout, he took £9,000 of his purse and invested it in the house where he still lives, which is now worth in the vicinity of £350,000. He eventually invested other money in a nightclub, in partnership with a friend, and dubbed it the 007. London never drank, which made him a better prospect as a bar owner than many former athletes. His first wife did, however, and even as the business thrived, even as the club became the hippest place in town, London's marriage collapsed. For years, he and his partner and their wives had been a social foursome—though the partner's wife, a refined sort, didn't have much time for London, finding him a little too rough around the edges.

Eventually, over time, that impression changed dramatically. "It took me a while to start to like him," says Veronica, who was that partner's wife, who later came to like and love and marry Brian London. They now live happily together at Be Lucky. "I've got a lovely home, a wonderful lady and a few bob in the bank," London says, as Veronica brings more tea.

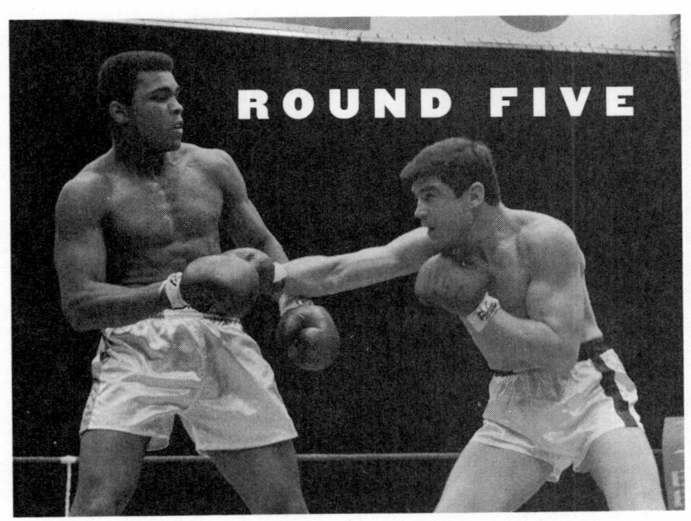

KARL MILDENBERGER

Kaiserslautern, Germany

THE MEETING HAS THE FEEL of a minor political summit. We are summoned to a *seehotel—see,* in this context, means lake—tucked away in a quiet, scenic corner of southern Germany, a resort area in the warmer months, which is not right now. The place is deserted. Karl Mildenberger, as he later explains, actually lives above the town, in the white house below the castle (there are several white houses below the ancient ruin, and all of them look quite nice). But he couldn't possibly do the interview there because we haven't really been properly introduced, and so it was much better to meet here, on neutral ground. Coffee and soft drinks are on the table, and off in one corner there is some sort of grey-brown mousse-like substance molded into the shape of a fish, which may or may not be intended for us. It seems the sort of thing that ought to be refrigerated, but isn't. Not surprisingly, then, the place smells faintly of old tuna sandwiches.

Prolonged negotiations have been necessary to schedule this interview, all of them taking place through Mildenberger's manager, Ulrich Hirsch, who in his other life is the proprietor of a printing house. "Yes, yes, we understand," he says. "Muhammad Ali is very big in America. But you have to remember that Mildenberger is very big in Germany." So there is the matter of protocol. Not to mention remuneration.

The Mildenberger delegation arrives a few minutes late. First comes Herr Hirsch, who wears a homburg hat, and has the sub-regal bearing and manner of a small-town mayor. Then his wife, who says very little, but counts the money. There is the second Frau Mildenberger—Miriam—who is deeply tanned, displays ample cleavage and who comes bearing gifts for the visitor from afar (wine bottles with a special Mildenberger label; a jersey from the local Bundesliga side). Finally the man himself arrives, wearing a four-button grey suit in a contemporary style, sporting a jaunty shock of snow-white hair and looking remarkably fit, just two kilograms over his fighting weight. In photographs from his boxing heyday, Mildenberger always seems a bit grim and heavy-browed, but now he simply appears distinguished, with a warm, open smile. Despite the entourage, he is apparently free of the taint of celebrity, or worse, the taint of faded celebrity.

"He has a huge name," Herr Ulrich says. "And just after Max Schmeling, it is Mildenberger. Schmeling is a boxing legend. Mildenberger comes behind Schmeling. Karl Mildenberger has reached the advanced age where he has 'charisma.' It is because of his success. Because of what he is as a man. Ali is a legend. Now Mildenberger, because of this fight, it also a legend.

"There are always people who say, 'Look, he fought Muhammad Ali.' I meet a lot of people who say to their children, 'He fought Muhammad Ali.' So it goes from one generation to another."

In fact, in Germany, the single iconic boxer is Max Schmeling, who remains the only one of his countrymen to hold the heavyweight championship of the world. He won the title vacated by the retirement of Gene Tunney, declared the victor on a low-blow foul against Jack Sharkey in 1930, and then lost it to Sharkey by decision in 1932. But he is best known for two fights that took place long afterwards. In 1936, Schmeling came to New York in the role of grizzled veteran to meet a young, undefeated heavyweight sensation from Detroit named Joe Louis, already widely considered the champion in waiting. Though he was supposed to be merely a stepping stone, part of the seasoning process for the rising star, he instead dealt Louis the first loss of his career, knocking him out in the twelfth round.

Two years later, the world was on the verge of war. Schmeling, billed as the Nazi poster boy, as an Aryan superman, returned to America for a rematch with Louis, by then a world champion who would become the first African-American athlete to be viewed simply as an American, as a patriotic symbol. At Yankee Stadium, he gave Schmeling a savage, one-round beating, which seemed to resonate far beyond the ring.

Though Schmeling would be identified with the Nazis, he also secretly helped Jews to escape the terror of Kristallnacht. After the war, he began a successful career working for that most American of companies, Coca-Cola, built himself a tidy fortune and, at the time of writing, was still healthy and active at age ninety-six, enjoying a quiet life as Germany's most revered sporting hero.

Mildenberger is the product of what was then a very different, divided Germany in the post-war rebuilding years. In fact, he began boxing as an amateur in an occupied nation. His father's cousin had been a Reichmeister—a boxing champion of the Third Reich—and was the first to give young Mildenberger some pointers. His interest grew enough that he joined a boxing program run by FC Kaiserslautern, the local football club. "When I went there, I found out I had a bit of talent," he says. "Then I went to Mannheim for the training. I was living in the French sector, and fighting was not allowed there. Mannheim was in the U.S. sector, and there we could box."

He finished second in the German amateur championships in 1957, and then won the national heavyweight championship a year later. A natural southpaw, Mildenberger was never converted to conventional style—significant in that, to that point in history, no left-hander had ever challenged for the heavyweight title, let alone won it. (To date, only one—Michael Moorer—has ever claimed the belt.) Left-handed heavyweights, who jab with their right and carry most of their power in the left, are still rare and can be all the more confusing to fight, as Ali would later find. "Being a southpaw, I used my quickness," Mildenberger says. "I was quite nimble on my feet. My style was always built on speed. Then, if I had my opponent where I wanted him, in the right spot, I could finish him off with the left hand.

"When I was the amateur champion, the offer came from a guy in Stuttgart to turn professional. I was young—a young boy. There was not too much money. So I did it. I had three or four fights, a string of good wins, and then I had a final eliminator for the German light heavyweight championship against Helmut Ball. I lost that fight, and they said about me, 'He will never be anybody. Forget about him.' That gave me the inspiration. I fought myself up through the ranks internationally and I went for the European championship in Dortmund."

That was in 1962, in Dortmund, and the opponent was the Englishman Dick Richardson. Mildenberger was knocked silly inside a round. "I lost the fight against Richardson because I was inexperienced. I was too young. I was unprepared," he says. He doesn't mention it during the interview, but that loss earned him a cruel nickname at home: Karl der Flache—Karl the Flat. The German fans, and the German sports press, wrote him off as a pretender. "It was the same as after the loss to Ball," he says. "All I heard was 'Karl is nothing.'"

Mildenberger retreated following the Richardson fight. His manager, Bruno Muller, kept him locked away in the gym. "Muller said, 'No fights. Just train, train, train,'" Mildenberger says. When he was finally deemed ready, there was a series of fights leading up to a challenge for the European championship, against the Italian Sante Amonti on October 17, 1964. (Henry Cooper, who held the title, had been stripped of the belt when he couldn't defend it because of injury, and the championship was declared vacant.) In front of a huge, partisan crowd in Berlin, Mildenberger knocked out Amonti in the first round, and won back the affection of German fans.

As to just how talented Mildenberger was compared to the best heavyweights of his day, that remains a matter of opinion—or perhaps more accurately, a matter of perspective. In America, his reputation is based almost solely on the Ali fight, which was the first bout ever shown live and in colour on television from Europe via satellite. Because he gave Ali trouble at a time when few fighters could, he was regarded as, at the very least, a tough, awkward opponent.

At home, he is one of the premier sports heroes of the post-war generation because of that same fight and is routinely saluted as "the toughest opponent Ali fought" (at least during the pre-exile phase of his career). The bout itself is recalled in Germany as a classic almost on the level of Ali–Frazier.

Herr Hirsch offers a history lesson: "It was after the lost war, and they had something to look up to. It was a terrible situation then, and he brought light in this time—because Germany was in tatters." He then goes on at some length about the events of the second half of the twentieth century. "But, to make a long story short, people like Fritz Walter [the star of West Germany's football team, which won the 1954 World Cup] and Karl Mildenberger should not be forgotten."

He goes on.

"Of course sports and politics don't mix. Party politics, we have nothing to do with it. We are not qualified."

In England, where even the sports press still makes too frequent reference to The War, and where they saw Mildenberger lose to both Richardson and Cooper, the memories are somewhat different. Consider this passage from a profile in the British *Boxing News*: "Mildenberger's record of only two losses in fifty-five bouts [at the time of the Ali fight] looked highly credible. There were some extremely good names in that record, too. The trouble started when you looked beyond the result to the actual story of some of the fights. All but one of Mildenberger's bouts had been in Germany. There were three draws on Karl's record, against well-known Americans—Archie McBride, Amos Johnson and leading world contender Zora Folley—good results in themselves, but when a visiting fighter drew with a German in Germany, most people took it that the visitor well won. . . . Some of Mildenberger's points wins over visiting fighters seemed a bit dubious too—and the majority of the bouts did go the distance. Most notorious was his win over American David Bailey—certainly no world beater—in September 1965. Mildenberger was down three times in the ninth round, and Bailey's corner was to protest the session was cut short. The German survived the final three minutes and took the decision."

All of this places Mildenberger's own interpretation of his career in a slightly different light. "[After the Amonti match] I really started fighting Americans," he says. "I wanted to build myself up as a name in the United States by fighting Americans. I really wanted to fight for a world championship. That's why I needed the Americans."

There's no denying that in September 1966, he was a natural opponent for Ali for several reasons. Mildenberger had worked his way up to the number-one contender's position in the *Ring Magazine* ratings. And Ali, who had been forced to fight outside of the United States earlier that year because of his refusal to enter the draft, was on something of a world tour: first George Chuvalo in Toronto, then the rematch with Cooper in London, then Brian London, and finally Mildenberger, in the first world heavyweight title fight ever contested on German soil. "Because I became German champion, European champion, because I fought the Americans, I was the logical challenger," Mildenberger says. "Of course, if the fight would have been in America I would have gone there. I was recognized as the official challenger, so I would have gone anywhere. I wanted to be the champion."

The buildup to the bout was like nothing he had experienced before, having hardly fought outside of Germany, and having never ventured outside of Europe. In order to drum up a bit of interest, Mildenberger was flown to the United States to make an appearance for the press. He was allowed to get on the plane in Frankfurt without a passport only because he persuaded the German customs officials, "I have to go there because I have to become an opponent for Muhammad Ali." The Americans were a slightly tougher sell, threatening to send him home immediately from O'Hare Airport, until he told his story to a member of the local constabulary. "He put me on the back of his Harley Davidson and drove me to my hotel," Mildenberger remembers with a laugh.

It wasn't until Ali fought Cooper for the second time, in London, that Mildenberger actually saw the champion in the ring. "He said, 'You are a nice boy, you look good, you're going down,'" Mildenberger remembers. "He once said, 'I will shoot him to the moon.' I told him, 'Then you will need two extra men.'"

At this point, Herr Hirsch is again moved to interject.

"I would like to tell you this, but of course you are in the profession much longer than I am, so you know this as an experienced professional. You must know when two men are to face each other in the ring sometimes there are sympathies or there are no sympathies. In this case, there were sympathies. It was love at first sight."

Frau Mildenberger chimes in. "Ali claimed to be the most beautiful black athlete," she says. "And he said [to Karl] 'You are the nicest white guy. And as a German, you don't look bad either.'"

Having watched Ali tear Cooper to shreds, Mildenberger understood that he faced a daunting task. "Can you do it?" his manager asked him. "Yeah, I saw him fight," Mildenberger said. "I see his style. Yeah, let's go on. We'll try it. We'll do our best."

"I really worked on speed," he remembers. "To fight Muhammad Ali, you've got to have speed. If you're not moving, you're finished. I trained on speed, and I felt that if I had him in the spot where I wanted him, I could execute. I sparred with lightweights for the speed."

Mildenberger trained for twelve weeks, in the hilly countryside near Frankfurt. "Every morning I could run in the woods, breathe the fresh air." His managers brought in better sparring partners than he was used to. "It doesn't come every month, the possibility of fighting for the world championship," he says—especially for a European, especially for a German. This, he knew, would be his one and only shot. But did he honestly think he could win the fight?

"Yes," Mildenberger says, without hesitation. "I had the will and I had the courage and the guts to win. But I was especially motivated by the press, the part of the press that wrote me down. I thought, I will show you something. They wrote and wrote and wrote and wrote, article after article. 'This is it. This is the big event.' But nobody ever thought about me winning the fight. Everybody said three or four rounds, then I would be finished."

At the weigh-in for the fight, there were 140 reporters present, most of whom still insisted on referring to the champion as Cassius Clay. Mildenberger made a point of addressing him as Muhammad.

"Ah," Ali said. "You know my name."

"He really appreciated the fact that I called him by his new name," Mildenberger says. "Everyone was calling him Cassius Clay. Ali didn't want to know anything about this Cassius. I called him by his chosen name, Muhammad Ali, and he appreciated that very much."

At that point, Mildenberger says that he still felt confident about his chances. But as the fight neared, he began to feel the full weight of the occasion, and of his countrymen's expectations. He was fighting a great, young undefeated champion. He was in way over his head—though for a fighter this is nearly impossible to acknowledge. "It was absolutely different from other fights," Mildenberger says. "Even during my amateur days and my early professional days, I fought guys from every country, but this was different. Like every superstar, when he goes on the stage, I know my lines. I know how to fight for championship fights. But this was different. Even though I knew my lines. I still had a bit of stage fright. Fear I didn't have. Because if I had any fear, I would have stayed at home. I was a very healthy guy. Nothing could happen because I was well-prepared. I was in the prime of my life. Twenty-eight years old. I knew I had to fight on my speed and my craft."

When he made the walk to ringside, Mildenberger noticed the celebrities in the crowd. Jean-Paul

Belmondo. Ursula Andress. And, most significantly, Louis and Schmeling, sitting side by side. "My horizon was a little bit narrowed, but I saw it. It didn't get to me. It was different in my amateur days. But I was a very inexperienced guy as an amateur. I didn't see anything else. I was only seeing my opponent. But once I gained experience, I was getting older. I could focus on the fight and yet see a little bit more around it. On the ropes, I could take a look around."

The champion arrived last, as is the tradition. From then until the opening bell, says Mildenberger, it's a bit of a blur. The instructions are given. The seconds leave the ring. The only two men who really matter are finally standing alone. "I had seen him fight in London," Mildenberger says. "He made quite an impression on me. He had a great reaction. His speed was good. His legs were good. I knew how he would attack. Quick flurries. Left-right. And then he'd slip. I had to move with him so that he couldn't go his way. He had to go my way. I had to cut the ring. And when I had him a little bit cornered, then I punched with all of the power and speed that I had. Ali was very clever. He was very shrewd. About two or three rounds he let me go. He tried to figure out my style. I went after Ali, but in the meantime, Ali adjusted to my style. In the last thirty seconds, it was boom boom boom, and he stole the round. After ten rounds, it was more or less even on points."

In fact, Ali was comfortably ahead, despite having all kinds of trouble with Mildenberger's southpaw style. In the eighth, Mildenberger landed a hook to Ali's liver, and the champion was obviously hurt—which is saying something, considering how much punishment to the body Ali absorbed both in sparring and during fights, apparently without much effect. In 1974, when Ali fought Richard Dunn in Munich, Angelo Dundee came up to Mildenberger and told him, "Another left hook to the liver and you could have finished him."

"You should have told me that then," he replied, laughing.

Coming from Dundee, one of the more generous men on earth, the sentiments might not have been entirely accurate, but still, that punch is remembered in Germany as the near equivalent of Joe Frazier's left hook in 1971.

Against Mildenberger, Ali also demonstrated occasionally dirty tactics, which were part of his arsenal, though they tended to get lost beneath the artistry. Several times, he seemed to thumb him in the eye. "He had a few warnings not to misuse the thumb," Mildenberger says, albeit without a trace of bitterness. "And, oh yes, I had trouble with it. He tried a couple of times. Because he was bigger, he punched a little bit downwards. I tried to move in the ring from the left or the right side. In the tenth round, I was briefly on the floor. And then the stadium erupted. 'Milde! Milde! Milde!' they were cheering. To give me an extra boost. By the twelfth round, I couldn't see anything. I was cut around the eyes badly. I indicated that I had big trouble. And then the referee stepped in. There were another three [rounds] to go."

"It was not really a knockout," Herr Hirsch says. "But he was softened up. Ali worked him over. It was a stoppage because of the cuts."

"I was standing in the corner," says Mildenberger.

"That's the nice thing about Ali," Hirsch says. "Ali never tried to make things look better for himself after the fight. He didn't belittle Mildenberger's efforts. And Mildenberger stood tall in that fight."

No one argued with the stoppage. Mildenberger was finished. Still, the German fans that had treated him so cruelly in defeat earlier in his career immediately understood, this time, the nobility of his effort. For the first time since Schmeling, one of their own had nearly reached the top. He hadn't been flattened in a round or two. He hadn't surrendered. He had given Ali trouble. He'd hit him with that one great shot to the belly—not victory, but moral victory. And a new national hero was anointed. "I wasn't disappointed," Mildenberger says. "People gave me three or four rounds, and I went twelve with the loudmouth. If I had not had any cuts, I could have gone fifteen rounds. I proved to myself and I proved to him that I could stand up to the loudmouth. Ali came into my corner and gave me a tap on the shoulder, in recognition.

"It was absolutely great when the fans hoisted me in the air. I lifted my arms, in a token of victory. In this case, it wasn't a victory over Ali, but a victory over myself. I was always faithful to my town and my country. I was born here, and I was a hero here. The older generation, they still recognize me. Nobody talks about my being European champion. They talk about this fight."

Mildenberger fought on for a little while longer, retiring, finally, after losing a European heavyweight title fight to Henry Cooper in 1968. "If I had retained the title, I would have relinquished it," he says. "Win, lose or draw, I would have retired anyway. I fought as a professional for ten years, ten years as an amateur. This was the end. I was unharmed. No terrible things had happened to me. No wear and tear." Initially, he says, he missed boxing. "It was difficult to find the rhythm. Because I had done twenty years of the rhythm—up in the morning, running, the daily schedule of training. Now I had time on my own. I was available to do what I wanted to. I was free to do what I wanted to. Not to watch my shape.

"Eventually I started to live life as a human being. I didn't have the mental pressure. I had a more relaxed life. I wanted to enjoy myself. Just enjoy life, and visit the places where I've been as a fighter. Because as a fighter, I just had to concentrate on the fights."

Here, the manager again decides to elaborate.

"This is perhaps also interesting," Hirsch says. "After his fighting days, things were quite good for Karl Mildenberger. He got offers from industry. I had my autograph-signing sessions. If I may say so, this was quite positive. He has not fallen by the wayside. He was never down. There are too many stories about fighters who ended in a bad way. That's why working with Mildenberger is quite easy. He is a very, very modest man. Down to earth. He is very honest. Apart from representing his business, we have become friends. He's not a difficult man. The good thing is, you can go places with Karl. You don't offend people. He is a nice guy. If there is a party with important people, you can go without worrying. You're always welcome."

The fact is that in later years, Mildenberger was a bit lost in the shuffle. German reunification coincided with a huge boxing boom in the country. Fighters from the former East Germany, like the light heavyweight Henry Maske, became world champions and symbols of the new Germany, embraced on both sides of the old ideological divide. Other fighters—ethnic Turks, Bulgarians, Romanians—arrived and adopted German surnames to enhance their marketability. "In this time, there are no real Germans who fight," Mildenberger says. "They couldn't qualify in their own country. And all of a sudden they're fighting for a world championship. Whereas in my time, first you had a national title, and then a European championship. And with that European champ in your pocket, perhaps you fought for a world championship. Today, all of the fights are shown on television, with big purses. I was happy in my time, when I fought, that there was a small line on national television and it said, 'Karl Mildenberger last night won a fight.'"

No great new German heavyweights have emerged, but a relatively mediocre one, Axel Schulz, was picked as a soft-touch opponent for George Foreman after he'd regained the title in his dotage. They would fight in Germany, and most agreed that Schulz deserved the victory, though Foreman was awarded the decision and kept his title. That fight might not have had the sheer celebrity wattage of Ali–Mildenberger, but because of modern television technologies, because of the intense promotion, it must have felt nearly the same. And, of course, many of those who looked on and cheered the German champion had only vague memories of Mildenberger if they had any memory of him at all.

"Recently, they made a poll among youth in Germany," Herr Hirsch acknowledges. "There are still people who recognize him. But it's the guys who are interested in playing video games who are not interested. Of course even at that time, there were people who were absolutely not interested in Karl Mildenberger, as there are people today. But now they say, 'Mildenberger, wasn't he a boxer?' That's what I found out, because it is my job to sell Mildenberger to the public, to make something out of it. To see who recognizes him and who doesn't. You know Max Schmeling? He had a huge name. And just after Schmeling, it should be Mildenberger."

Though it is not yet so, this is a wrong that Hirsch is hoping to make right. He and the fighter have collaborated on an autobiography, which he is hoping to publish. "We were at the Frankfurt Book Fair," he says. "In the hall, people approached him many times, and they asked for his autograph. There were people from show business, actors, singers. People from the publishing business, they approached him to sign pictures.

"Please allow me to say something extra. I am in the book business. I have to deal with young authors. Every year there are ten thousand new books on the market in Germany. About every aspect of life. I have found out one thing. That Mildenberger still is a man with a name. As *the* great sportsman, *the* great boxer in Germany. He equals absolutely four good, best-selling authors. You certainly have to write three best-sellers in Germany to have a name. But in Mildenberger's case, if Mildenberger publishes a book about himself next week, "My Story, Karl Mildenberger," it would be available in every bookshop in Germany.

"You intend to make a book?" he asks me.

"Yes."

"You make this book. Then we, in the meantime, are putting a book on the market of stories in and around the ring with Karl Mildenberger. Hirsch is my name. They are his stories, but I'm writing the book."

At this point, after sitting silently for quite some time, Mildenberger is moved to finally interrupt his manager. His own, innate sense of modesty has been offended. "But it's over thirty years ago," he protests. "There are a lot of press people now who don't even know me."

Frau Mildenberger jumps in before her husband can say anything more. "I look after his mail," she says. "I look after his signing sessions. And the fans always say that they love him because he fought for Germany, because he fought for the honour of his country."

"I fought for myself," he corrects. "But I judged it as being an honour to represent my country at the world level."

The fact is, interest in Mildenberger in Germany has been revived, albeit indirectly, as a new generation discovers Ali. Every retelling of the Ali story, every book, every film, includes Mildenberger, at least as a footnote. Twice, Ali had returned to Germany on promotional tours, in 1986 and 1998. At every stop, he was asked the same question: What do you like best about Germany? Almost without fail, he'd answer, "Karl Mildenberger."

That, Mildenberger understands, will be his legacy, though of course Herr Hirsch would like to also add a few thoughts. "That's our final word," he says. "But we will also write in the book that we want peace in the world. No wars. Though we cannot prevent wars. And a good life for everybody. They can have their peace, they can have their quiet daily life."

"It is so painful to read what the press writes about Muhammad Ali," Frau Mildenberger says.

"I suffer with him," Mildenberger adds.

"In every possible interview," Frau Mildenberger continues, "my husband wants to make it clear how he thinks about this."

"As a friend, I cherished him," he goes on to say. "I put him on a pedestal as a boxer."

"A lot of people say hallelujah one day and crucify him the next day," she says. "When he lit the Olympic flame in Atlanta, our phone started ringing constantly, reporters asking for interviews. They wanted to know the personal opinion not only of Karl Mildenberger, but also of his wife. They asked me, 'Would you accept having your husband in the public eye if Karl had been affected by Parkinson's?' I said, 'Ali is my friend and he will remain my friend.'"

"There are many Germans who have Parkinson's disease," Mildenberger says. "Actors. People who have nothing to do with boxing. He is a sick man. People always talk about the fights, that he had too many, as the reason for his illness. But the ones who write about Muhammad Ali, who put him down with his disease now, are the same ones who used to wake up in the middle of the night to see his fights."

Herr Hirsch, for the final time this afternoon, interjects.

"In society and this world," he opines, "we have to give to the people who are affected by disease like this Parkinson's. We have to live with them as being like everyone else."

Mildenberger himself cuts in. Enough of the gloom, enough of the profundities. He clearly wants to lighten the mood, to end things on a happier note. "Don't worry," he says. "Ali is okay." Then he tells a little story. During his last visit, Mildenberger and his wife were invited to Ali's hotel suite. The moment they opened the door, Ali, without comment, walked up to Frau Mildenberger, took her by the arm and, as a joke, began to lead her towards the bedroom.

"What did you do?" Mildenberger is asked.

He smiles a great, broad smile and says nothing, but raises his clenched right fist.

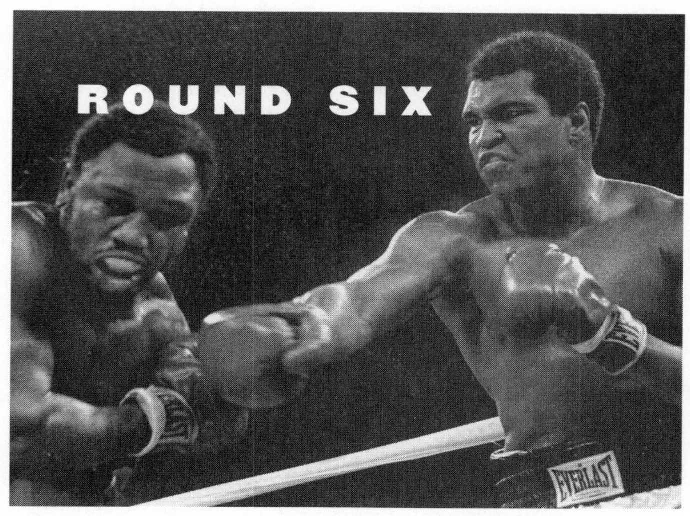

JOE FRAZIER

Philadelphia, Pennsylvania

SITTING IN THE RAMSHACKLE back office of his gym in North Philadelphia, Joe Frazier has just wrapped up more than one hour of what is, for him, enormously restrained conversation. Over the years, his interviews have tended to bend towards bitterness, peppered with words that, especially when taken in isolation, sound like sentiments that a more careful, considerate man would leave unuttered. What was it Frazier said after the opening ceremonies of the 1996 Summer Olympic Games in Atlanta?

That he wished Muhammad Ali had tumbled into the cauldron immediately after lighting the flame? No publicists worth their salt would have allowed that to reach print, so these days, Frazier has people carefully guarding his interests—especially his commercial interests. That's why the question keeps coming up, both from Joe and his son Marvis, a former fighter and sometime minister, who is also his father's number-one guardian: "You're not going to make a movie, are you?" they ask. Michael Mann's film *Ali* is still in the theatres, and it's clear the Frazier interests hope their own Hollywood story will someday reach the silver screen. (Frazier wasn't consulted at all on the Ali film, in which he was played by the fighter James Toney—no surprise, since it was an Ali-approved production, and since the rift between the two remains wider than it was in 1971.)

Still, even the new, polished, packaged Frazier has his moments. The night his daughter, Jacqui Frazier-Lyde, fought Ali's daughter, Laila, at a casino near Syracuse, New York, he ambled by the ringside-press row just a few minutes before the main event, and was asked by someone in search of one of those juicy quotes whether he knew where Ali was, whether he knew how he was. "I don't think nothin' about him," Frazier said. "But I know one thing. He thinks about me. He thinks about me every day when he gets out of bed." The reference was to Ali's infirmity, to his Parkinson's syndrome, and the part Frazier's left hook might have played in causing it.

This time, though, the slip is gentler and more poignant. Looking around a room jam-packed with memorabilia, he points to a poster-sized photo enlargement hung on one wall. It shows a *Life* magazine cover that appeared just before their first meeting in the ring, the bout that, promotional clichés aside, might well be considered the most important fight of the twentieth century. The two men are pictured together, in formal attire, the colours and the frills typical of the flamboyant styles of the times.

"Look at that picture," Frazier says. "You tell me. Who's more handsome? Who's the more handsome man? You tell me I'm not more handsome than he is."

Then it all comes back, all of the taunts, the slurs, that Frazier endured in near silence, in the interests of promoting the three fights that defined his career, and that are still, in so many ways, how the world defines him: "Ugly," "Ignorant," "Uncle Tom," "The White Man's Champion," "Gorilla." They slipped past Frazier's guard, like Ali's left jab. They found their mark. And the pain lingers.

To SAY THAT, OVER THE years, Joe Frazier has been misunderstood is a gross understatement. The fact is, he was never truly understood at all, at least not by the general public, because no one needed to perceive him beyond his narrowly defined role as the Other. Frazier was counterpoint, a secondary tune against which the main melody emerged. He was background and context and contrast. In three fights, Frazier and Ali were like partners in a dance, one always leading, the other always following, the rhythm of their very different movements somehow in perfect harmony.

Jab. Jab. *Left hook.* Jab. Jab. Right Hand. *Left hook. Left hook.* Forty-one rounds they fought, two hours and three minutes, every moment a variation on that theme, each fighter pushing the other towards greatness. For those who loved Ali, Frazier was the primitive danger that their hero parried with his skill and smarts. For those who hated Ali, Frazier was their surrogate, the one who came closer than anyone to finally giving him his comeuppance, to finally shutting his mouth.

Outside the ring, Frazier couldn't fire back, he couldn't drop that hook on Ali's jaw, or bury it in his liver. He just took the shots, over and over and over, occasionally offering a pathetic counter, occasionally boiling over in rage, more often silently absorbing the punishment. Ali told the world what Frazier was, how he looked, what he believed in. He was able to define Frazier because the dissenting voice was one in which no one was particularly interested. "Ali called him ignorant," Larry Holmes says. "That hurts your feelings, but you've got to know how to come back. Joe didn't know how to come back. You know, Joe don't want everybody to say he's dumb and can't read and write and spell. Joe had to come up with something like, 'Yeah, okay, I might be ignorant, but this ignorant man is going to kick your ass.' But he didn't know how to come back at it. He just took it. And it bothered him. And you can't let shit like that bother you."

It bothered Frazier. He seethed. And when, irony of ironies, Ali was struck nearly dumb by a condition that Frazier may well have contributed to with those heavy, thudding shots, suddenly there was another voice. But who wanted to listen to that, who wanted to hear that the silent saint wasn't a saint at all? Who wanted to hear unbridled, inarticulate hate? Nice people, civilized people, sensitive people wouldn't say those things, and certainly not about someone who had become, through illness, a tragic figure. Finally, Joe Frazier was speaking for himself, and it made people cringe.

You've got to go back to the beginning, he says over and over again during a long, twisting conversation. You can't start in the middle. People want to start with Ali, or with the Olympics or with Manila. They're impatient. They don't want to hear the story from the start. They don't really want to take the time to understand. "People don't understand where you come from," he says. "This is what I always tell Marvis. When I get into the business of making a movie, mine's going to be from way back when. Mine's going to go back to the woods. Mine's going back to cutting school, fighting in the street, hiding in the woods gambling. These things that need to be brought out with our heroes and our guys who are great in the world. Everybody wants to jump up from the beginning. And that's not really the way you lead the kids to be great guys and great girls. They've got to know where you come from. Not where you started in the middle of something. It's always in the beginning. If you look at it, it's always in the beginning."

THE BEGINNING IS IN South Carolina, in rural Beaufort County, where Joe Frazier—Billy Boy, they called him—was born the twelfth of thirteen children, and went back to being the baby in the family when his brother David died of diphtheria at nine months. His mother and father, Dolly and Rubin, were field workers. His father augmented the family income by making moonshine. "In the neighbourhood, my dad was the one that had the television," Frazier says. "Back in them days he was the man in the community. So we got a little more than most of the people."

More was certainly still not much. Their own ten-acre plot wasn't fit to grow much of anything. When Joe's father went on his rounds—which tended to include drop-ins on several local women with whom he had relationships—his youngest trailed along behind him. "I was daddy's boy," Frazier says. "That's what my brothers and sisters always said, because my daddy always gave me a lot of time with him. I went everywhere he went. I was, like, tailor-made for my dad. I was designed to stay close to him and learn everything about life, what he was doing, where he was going, who he was going with, how long to stay away, when to come back. I used to sit outside the room so he wouldn't get away with me. Me outside the door on my little pillow, so that when he come out he either fall down or he'd walk on me. So that's how I felt about my dad. I wanted to know everything that he was doing."

(Frazier did learn at least one thing from his father: As he readily admits—even to his long-time, and now ex-, wife—he spent time, and fathered children, with other women throughout his life.)

Watching the old black and white television that elevated his family above their neighbours, Frazier naturally saw the fights—in the 1950s, boxing was a staple of prime-time television. He saw Ray Robinson and the best heavyweights of the day, including Rocky Marciano, who would seem his natural role model: small for a heavyweight, with especially short arms, though doggedly aggressive and a devastating puncher. "I loved the fights," he says. "Especially the big guys—or the little guys that make the big guys fall. I liked that. I thought, wow, I can do that. But in the South it was a little different. If you were a white guy, you liked the white athletes. If you were a black guy, you liked the black athletes. So for me it was Joe Louis. Ezzard Charles. Jersey Joe Walcott."

Frazier says he decided early on that he was going to be a fighter. "I had one thing in mind: being the heavyweight champion of the world. And I was a little guy—but a little guy with a big mind and a big body, and big punches. I used to work in the country, with the sacks in the trees. They didn't have anything there to help me improve. So I said, I want to be champion of the world. I made my bags and hung them from the tree. In the country, you just develop power, punching them sacks. We filled them with Momma's slip, Daddy's old pants. Learned really how to whack. Some old boots. 'Corn cobs.' You know what that is? Spanish moss. And I made my punching bag. I hit that bag every day for an hour. I said, I'm going to be the champion of the world."

With Marvis's prompting, Frazier tells what is obviously a favourite family story. Back home in South

Carolina, the family kept a big boar hog, which it was Frazier's job to feed, and Frazier's hobby to torment. "I was a bad guy. I was always fooling around with this bull hog. I'd throw his slop to him, and I'd beat him all the time. One day, he broke out of the fence. Big scamboogah. He had tusks like that [holding his hands out from his cheeks]. He rooted me up and knocked me down, hit my arm, *boom*. I was thinking, Daddy going to get him tonight, don't worry about that. He'll be on the table a couple of weeks from now. But I fell on a brick and busted this arm up."

Frazier's left arm never quite healed and was forever frozen, it just so happened, at the same angle used to throw the hook.

"So I still threw that hook because it was something I had to do, because the elbow wouldn't stretch out no more. That's as far as it would go."

"He had hog-itis," Marvis chimes in.

EARLY ON, FRAZIER DECIDED that he had to leave the South. He had ambitions that would forever remain unfulfilled if he stayed in Beaufort County, especially as racial segregation remained a reality. "Let's just say the white water fountains," he explains. "Let's just say the back of the bus. These things were always there." In 1959, at the age of fifteen, with minimal education, he headed north, following the path of many of his family members. "The older ones, the aunties and the uncles on my dad's side, they migrated from the South to the North, where there was more opportunity for them: the opportunity to advance and do things, and make money, not seventy-five cents or a dollar an hour.

I wanted to get away from Mom and Dad and stand on my own. And New York was the place. New York was totally the place to go. So I grew up quick, grew up fast, and got out of there."

Predictably, he was not about to enter the land of milk and honey. He took a place with his older brother Tommy, and Frazier immediately learned that his options were still extremely limited. "Ever heard of paying for a job? I had to buy a job. I paid a guy for a job in a sheet-metal factory. Then, as soon as I got through paying for the job, they fired me and I had to find another job." So Frazier moved into a different line of work. "Once in a while, we'd steal a few cars. Push them to the junkyard. Back in them days, when you steal a car and push it to the junkyard, you got yourself fifty dollars. Fifty dollars was a lot of money back then. You could feed four or five families on that kind of money. They didn't have no locks on the hubcaps back in those days. They didn't have no alarms. They didn't have no lock on the steering wheel." Frazier was never caught. "I always tell my kids that the Lord helps the watchman and the thief. He helps you steal and he helps somebody catch you." But he came to understand that it was only a matter of time, that he had to move on.

"I had to get out of there because that wasn't going to last, and that wasn't what I came to the North to do. Not to get in trouble. There wasn't no trouble in the South. I moved from New York to Philadelphia. I didn't have to buy a job there, but it was awhile until I got a real steady job. It was a piece job here, a piece job there. Then I went to a relative of mine who was a butcher. A distant relative. He took me in to get a job with him, and I stayed there for quite some time."

Frazier took a position in a slaughterhouse, cleaning the floors, washing guts down a chute, sometimes butchering steers himself: unpleasant work, but paying work to support his young family. Perhaps Sylvester Stallone claims he found inspiration elsewhere, but Frazier's sure he was the model for Rocky, pounding away on sides of beef. Around the same time, Frazier also walked into a Police Athletic League gym. His weight had ballooned, and with steady employment, he was again free to dream about becoming a world champion. In the gym he met a retired policeman named Duke Dugent, who in turn introduced him to a trainer named Yancey "Yank" Durham, who saw in Frazier the raw materials of a great, power-punching heavyweight.

From there, it happened fast. Frazier won the Golden Gloves in 1962, 1963 and 1964, which made him a leading contender for the team that would represent the United States at the summer Olympic Games in Tokyo. In the qualifiers, though, he lost a decision to Buster Mathis, a strange physical specimen who weighed more than three hundred pounds, appeared obese, but fought with a quick-handed, quick-footed style. Frazier was invited to join the Olympic team at their training camp, where he would serve as Mathis's number-one sparring partner. When, during one of their sessions, Mathis broke his left hand on Frazier's head, Frazier took his place.

"I knew it wouldn't be any problem taking on the Russian, the German, the Ugandan or the Australian," he says. "The only guy who lasted with me was the German [Hans Huber]. The Russian was 231 pounds of muscle and bone. I set him down. I put him down with that hook." Against Huber in the final, Frazier fought with a broken left thumb and barely squeaked through to win a split decision. He was the fourth American to win the heavyweight gold medal, and would become the first to go on and win the professional heavyweight championship of the world. (Floyd Patterson won his gold at middleweight, and Cassius Clay at light heavyweight.)

"All I wanted to do was get back with my family," Frazier says. "I'd been gone six weeks, eight weeks. I wanted to get back to them and show my medal off. Because out of twelve guys on the boxing team, only one gold medal came out of Tokyo for boxing and that was me. All of the other guys lost.

"When I got back here I had to try and find me a job. I had a lot of mouths to feed. There wasn't no money offered to me. I mostly had to beg people to manage me. I had to beg them, man. I was a small guy for a heavyweight. What do you have to do to prove to the world that you can get the job done? That you could have done the job?"

Returning to the slaughterhouse with a cast on his left hand, Frazier found it difficult to work in the constantly wet conditions. "So even though I had a gold medal, my boss fired me. He fired me. I busted up my thumb in the Games and had to have an operation and couldn't really use the hand.

"My job was cleaning blood and flesh off the floor so that the guys wouldn't slide down and hurt themselves. With water and a cast, it didn't work. So they fired me. *Fired me*. Didn't have a job."

Professional boxing was the only option remaining. Today, an American gold medallist, especially a heavyweight, could count on being a millionaire before ever lacing on the gloves for money. Even then, many prospects were eased into the business. Clay had found immediate backing from the Louisville Group, and Mathis, the fighter who didn't make it to the Olympics, signed a management deal long before Frazier found anyone to handle his career.

"I tried to get an organization [of black businessmen] together, saying, 'Come on, I'm going to be a champion of the world.' About forty or fifty guys, $200 apiece, so I could stay away from the hard jobs and get down to the business of being the champion of the world. They didn't believe that," Frazier says. Eventually, following a newspaper article that painted his family situation as nearly destitute, a minister who was active in Philadelphia politics successfully rounded up a group of investors, which would be organized under the name "Cloverlay."

"It really was nothing," Frazier says. "I think they put up like $250, $500 apiece. And there were maybe fifty or sixty businessmen. It was really nothing to these guys. I said to them, 'I'll be champion of the world. I'll make you guys proud of me.'"

OF COURSE, IN 1964 AND 1965, there were other, bigger stories in boxing than Joe Frazier. By the time of his first professional fight—a first-round knockout of Woody Goss, for which he was paid $160—Cassius

Clay had defeated Sonny Liston for the heavyweight title, changed his name to Muhammad Ali, defeated Liston again in their controversial rematch and turned himself into a kind of sports hero entirely unlike the men Frazier had admired while growing up.

"He had a lot of lips," Frazier says. "A lot of mouth. I used to watch him on television. He called the round when he was going to take these guys out. I said, that guy's got too much lips. I'm going to shut it up for him. From that day on, my mind was focused directly on him. I said, watch him. He's saying stuff like 'Sonny Liston, I'm going to whup you, I'm going to whup you Sonny. Big bear.' What's this guy doing to people, man? I'm going to close his mouth."

Neither was Frazier impressed by Ali's political beliefs, refusing induction into the United States Army as a conscientious objector—a stand that would change both men's destinies, and set the stage for their first great fight in 1971.

"I loved the armies and navies and air force and marines," Frazier says. "I did try to go when I was a young boy in the South and I couldn't make it because I didn't figure out the puzzle that they put in front of me. I called the guy and said, 'Why did you try to fool me? All I want to do is go in the service.' He said, 'We want to see how sharp you are.' I said, 'Okay. Talk to you later.' I walked out. But then they reclassified me. But when they reclassified me, I had Marvis, Jacqui. I had a lot of mouths to feed. So if I go in the service, hey, I think I'd be making more money than a lieutenant. They paid you by your dependants back in them days."

Frazier had failed the same aptitude test that Ali had failed. He was later reclassified, as Ali was, because of the escalating war in Vietnam and the need for more warm bodies to throw into the fight. Unlike Ali, he might well have found himself on the front lines, since he didn't have the celebrity insulation that came with being the heavyweight champion. But because he was married, with children, he was exempted from service.

None of that made him any more sympathetic to Ali's plight, any more willing to consider the possibility that dodging the draft was the right decision. And while many others who opposed Ali's stand at the time would later soften their position, in light of what happened in Vietnam, Frazier believes now what he believed then.

"Of course he was wrong," he says. "I didn't even have to think about that. Of *course* he was wrong. We know every man in the United States is available to be drafted. He wasn't going to do nothing but probably entertain the troops or different people within the service. I thought it was a great thing to do if he ever wanted to go. If he'd have gone, I think he could do much more for the country; I think he could do much more for the brothers—for the white people, for the black people, whatever it is. He could bring people together more if he had gone and, like, served the country, as far as I'm concerned. But he didn't go."

Because he didn't go, he was eventually stripped of his title. Because he didn't go, two separate box-offs emerged to crown a new champion; one under the auspices of the New York State Athletic Commission (then the most influential regulatory body in the sport), the other engineered by the World Boxing Association. In March 1968, Frazier, who was undefeated in nineteen pro fights, knocked out his old nemesis Buster Mathis in the eleventh round at Madison Square Garden to claim half the title. A little more than a month later, Ali's sparring partner Jimmy Ellis won the WBA portion of the crown with a decision victory over Jerry Quarry.

It took nearly two years for the business and politics of boxing to bring them together to unify the belts. Frazier knocked out Ellis in the fifth round on February 16, 1970, to become the undisputed heavyweight champion of the world. "When I beat Jimmy Ellis, that was it," he says. "And Jimmy was one of the easiest fights that I had in my whole lifetime. Jimmy was a breeze. You know why Jimmy was a breeze? Because Jimmy wasn't no real heavyweight. You can make a car out of a truck, but you can't make a truck out of a car."

By then, Frazier had also enjoyed his first personal contact with Ali, who was continuing his legal battles and attempting to get his boxing licence back.

"I met him around 1968, when I was champion, after he was stripped of the title. I hadn't met him till then. He'd been in trouble with the law at that time. He never got a chance to say anything to me until he had something he wanted me to do—a hookup for publicity. So he can get some ink from the press. Because they didn't give a hoot about him. He was the guy that dodged the draft or whatever they called it. They didn't want to bother with him. The government seemed like it was more strict then than it is now. So they stripped him of the title. He just wanted to get back. And anything that I could do to help him to get back, that's what I done.

"He called me here in '69. He said he wanted to come down and come to the gymnasium, or we'd meet at the park and act up and make some noise. That's what it was all about. And I went along with him."

Frazier went along with the publicity stunts—including that staged confrontation at his gym in Philadelphia, which was followed by Ali challenging him to a fight in a local park—because he knew there was a tremendous payoff waiting if Ali could indeed come back. But there was also a streak of compassion in Frazier that's often overlooked—and that now he'll only barely acknowledge. Just as the scene in the film *Ali* suggests, he was quick to offer to loan the exiled champion money.

"Decent? I was more than decent," he says. "I'm the man that's responsible for him getting his licence back. There's no doubt about that. And he knows that. I rode to New York and loaned him some money. I wasn't scared of him. Scared of who? He's got two legs like me. Two hands. A little more lips. I wasn't afraid of the guy.

"Anything I had to do to get him in those four squares, I would have done it within reason. I went to Washington and talked to the president. I met him to campaign for this guy to get his licence. At a boxing dinner, they sent me around the table like the last supper—all of these guys from Jack Dempsey down to José Torres were there. All of the champions of the time, they were there at that dinner that night. And we discussed it."

In 1970, Ali's licence was reinstated, and that fall he fought Quarry in Atlanta to begin his comeback. The former champion, unfairly stripped of his belt, was returning to claim what was rightfully his. Frazier was a great fighter, or at least a great puncher, but was widely regarded as a secondary figure. Still, Ali's absence coupled with Frazier's ascension had created an enormous opportunity for both fighters: For the first time in boxing history, two undefeated, undisputed heavyweight champions would settle their score in the ring. And with Ali's controversial, divisive image, with the shifting, volatile politics of the time, it would turn into a promotion like no other, capturing the public imagination worldwide. There hadn't been anything like it since Dempsey's heyday, and with burgeoning closed-circuit-television technology, the money generated would be unprecedented, not just in boxing terms, but for any sporting event.

"Nineteen seventy-one was the year," Frazier says. "I made that New Year's resolution that I was going to dust that butterfly off. I was going to clip his wings. I was going to slow him down. I wanted to show him who was the greatest. It wasn't just the big payday involved. I wanted to close his lips. I wanted him to get that licence so I could shut him up. I know my ability as a young man. I thought, this guy has got to be dreaming. He thinks that he's going to whup me? No way. I just wanted to get him in the four squares. That was the drive. To get him in the four squares. To get him in that ring so I could quiet him down."

What Frazier didn't understand then was that the noise that would dominate his life had only just begun.

MAYBE ALI WAS JUST doing it to sell tickets. Maybe it was simply an extension of what had gone before, "the big old ugly bear," Sonny Liston; "the washerwoman," George Chuvalo; "the rabbit," Floyd Patterson; sneering at Ernie Terrell and demanding, "What's my name? What's my name?" During his first incarnation, he had set up his fights like a professional wrestler, playing to the cameras, inventing nicknames, hurling insults—though most always with a wink and a smile and at least the suggestion that it was all a harmless joke between him and the paying customers. And for most of those opponents, the shots simply rolled off. Some of the men on the receiving end might have been perplexed by Ali (as Liston certainly was), or annoyed by him, or even hurt by him, but they understood the game, they understood that every newspaper story, every sound bite or television clip, was money in the bank.

With Frazier, it was different—different because Ali, no doubt sensing vulnerability, went straight for his heart, different because Frazier was unequipped to fight back, at least outside of the ring. Ali called Frazier ugly, his own familiar, cartoonish preening lifted straight from the act of Gorgeous George. He called him stupid, and ignorant—though of course they'd both flunked the same army aptitude test. Later on, he combined the two insults, and labelled Frazier a "gorilla," echoing the worst racial stereotyping imaginable. But he also managed to have it both ways, casting himself as the champion of the people, especially of *his* people, of the young and the hip and the socially and politically aware, while turning Frazier into the proxy warrior of the oppressor, of the establishment, of the warmongers, of the ruling class. "Is Joe Frazier a White Champion in a Black Skin?" was the headline on a contemporary magazine piece written by Bryant Gumbel, long before he crossed over into television. To a large degree, the public bought it. Frazier as Uncle Tom. Frazier as the house nigger. Frazier, who had grown up dirt poor, in a segregated society, who had been burdened by far greater obstacles than Ali faced in working-class Louisville, was forced to surrender both his manhood and his racial identity. No one had ever given him a break, not even after he won a gold medal for his country, and here he was, defending himself against the image Ali created of him, that of a shuffling, deferential sellout.

And because he wasn't quick, wasn't verbally gifted, he couldn't get a word in edgewise. All he could do was seethe, and hate, and dream of that perfect left hook. Only later, much later, after Ali had been struck nearly mute, did anyone have much interest in what Frazier had to say. It makes for uncomfortable listening.

"Muhammad just wasn't right as a black man. He just wasn't right. I didn't even see him as a black man, the way he runs his lips and carries on. What kind of black guy is talking like that? Look at him. He's light, bright, almost white. You and him look alike. The whole family was light bright on the mother's side.

"Anything that come to his mind about me, he said. And he meant every word that he said. It did not just hurt then. It still hurts. Every time he got a chance to do something, to disturb his opponent, he done this. It didn't quite bother me, but it bothered me when it started coming to my kids. That's when it started bothering me. Because they had to have bodyguards at school, they had to have bodyguards to go out. And it cut down their fun, all because of those names. He started this thing. I just wanted to be the champion of the world and represent the people in the right way. Not a Tom, or a yes-man or the white man's champ. I represent the world. That's how I looked at it."

On March 8, 1971, Frazier claimed some measure of revenge. "He was Goliath, I was David. And I had a repeat slingshot," he says, laughing. "My slingshot just kept coming back over and over, you know what I mean? Not just in the fifteenth round. In every goddamned round. Every round. *Every* round. This guy got hurt every round. Look at the fight.

"It was great. My dream came true. And I lived up to my word. I said I was going to help him get a licence, and then I was going to dust him off. I used to sit back and watch him on television. I said, 'Lord, I'm going next week or next month against this man. I'm not asking for something unworthy. I want you to help me kill that scamboogah.' That's what I said to the Lord. I said, 'This guy ain't right. This guy just ain't right.' Anything that he ever done, it seemed like it was so gloriful or so great. What has *the* greatest ever done that's so great? What have he done so great for this world? I want everybody to sit back and look at it. What have he done so great for this world? Everything that he has done was against this country. When are we going to open our eyes up and see? When are we going to start seeing? You all ask the Lord. Don't ask me."

Twice more they fought: Ali won a rather dull decision victory in a non-title fight in 1974. And then, a year later, came the Thrilla in Manila, in so many ways the defining moment in both men's careers. Ali was riding high after his upset victory over George Foreman in Zaire, in which he'd reclaimed the heavyweight championship, while Frazier, though two years younger, seemed finished, an old contender in his last days trading on the past in search of one last big purse. During the pre-fight build-up, Ali mocked him, nastier than ever, dubbing Frazier "the gorilla" and smacking on a rubber toy monkey to bring his point home. Apparently feeling little threat, Ali also trained indifferently, distracted in part by the presence of his girlfriend, Veronica Porche, whom he'd brought along to the Philippines, introducing her as his wife. When news of that filtered home to Belinda, the woman still married to Ali, she flew to Manila to confront him. Always a bit chaotic, this time the Ali camp was a circus.

The fight took place at ten in the morning, Manila time, in oppressive humidity and with temperatures in the ring rising beyond 110 degrees Fahrenheit. Ali mugged during the pre-fight introductions, grabbing a huge, spectacularly ugly trophy that was to be awarded to the winner as a gift from the Philippine president, Ferdinand Marcos. When a few in the crowd booed as Ali's name came over the loudspeakers, the fighter broadly pantomimed anger, then tears. Frazier, all business, bounced up and down in anticipation of the opening bell.

The early rounds did nothing to shake Ali's confidence. Near the end of the first, after cruising through the first two minutes, he nailed Frazier with a right hand, and hurt him. But through the first four rounds, Frazier kept pressing forward, his own bobbing, weaving rhythm setting the pace of the fight. He pounded Ali to the body while in close, and ripped shots through Ali's guard to the head. By the sixth round, as magnificent as any in Frazier's career, he seemed to have ground Ali down, doubling his left hook to the body and head, throwing each punch with savage intent. Through rounds seven, eight, nine and ten, Frazier continued his assault, and though Ali rallied for a minute or two at a time, catching his opponent with clean punches as he surged in, he just couldn't slow Frazier down. After the tenth round, Ali slumped in his corner and told his trainer Angelo Dundee, "This is the closest that I've ever been to dying."

What followed were the rounds that, more than any moment in the Foreman fight, stand out as the peak of Ali's post-exile career. Even as Frazier sensed that the kill was near, even as Ali seemed physically spent, the tide turned—first subtly, then emphatically. In the twelfth, Frazier's pace finally started to slow, and his left eye began to swell shut. No longer could he see Ali's right hand coming, and over and over again it found its mark, appearing to resculpt Frazier's face as it landed. In the thirteenth round, Frazier staggered backwards, and in the fourteenth, after Ali rested for the first minute, he beat Frazier mercilessly. With thirty seconds left, Frazier threw a wild left hook in the direction of Ali's head and nearly fell over at the effort. With three seconds remaining, he sunk one final weak left to Ali's mid-section—the last punch he'd ever land against him.

Would the exhausted Ali have continued if trainer Eddie Futch had let Frazier come out for the fifteenth round? Like the Dempsey–Tunney long-count, that remains one of boxing's great unanswered questions. What's certain, though, is that Frazier would have fought on if given the chance, and that after Ali's victory was announced, the champion stood for just a moment before slumping to his stool, every bit of bravado beaten out of him. An interviewer fought through the crowd and asked him about his opponent. "He's the greatest fighter of all time," Ali gasped, his voice barely audible. "Next to me."

Frazier thinks he won their second fight. He thinks he could have won the third, if Futch had allowed him to finish it. He thinks that every round, every minute, demonstrated that he was the better man if you looked at it objectively, if you refused to be blinded by Ali's trickery.

And, even if the record doesn't show it, he thinks that scores were settled, debts were paid, and that now, on the cosmic scale, he's getting even.

"IT WAS THE WILL OF GOD," Joe Frazier says. "All of the things that happened to this man is the will of God. . . ."

Not so long ago, they still appeared together when necessary for commercial purposes, Frazier doing all the talking, Ali sitting silently by. But that rarely happens now. On the thirtieth anniversary of their first fight, Frazier and his family took the opportunity to argue for greater recognition, to at least make people remember who won, and to try and make a little money in the process. That plea was lost in the hype for the upcoming Ali film, in the celebrations of Ali's sixtieth birthday, in the continuing deification of the man and the persisting public unease with Frazier's raw, unvarnished anger. Frazier demanded an apology for all of the past slights, and Ali offered one—in a piece published on the op-ed page of *The New York Times*. Frazier chose not to accept it since it wasn't delivered in person, believing its true authorship remained in question.

In conversation, Frazier tries to avoid saying the worst things, the things that make people wince, because he's apparently aware of how they play, of how they make him appear, because somebody probably had a talk with him about image and public relations and how they relate to earning potential. Inevitably, though, the talk turns to Ali, and the struggle between saying what's savvy and what he truly believes, begins.

"He still thinks, 'I am *thee* greatest.' And he can't be *thee*. He can be *the*, but he can't be *thee*. There's only one *thee*.

"So the Lord got tired of his mouth, talking about 'I am *thee*.' 'What are you doing, boy?' the Lord said. 'You *thee?* Ain't but one *thee*. I'm up here. Look up here.' He didn't look up there, you understand? He kept saying, 'I am *thee*. I am the people's champ. I am the world's champion.' You know what the Lord's done to him now? Shut him down. The Lord shut him down because God's a mean guy if you keep on doing things that are slapping Him in the face. You've got ten commandments. You're not going to live by all of them, you understand. But there are some things you just don't ever do. You can't be *thee*. You can't believe that you're greater than God. [Ali] told me in the ring he was God. I tell him, 'You're in the wrong place tonight.' 'Joe Frazier, I'm God,' he said. I said, 'Okay God, you're going to get your ass whipped tonight.'

"How many guys you know within your time of being a sportswriter, how many announcers or athletes have the Parkinson's? You give me one guy. Now there was two guys that drank out of the same glass together—him and Howard Cosell [who also suffered from Parkinson's disease]. I don't know what they was drinking. They might have had champagne. They might have had a little water. They might have had wine. I don't know. But I don't feel like it's really the fight game that done this to him. I think the Almighty Lord shut him down.

"So he's in the Lord's hands now. Some people feel like he was the greatest guy in the world. I feel about him today like I felt about him yesterday. I helped him get on his feet and get his licence. I have no problem with the guy. If he had all of the crazy ways about him like it used to be, he would be more fun. But now you know he's not well. I wish him the best. If there's anything I can do, maybe I'll try to help. But like I say, he's in the Lord's hands now. There ain't nothing that you or me can do now."

Do you think Ali wants to make it up to you? I ask Frazier.

"I would say that the people that work with him—I imagine they try to be fair. You know, they're working for love. Do you know how you spell love? M-o-n-e-y. They are the people that are making this happen for him, for *love*. It's all right. But bring the truth out some time. It sets you free. It can probably get you killed. One or the other.

"It's just to the point that I wish the guy the best. If he wants to apologize to me, it's okay. And if he don't want to, it's still okay. Number one, he's got to be right with himself. If he thinks with his mind that he's going to push heaven's door down, he'd better have another thought. If he thinks heaven's door is going to open for him whenever he gets out of here, he have another thought. I don't know if he's asking for forgiveness for the things that he's done, the people that he's gone around and hurt in more ways than one. I don't know. But it's up to him. He's the man. I mean, you can't do it for him. And like I say, man, there's forty-million-eleven—you like that number?—there's forty-million-eleven boxers in the world, and he's the only one I know that's got Parkinson's. So if you've got a question to ask, you'd better ask the Lord. I don't have an answer.

"If I could do something for him, I would do it. But it's out of my hands. It's totally out of my hands. I just hope that one day he could walk, and we could go out boogying. You understand. I don't know what's in his mind. People question me. I reckon I'm the closest they can get to him. But I don't know how he think. Me and you can't think for him.

"We had good fights. We had bad fights. We fought each other forty-seven rounds."

At this point, Marvis prods his father back towards the path of diplomacy. "What would you do with him today if you could?"

"Go around hugging each other probably and show the world that we can make the adjustment and get along," Frazier says. "Quit fighting, man. I'm tired of it. It ain't going to ever change until we do that. It might be a shining light maybe for the whole world."

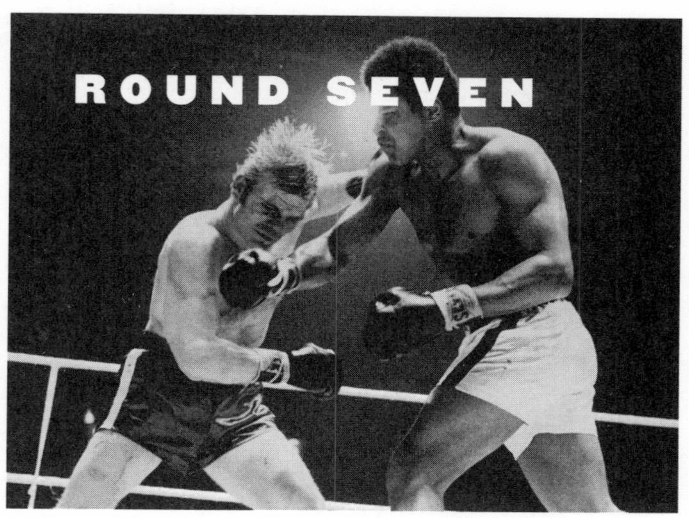

JURGEN **BLIN**

Hamburg, Germany

THIS IS THE SUBTERRANEAN section of Hamburg's main *bahnhof,* the railway station in the city centre. It is a port town, a tough town in places, and down here the drugged and the dispossessed mingle with those rushing to catch the subway, or the high-speed trains to Frankfurt and Berlin. Tucked away in one corner is the Jurgen Blin Bier & Snackbar, where there are perhaps fifteen seats arranged in the shape of a horseshoe. Early on a Friday afternoon, each of these seats is occupied by a man, hunched over the bar, drinking intensely, smoking intensely, saying precious little. No one seems the slightest bit interested in the gambling machines, which blink and flicker on one wall. So much beer is sold at this tiny bar, in fact, that the proprietor now has an open invitation from the local brewery to sit in its private box at the soccer stadium in town.

"My son," Jurgen Blin says, in English, pointing to one of the photos on the wall. Blin looks fit, young, remarkably like the boxer pictured in the modest collection of fight memorabilia that decorates the walls (and includes, over to one side, a small shrine to Muhammad Ali). Intense of gaze, heavy of brow, just a kilogram or two over his fighting weight: Thirty years on, and only his slightly thinning hair exposes the passage of time.

But the picture Blin wants to show off is of a different boxer, young, blond, wildly handsome, posing in the ring after a victory, smiling broadly, his gloved hands held high. "My son," Blin says. "Knut."

"Is he still fighting?" I ask Blin.

"*Nein, nein,*" he says. His eyes change in that moment. The life goes out of them. The hint of a smile disappears. "Ill," he says. "Ill." Then, in German, "It's bad with my son, now. It is very bad."

We leave to find a quieter, or at least less smoky, place to talk. Blin points to another small restaurant next door, an upscale coffee and croissant place. "That's mine," he says. And to another corner, where the fast-food stall specializes in varieties of wurst. "Yes, this is mine as well." It becomes clear that he is the king of this particular piece of the world, below the streets of Hamburg. Even the quiet bar in which we settle was once his, before he decided to sell.

Not bad for an old fighter who was, by his own admission, nothing special, who fought forty-eight times in eight years, winning the German heavyweight championship, holding the European title for all of four months and a day, and who fought an out-of-shape, disinterested Muhammad Ali on Boxing Day 1971, and was knocked out, easily, decisively, in the seventh round. So many in the game, who had so much more, wound up with so much less.

When Blin starts to tell the whole story, though, his business success seems beside the point. He leans over the table. His words are filled with anger, with passion, with a profound sadness. There is no pretence, no ego, no self-mythologizing, none of the usual old athlete's conceits. His memories are raw, honest, and very obviously, the remembering hurts.

"I HAD TO START FROM ZERO," Blin says. "I came from nothing." He was born, in fact, in the town of Grossensee, a tiny place in the far northwest of Germany, just below Denmark, on the Ostsee, in the war year 1943. But he and his family never really settled there, or anywhere else. Blin's father was a *milchmeister,* who went from farm to farm, milking cows by hand, collecting for the local dairy. Or at least that's what he did when he wasn't too drunk, back when he could still manage, if temporarily, to hold down a job. "The first fifteen years of my life, I don't want to talk about it," Blin says. "It was terrible. Terrible." But then, he talks.

"My father would be too drunk to do the work," he says, "so my mother and the children would have to milk the cows. We could go to the farm at four o'clock in the morning, and then work until seven. Then we had to leave for school. At school, the other children called me 'cowshit.' 'You smell like cowshit,' they'd say. To work all morning, and then they make fun of you. Many times I went to the woods alone to cry. Every two or three years, my father would get sacked, and we would have to move to another place.

"I never had a father who would pat you on the shoulder and say, 'Well done,' or 'Good job,' or 'Maybe you should have done it like this.' I never had that. I never had anything."

Blin finished elementary school at fourteen, enrolled in a couple of courses in the equivalent of high school, and soon after decided he had to flee. He was not yet fifteen years old. "I had to go away. I had to leave it. I couldn't stand it any more. I was determined to get out. I needed the money. I was really obsessed with getting away from the trouble." When he says this, he leans almost across the table, his voice rising at the memory. Blin moved to Hamburg alone and was apprenticed to a local butcher, with whom he also lived. Across the street from the butcher's house, there was a boxing gym. One day he gave it a try. He liked it, and he was encouraged; they said he had some ability. And so by day, he worked cutting meat, and at night he began to train. "I couldn't do roadwork in the morning, because I worked," he says. "So I would run after work, and then go to the gym. Home at eleven, and then up in the morning again."

From those early days until his retirement in 1973, following a knockout loss to Ron Lyle in Denver, Colorado (his only fight outside of Europe), Blin never gave up his day job. Before and after he fought Ali, he was a master butcher in a sausage factory. Only when there was a big bout on the horizon would he book three or four weeks off work, without pay, to train full-time.

Blin's strength as a fighter was his determination and his work ethic, certainly not any natural gift. "If I had had a punch to go with my dedication, I would have been pretty good," he says. "I just didn't have the talent." Still, he won local championships as an amateur, and then the German title. In 1964, he fought for a place in the Olympic Games. That year, East and West Germany sent a single team. Blin lost, in the end, to the East German Hans Huber, by a narrow decision. Huber went on to win a silver medal, losing in the Olympic final to a promising young heavyweight from Philadelphia named Joe Frazier.

At the age of nineteen, Blin decided to turn professional. He already had a wife and three children to support. "I wanted to get out and do something for myself," he says. Two men in the local fur business took an interest in him and offered to manage his career. He was given nothing to start, and for his professional debut, a first-round knockout of Fritz Mayr in Dortmund, he was paid eight hundred Deutschmarks.

A quick glance at Blin's career record shows few names that would be familiar to North American boxing fans. In his fifth pro fight, he lost a decision to Ray Patterson, brother of Floyd. He took the German title from Gerhard Zech, lost a chance to fight for the European title when he was disqualified against the Italian Pietro Tommasoni, and finally lost a controversial decision when challenging Jose Miguel Urtain for the European title in the champion's home country, Spain. Blin beat the odd American journeyman, such as Charlie Polite, but he couldn't raise his game even to the level of the better Europeans, such as Joe Bugner. He was too small, he admits. He didn't have knockout power. He wasn't especially fast. "I didn't have the talent. I didn't have the size. I didn't have the punch. All of the assets that make up a good fighter, I lacked. I could make up for it somewhat with my dedication, and an absolute desire to make something of myself. I just did the best with what I had."

In May 1971, Blin lost a fifteen-round decision to Bugner in London for the European title. It was his eighth loss as a professional. He had clearly established his level. But the pool of heavyweight talent was relatively shallow, world ratings were typically illusory, and the former heavyweight champion of the world was looking for an easy night's work, something to help build him back up following his loss to Frazier in March of that year. Ali's handlers looked around for just the right kind of opponent. "They wanted somebody," Blin says, "who could make him look good. They needed a guy against whom Ali could have a good fight. I think that's why they picked me."

THE FIGHT WAS SCHEDULED to take place in Zurich, on the day after Christmas. In an attempt to build up interest in America, Blin, who had never fought outside Europe was persuaded to fly to Houston, to watch Ali's awful engagement against the rotund Buster Mathis. "I didn't want to go," Blin says. "I'd seen Ali fight many times before. I knew what he could do." Still he made the trip, and then returned to New York for the press conference announcing Ali–Blin. The matchup didn't even inspire Ali's best doggerel: the most he came up with was something along the lines of "Fee, fi, fo, fin, I'm going to knock out Jurgen Blin."

Blin's purse would be 180,000 Deutschmarks, by far the largest of his career. And something else was different as well. "In all of my other fights, I knew I could win," he says. "I didn't care who I fought. If the money was good, I would go fight them. And before, I always believed I could win. But this time, I knew I didn't have a chance. I knew I couldn't win. Well, maybe if Ali tripped over his own feet. Otherwise, I couldn't beat him."

He remembers being more jittery than usual in the dressing room. "I was always a little bit nervous before fights. A healthy nervousness. But this was different. It was because I was up against a guy I knew I couldn't beat." From the opening bell, Blin came out fighting as fast and furiously as he could. "I fought at such a terrific pace, I couldn't last. But that was my only chance," he says. Ali toyed with him. The American boxing writer Mike Katz, who was watching Ali live for the first time that night, remembers him landing a remarkable triple hook. The point is that even though he wasn't particularly motivated, even though he was far from peak condition, he could have done pretty much anything he wanted.

In the third round, Blin remembers, he felt Ali turn up the pressure. "I could feel that Ali was trying to knock me out. Then in the sixth round, I went down, but I managed to get up. But in the seventh, I got knocked down again.

"I could have gone on. Maybe I should have. But then I would have been knocked out in the ninth or tenth in a bad way. So I live to fight another day."

Blin surrendered, in other words, which many fighters do, though almost none will admit to it. After the fight was over, he quickly left the ring, escaped from the hoopla, and went back to his life. "I went into the dressing room, packed my bags and went home, because I didn't have any business there any more."

The next week, he was back at work in the sausage factory.

Did the Ali fight change his life? I ask him. "Maybe it opened a few doors," he says. Did they treat him differently back in Hamburg? "Perhaps I was a little bit well known." Not famous. Carefully, he chooses not to use the German equivalent of the word. Just "well known." "They know me, they recognize me, and that's okay."

Blin fought on for a year and a half and actually enjoyed his greatest triumph—in 1972, he went back to Spain but this time managed to beat Urtain and take the European championship. "It's funny," he says. "Nobody remembers the European title. They only remember the Ali fight." Even against Urtain, he knew he was near the end of his career. "You only have so many cells in your body," he says. "And when they start to go, they go. In every fight, it took so much out of me that I was burned out." And they did go—in his next fight, when he lost the title to Bugner. They were entirely gone by the time he was knocked down, and decided to stay down, against Lyle. "It was a no-win situation," he says. "I could have stood up. But I knew that was the end."

He had earned a total of about one million Deutschmarks in boxing. "Looking back, I did all right," he says, though of course thirty per cent of that went to his manager, and his trainer had to be remunerated, and his taxes had to be paid. After the Lyle fight, Blin retired from the ring, and then quit his day job as a butcher. He took 250,000 Deutschmarks from his savings, and bought the first of his *bahnhof* restaurants.

"I should have done a lot of things differently," he says. "I didn't have enough of this [he rubs his hands together connivingly] to be a businessman. I'm too transparent. As a good businessman, I shouldn't always put my cards on the table. People know what I want. And in business, that is not so good. But I do it my own way. Nobody coached me in this, and that's a pity.

"In the beginning, I didn't even know how to calculate. I had to get people to help me. I didn't have a guy who could guide me, who could tell me this is right, or perhaps you should do it another way. I learned a lot of things the hard way."

Now, he works seven days most weeks, from seven in the morning until midnight, and the business appears to be thriving.

Not so for the businesses started by two of his sons, Knut's twin and a third brother. They followed their father into the restaurant business, opened five establishments, got bigger and bigger and bigger, employed one hundred people and then went bust, leaving behind debts of four million Deutschmarks. Now they operate a disco, which, because they declared bankruptcy, is held in the name of Blin's ex-wife.

The couple split ten years ago, though it's apparently an amicable parting. She lives on a property they share, in one of three houses built in Schwarzenbek, where Blin used to train for his fights. He lives in an apartment in the city. The marriage ended not long after Knut's troubles began.

"HE DIDN'T HAVE TO FIGHT." Not like his father did, Blin means. He didn't have to fight for money. He didn't have to fight for recognition. He didn't have to fight to express his pain and anger. Instead, he stepped into the ring because he wanted to, because he was free to make a choice. And unlike his father, for Knut Blin, it came easily. "This guy had everything that I didn't have," Jurgen Blin says. "He had size. He was very strong. He had talent. And he could hit. He won his first ten fights by knockout. When he hit guys, they were going down."

He also had a father who could show him the ropes, who could tell him what to do, and tell him what he probably shouldn't do, who could tap him on the shoulder and show him the way.

Then, at twenty, he quit the sport cold. Knut joined a cultish religious sect and gave up boxing, gave up everything else in his previous life. The "illness" came soon afterwards, a particularly devastating form of depression, which has left him, now, confined to a psychiatric hospital.

"It all went wrong," Blin says. "It has been twelve years of complete agony. He is in a very, very bad way. He has rages. Sometimes they have to tie him to his bed with ropes. Sometimes they have to give him tranquilizers. Sometimes he gets so many drugs that he just sits in his chair, looking but not seeing anything. They say that it is something that could happen to anyone.

"Three times already he has tried to kill himself. God help me as a father, but sometimes I hope that the next time he tries, he succeeds."

THOUGH HE STILL TRAINS three times a week—"It's a good way to find your relief," he explains—Blin rarely goes to the fights these days. Too many painful memories of his son. But the next night, there is a small boxing card at a hall in the outer reaches of Hamburg, and he's there, sitting not at ringside, not among the local celebrities, the guests of the promoter, but halfway back in the crowd, by himself. It's not a great evening for the sweet science. The entire show features local heroes, house fighters, beating up opponents who clearly understand that they're being paid to lose. For some of the spectators, that's entertaining enough, but Blin just shakes his head in disgust, as each of the "opponents" is counted out.

During a long intermission, a full dozen fighters are asked to come to the ring to be introduced. One is a world champion, the rest are obscure. Not among them is the only man in the house to have seen Muhammad Ali up close.

When the last bout ends, an Uzbek who has made Hamburg his adopted home is carried victoriously on his supporter's shoulders. Blin heads for the exit quickly. From far on high, in the cheap seats, a single voice hollers in his direction. "Jur-gen. Jur-gen."

Without looking up, he raises his hand, and waves, and walks out the door.

ROUND EIGHT

JOE BUGNER

Sydney, Australia

THE BOXING COMPETITION at the 2000 Olympic Games is held in the sterile confines of a convention centre, too clean and too shiny by half, not a place that seems a good fit for the fights. Perhaps that's intentional, given that the amateur version of the sport has had so much of the bloodlust squeezed out of it, transformed now into something akin to fencing with fists, and given that those who run the Olympic franchise operation are increasingly ambivalent about whether it ought to be part of the Games at all.

But despite all of that, despite the surroundings, the Australians clearly love a good scrap, and especially love cheering for those who wear their colours. Boxing here is alive and well. As was the case in America in the early part of the twentieth century, the sport is driven largely by the waves of immigrants who were forced to fight their way from the bottom up. Australia's greatest boxing export was Bob Fitzsimmons—Ruby Robert, Freckled Bob—a bald, speckled Cornishman who came here at the end of the nineteenth century and eventually won the world middleweight, light-heavyweight and heavyweight championships. He is English according to the record books but was Australian, in fact, having never even laced up the gloves in the UK during his long professional career. Similarly, the best Aussie boxers of modern times, three-time world champ Jeff Fenech, the son of Maltese immigrants, and Kosta Tszyu, the Russian-born junior-welterweight champ, had roots in the Old World but found opportunity in the New.

Tonight, Fenech is at ringside, and the crowd greets him warmly. When the former heavyweight champion Evander Holyfield is introduced, the ovation is even louder, fitting for a fighter who has ensured himself a place among the all-time greats. But the object of the longest, loudest cheer is surprising, at least for those recently arrived on the great island. When Joe Bugner stands from his ringside television position and waves towards the stands as he is introduced every day of the tournament—with familiar blond, curly locks and strong facial features, he remains a cartoonist's dream—he is greeted as the favourite of all favourite sons. The chant goes up: "Aussie Joe, Aussie Joe, Aussie Joe."

Technically, that would be Aussie-Hungarian-by-way-of-England-with-a-long-stop-in-California Joe, but none of that particularly matters. Not that Australia is a classless society. Degrees of wealth and poverty, as in North America, are the points of demarcation. Race is also an issue, most obviously in terms of the aboriginal peoples, and there's no veneer of politesse, of correctness, to cover the rough, nasty edges of bigotry. But this is also a place where it is clearly possible to arrive on a Tuesday, and on a Wednesday be Of The Land, especially if you bring something to the table. Bugner came with an Australian wife, a list of B-movie credits, a reputation as a former contender for the heavyweight title and, especially, with credentials earned by going twenty-seven rounds with Muhammad Ali. Hence, the welcome, the adulation; hence instant Aussie Joe.

When the day's competition is over and he stops to talk, autograph seekers and well-wishers interrupt every few minutes, all smiles and backslaps. Bugner's accent is unplaceable at this stage, hardly surprising given the long, winding road that brought him here. He has the confident-bordering-on-cocksure air of someone who has enjoyed varying degrees of fame for the better part of three decades and likes it an awful lot. His physique up close is remarkable, a huge chest and narrow hips, built by nature, not in the gym, which immediately brings to mind the famous line written by Hugh McIlvanney, the superb British sportswriter. Bugner, wrote McIlvanney, "is built like a Greek statue, but with fewer moves." Of course that was penned long ago, back when Bugner was trying in vain to win over the public in his first adopted home. It was so very different there than here.

Bugner was born in 1950 in Hungary and arrived with his mother and three siblings in England in 1956, refugees from the failed Hungarian revolution. They settled in Bedford, a working-class borough fifty miles north of London. "The necessity to box came from the fact that we were very poor," he says. "My mother couldn't speak a word of English when we arrived in England. In those days, European people were sort of scorned upon. So it was very, very difficult to get by. She took the most menial jobs that you could find. One she took was washing cars. I don't know if you've ever been in England in the wintertime, but it's bloody cold. What an awful job.

"As time went on and we got older, I started working as an apprentice engineer. I was learning to be a turner-fitter. Working with lathes, making cogs and things. I was working for a company that was making gas turbines for nuclear submarines. But I hated it. I hated being locked up in a factory and clocking in, clocking out, smelling the oil and all that. That was just not me. I'm an outdoors person. My first love always was athletics. I loved track and field. One of my favourites was throwing the discus. I was in the junior *Guinness Book of World Records* at the age of fourteen. I broke the schoolboy record by some ridiculous distance. For twenty-two years, my record stood."

Discus throwing, though, had little income potential, and money—then, as now—was the object. Bugner is nothing if not pragmatic. A friend at the factory looked at the huge, athletic kid and suggested a couple of ways that he might turn all of that muscle to cash. Why not try professional wrestling? he suggested. Or maybe boxing. "I was a bit of a weakling—a weakling in the sense that I didn't like brawling," Bugner says. "I didn't like the idea of going in there and getting your head punched in. I thought it was inane and stupid. I really did. And I thought people who did it were also inane and stupid. Really. When boxing was thrown in my way, I wasn't too impressed." But as a Hungarian, he had heard of the great amateur and Olympic champion Lazlo Papp and, most significantly, he understood the alternatives. "I thought about it very carefully. Then I decided that I'm going to achieve a lot more in boxing than I'm going to achieve being a plain old engineer in a factory." He was introduced to his first trainer, Andy Smith, in 1966, and had his first amateur fight in 1967. "I fought one season as an amateur—nothing to boast about. But you can't eat medals. You can't do anything that's worthwhile being an amateur boxer."

So that same year, Bugner turned professional. He was matched against a fellow novice, Paul Brown, on a card staged at the Anglo-American Sporting Club located then in London's Hilton Hotel. The payday was enormously satisfying. "In my very first fight I earned more than some of these guys in the factory earned in two weeks. I'm talking about fully qualified engineers. Forty-five pounds in 1967. In those days that was worth about a hundred bucks. I'd never seen forty-five pounds. And of course when I gave it to my mother, she'd never seen that much money in her life."

The outcome was not quite so satisfying: Bugner was knocked out in the third round.

Many a career would have ended right there. "I thought about packing it in," Bugner admits. "I thought maybe I should go back to engineering." But in his dressing room after the fight, the venerable London fight promoter Jarvis Astaire dropped by and offered some encouraging words, understanding, if nothing else, the commercial possibilities of a young, statuesque Caucasian heavyweight. "He said, 'Son, for whatever it's worth, what you did was great until your head started wandering, looking down into the crowd to see what celebrity or star was there.'" The great Jack Dempsey, Astaire told him, had also lost his first fight. This was no time to quit.

It is indeed true that Dempsey lost his first recorded professional fight, and it's true that Bugner did the same, but the comparison ought to end there. While Dempsey was famous for the savagery of his style, most notably when he beat Jess Willard to a bloody pulp in Toledo, Ohio, to win the heavyweight title, Bugner's calling card would be his relative passivity. Though he was more physically imposing than virtually all of his opponents, he never had much taste for actually *fighting*. Instead, he preferred the manly art of self-defence, with the emphasis very much on self-protection. Some say that he changed after one of his early opponents died following their fight. Others, including McIlvanney, scoff at that notion, saying the aggression was never there in the first place, that Bugner simply lacked the mean streak that is a hallmark of all the great ones, including Ali. It would be a tough image to live with, a tough style to explain away: someone who looked like he ought to be a knockout puncher instead taking a safety-first approach. That's part of the reason the British public never really warmed to him. The other, of course, was what he did to Henry Cooper.

When Bugner returned to the ring following that initial defeat, he managed to put together a string of victories. Then he asked for Paul Brown again, and this time knocked him out. "His claim to fame would be knocking out Joe Bugner in his very first fight," he says. "And I never looked back again until I fought Cooper. That was the turning point of my career."

Turning point, and sore point. By 1971, 'Ammerin 'Enry was nearing the end of the line as a boxer, though at thirty-seven he still held the British title. His thinning hair made him seem older than that, and he was the obvious sentimental favourite. (Even forty-year-old heavyweights now are hardly a novelty; George Foreman regained the title as a forty-five-year-old.) The British fans still loved him for dropping Cassius Clay back in 1963, and they especially loved him for his humble, cockney persona. It didn't matter that he had never been quite good enough to beat the best. Cooper was still a national hero, even as a loser, a role Frank Bruno would fill twenty years later.

And Bugner was the young upstart, bigger, stronger and not nearly so self-effacing. Neither then nor now was he willing to worship at Cooper's shrine. "The biggest claims of Cooper's career was that he put Ali on his backside with that lucky punch," Bugner says. "Ali put his face out and said, 'Hit me here, hit me here, hit me here,' and Cooper threw that lucky left hook. As far as his three Lonsdale Belts [awarded for the British championship], he fought the same people over and over again, so it was a boring affair anyway. He fought one guy four times, he fought another guy three times, and he fought another guy twice. I don't dislike Cooper. I just dislike the people who have put him on a pedestal that he doesn't deserve. As soon as he stepped out of his bracket and he started fighting Americans who were just about an inch higher than him as far as status is concerned, he got knocked out. Cooper's record is that he got stopped nine times. Knocked out and stopped. And if that's something that you boast about, then shit. I think they put him on a pedestal that I truly don't think he deserves. That's my opinion. I don't know him as a man. I don't want to know him as a man."

Their fifteen-round clash for the European, British and Commonwealth titles was, by all accounts, a very close fight, and there were certainly some in attendance who thought that Cooper deserved the decision, even factoring out the sentiment. But it was Bugner who got the referee's nod. "Cooper said to the world, in a very nice way, that he was going to knock me out. 'Joe is too young, he's too immature. He's got no ideas.' All nonsense talk. When the fight was over and they lifted my hand up—and the verdict was soundly blown out of proportion by the fans and by the media—I was never forgiven for that. I took out Old Henry." Not lost on Bugner was the fact that Cooper actually became *more* popular after the loss in retirement, and that Bugner himself became more despised. "The fact that Cooper put Ali down and the fact that I beat Cooper made him the most famous man in Britain," Bugner says. "Henry Cooper is still idolized by the British sports fans."

Bugner had actually come to understand the commercial potential of wearing the villain's black hat a couple of years before the Cooper fight. In 1969, while being hailed as a bright young heavyweight prospect, he flew to New York for an encounter with a man who very much understood the duality of the bad guy/good guy act. Muhammad Ali was in the midst of preparing for his comeback fight against Jerry Quarry following three forced years of inactivity. As a publicity stunt, the *Daily Mirror* tabloid offered Ali the princely sum of $10,000 just to spar with the new British heavyweight hope. Bugner flew to America for the first time, arrived in New York City and checked into his hotel. "It was a real fleabag, I'll tell you," he remembers. "We were in the hotel having breakfast, and I started to hear people talking, saying, 'Ali's here, Ali's here.' Being nineteen years old, I was petrified. Here was the great man coming in, and I'm actually going to confront him. Don't forget he's been my idol since I was a young fellow. He's seven years older than me, so there is that age difference. He comes into this restaurant, and he's got a whole heap of people with him. Ali draws flies like honey does—or should I say bees. And it was incredible. We're about thirty or forty feet apart. And he shouts across the room, 'You called me a nigger!' And I thought, oh my god. This place is full of black people. Waitresses, waiters. And they're all looking at me. I'm quivering. What the bloody hell am I going to do? What am I going to do? So he wanders across. And he's got that cheeky smile. And of course he's screaming, 'If you think you're gonna lay a glove on me, you'd better apologize.' And he gave me all this razzamatazz. I haven't said a word yet. My manager is nudging me and saying, 'Don't worry, he's only play-acting.' I said, 'Bullshit.'

"Ali saunters across. And he puts his big hand across my shoulder. Bang. He says, 'How ya doing, kid.' Big smile. He never stopped smiling. We sat down and we had breakfast together. I've never seen a man eat so much food. I said to him, 'How can you eat all this?' He said, 'You'll find out when I'm beating the crap out of you.'

"We finished, we got in the cars and we're heading down to the gym. He has got this little elevator to go upstairs into the gym. The elevator's got to be maybe five feet square. It's one of the smallest elevators I've ever seen. Ali's in one corner and I'm in the other. And we've got two British journos. Muhammad, as soon as journos are around, he starts firing. He's like this [throwing jabs]. He's this far from my nose. I thought to myself, maybe he's getting serious because we're getting this close to the sparring session or something. And I'm standing there. I was in the corner and I couldn't go any further. He was getting closer and closer and closer. The elevator ride seemed like it took an hour."

The sparring session took place in a gym owned by the legendary trainer Gil Clancy. The fighters went six rounds in front of an audience of reporters, with Ali concerned as much with putting on a show as in putting in serious work for his upcoming fight. Bugner, though intimidated, held his own. "It was the greatest experience I ever had," he says. "Everyone was impressed with him and everyone was impressed with what I did."

Afterwards, Ali was asked what he thought about the kid. "Yeah, he's cool," Ali said. "He'll be good. But he'll never be a world champ as long as I'm around. Maybe after I retire."

Then Ali looked at himself in one of the dressing-room mirrors.

"Damn," he said, examining his reflection. "I've never had a white eye before."

It took awhile for the British writers to catch the joke.

Later, privately, Ali offered Bugner an enormously valuable piece of advice about how the boxing business worked. "I'm the bad guy in America," he said, drawing on his experience as the most famous draft resistor of all time. "They hate me. That's why they come to see me get bashed, to see me get beat up." Bugner recalls his reaction: "I thought about this and thought, hey, this is not a bad system. I said, hey, this is not bad for me."

After beating Henry Cooper, Bugner remembered Ali's words: "With that win, everybody from that moment on came to see me lose," he says. "And that filled the halls. That's what I wanted. I wanted to earn money. I didn't want to be a famous man with no money in the bank. I wanted to be a famous man with a lot of money in the bank. From that moment on, every time I fought, I would imagine sixty to seventy per cent of the people came to see me get beat, and it never happened."

Following the Cooper fight, Bugner had a modestly successful run in the ring, defending his European title twice against future Ali opponents Jurgen Blin and Rudi Lubbers, while losing a decision to fringe contender Larry Middleton. The Lubbers fight, in January 1973, landed him a non-title bout with Ali, who was then in the process of fighting his way back after losing his titanic first encounter with Joe Frazier in 1971. (Six days after Bugner's bout with Lubbers, Frazier had shockingly lost the world title to George Foreman in Kingston, Jamaica.) The Ali–Bugner fight would be held at Caesars Palace in Las Vegas, on Valentine's Day. The winner was supposed to be guaranteed a shot at the world championship. Both men appeared first at a pre-fight press conference in Chicago. "He was brilliant," Bugner remembers. "As soon as he saw me, he started hollering, 'Where's that honky? I'm going to kick his ass.' I learned a wonderful thing from him. He said, 'Bugner, remember one thing. It don't matter how good you are. If you can't put bums in the seats, you aren't worth nothing.' I thought about that. And I thought, geez, you know, he's right. I kept watching his antics. I kept watching his tactics. And I understood."

It was certainly not vintage Muhammad Ali. In his very next fight, he would suffer a stunning upset loss to Ken Norton, and have his jaw broken. Still, for Bugner, this Ali was plenty intimidating enough. "When you're sparring with Ali, it's one feeling," Bugner says. "When you're actually fighting him, it becomes a bit of a terror. Because you never quite know from this to that. We're talking about business here now. Ali and I on the many occasions when we did meet, he said, 'Joe, I look at things not personal, it's always business. I do this because it's business. If people think I do this because I love this, they're crazy. I do this because I'm great, I'm the best, I am the greatest. It's nothing personal.' A lot of the stuff that Ali used to say in his heyday, when he was out of the limelight, he was a very sensible, very straight-shooting guy. He said, 'Whatever happens, boxing is like business.' And that's how I looked at it. But at the same time, I was nervous. Was I going to be able to perform? Was I going to be able to live up to that standard?

"The bell goes, first round. He starts dancing. He throws a right hand. Boom. Fifteen stitches. I've got a great cut man in Harry Gibbs—he was Henry Cooper's former cut man. He seals it. No one believes that he can do this. He seals it. The fight goes the full twelve rounds. Nobody could believe this. The eighth round—that was one of my best rounds. Ali's coming towards me. He throws this beautiful right, and as it was coming I hit him with a right hand. It stunned him. He says, 'Damn, good punch.' He grabs hold of me. Even during the fight we were able to converse.

"The fight did go the distance, and of course they lifted his hand up. I honestly thought I'd beat him.

But that's neither here nor there. I tell you what it did mean. It meant more money in the bank. Because it proved to the world that here was this kid coming out of Europe—because Americans had this horrible attitude saying that all Brits were horizontal heavyweights. Up until that point, every British fighter was laid out. Brian London. Henry Cooper. Richard Dunn. You name 'em, they were laid out. Other than Tommy Farr, the rest were all laid out. Farr was the only one that actually stood up to a world champion.

"From that moment on, the English press were more on my side."

By surviving against Ali, Bugner earned another big payday against Joe Frazier in his next fight, a bout staged at Earls Court in London. Again, he managed to complete the twelve-round distance in a losing effort, winning credit for bravery after getting up from a knockdown, and finished the fight with one of his eyes swollen nearly shut. (It was Frazier's first fight back after being knocked out by Foreman.) Following those consecutive losses, Bugner embarked on what was, in hindsight, the best stretch of his career. He beat Mac Foster in 1973, had two more wins in 1974, and then in 1975 put together a string of five victories, including knockouts of Jose Luis Garcia and Jimmy Ellis. Thirteen days before the Ellis fight, Ali had miraculously reclaimed the world heavyweight championship with his win over Foreman in Kinshasa, Zaire. He followed that with relatively easy defences over Chuck Wepner and Ron Lyle, but the big fight on the horizon would be a third fight with Frazier, what would become known as the Thrilla in Manila.

They actually announced the signing of that bout just before Ali met Bugner in a rematch, this time for the title, and this time in Kuala Lumpur, Malaysia. Rather obvious, then, was the fact that Bugner wasn't perceived as much of a threat. "Ali was running out of opponents," Bugner acknowledges. "So they said, 'Shit, let's give this kid from Britain another crack.'" He chose not to take the slight personally and began to prepare for what would be his one shot at a world championship. Arriving in the strange land, though, he soon had other matters on his mind. "That was a pretty scary affair for me," he remembers. "There was a lot of shit going around about an assassination—of me. When we arrived in Malaysia, there were some radical Muslims coming through at that time. The word came around to us in the camp that if Joe Bugner thinks he's going to beat Ali, he will be assassinated. The Muslims would not put up with this.

"This put the whole government in a defence mode. They sealed off the hotel we were staying in. They had security guards everywhere, army everywhere. It was just bloody pathetic. Ali was in the Hilton hotel, and I'm in a bloody prison." Bugner was forced to do his roadwork at the local racetrack because that was the only place the security forces would be able to keep an eye on him.

The night of the fight, there were forty-five thousand fans in the outdoor stadium, joined by fifteen hundred Malaysian troops. "When you see that kind of protection around you," Bugner says, "there's got to be a reason." As it turned out, though, the only casualty of the night was Bugner's reputation. The fight is remembered as one of the dullest of Ali's career, largely because Bugner refused to mount any kind of offence. "The fight was much closer than the American commentators stated," Bugner claims. "At the end of the day, the Americans were very unkind in some of their comments. But if they looked at the fight now, and they listened to the imbecilic, stupid—and you can quote me on this, by the way—the imbecilic, stupid things they were saying during the fight, I think their heads were up their asses. They don't know boxing from their asses, they really don't. Joe Frazier is no lover of Muhammad Ali, I can tell you that now. He was the only one that was fair in his judgment as far as I was concerned. He said I wasn't doing enough work to get this fight, and I wasn't trying hard enough. That's bullshit. It was 118 degrees and 100 per cent humidity. You know perfectly why you're there: because it was planned. Here was a kid out of England that had no idea how to deal with this weather. It was pre-planned. It was political. It very tactical. So anyway, Ali won again on points."

Though he thought he'd learned all he needed to know about playing the press from watching Ali, Bugner would learn another, painful lesson, immediately after the fight. "I'm in my hotel room, lying in bed, totally bagged, literally totally out of it. I get a call a couple of hours later, Joe, come down, we've got the whole of the British press. They just want to see how you're feeling, mate.' Like an idiot, I did.

"They asked me to stand in the swimming pool and then handed me a glass of champagne. You know what they had in the paper the next day? 'Joe Bugner is so fresh and refreshed and smiling away. He didn't even try winning the world title. Da, da, da, da, da.' I thought, you fucking mongrels. I was so upset. I thought to myself, this is wrong. We were back in 1971 again. I thought, screw this, and I moved to Los Angeles.

"[The English press] just couldn't help themselves. They'd never had it so good. I was their best export. And they blew it. But we're still friends. And I still support the country in many ways."

In 1975, Bugner bought a house in California, where he married his second wife, Marlene, and remained for ten years, occasionally commuting back and forth to England when business required. He won back the British, Commonwealth and European titles by knocking out Richard Dunn in one round at Wembley Arena in 1976, lost a decision to Ron Lyle the next year and slowly faded out of the heavyweight picture. Like many boxers before him, he also tried to break into the movies and with his strongman physique managed to land a number of small roles in spaghetti westerns, fantasy epics and the like. In 1985, long retired from boxing, and at a bit of a career dead end, he and Marlene packed up and moved to her homeland, Australia, where Bugner went about the business of reinventing himself once more.

"Strangely enough it didn't take a lot to do," he says. "When I arrived over here in '85, these people took to me instantly. Not because I was any different from when I was in England; the only thing was that

I was as straight as I was, and they like straight-talking people here. They don't like bullshit. And there's no distinction between what school you went to and what school I went to. When you talk to John Howard, the current prime minister of our country, he looks at you like you're a human being. Whereas in England, if you're from the wrong school, they say, 'Piss off, you're not invited.' And that's true. We don't have class distinction here. We have distinction as far as how much money you've got. I may drive a Jaguar and you may drive a Ford. But that's where it ends. We still go into the same pub and have a drink. Eighteen months after I arrived here, I was an Australian citizen."

Bugner says that he had to be talked into his first boxing comeback, in 1986, but whatever the case, the rationale wasn't tough to decipher. He still looked to be in decent shape. George Foreman, a year older than Bugner, was embarking on his own comeback in America, and while it was originally ridiculed, it looked like it was going to be a money-maker. And Bugner needed the dough because a history of old tax problems awaited him back in England. His first three fights were against a couple of faded fringe contenders, James "Quick" Tillis and David Bey, and against an even more seriously faded former world champion, Greg Page. All of them were "names" though, and all of them Bugner dispatched with relative ease. "I whipped all three of them," he says. The Australians, who loved boxing but who hadn't produced a serious heavyweight contender since Fitzsimmons, seemed to enjoy the show, and a few of them even bought into the notion that Bugner might have a legitimate shot at winning a title.

Promotional logic dictated that it was time to cash in, time to secure a big payday. Though there was talk that the sensational young heavyweight champ of the time, Mike Tyson, might travel to Australia for what figured to be an easy defence, that soon proved to be a pipe dream. Instead, Bugner opted to make a long, not at all sentimental, journey home to England. He had taken to heart Ali's advice that playing the bad guy could be nearly as lucrative as playing the hero. Given the bad blood going all the way back to the Cooper fight, Bugner knew he wouldn't exactly be welcomed with open arms; but it was his choice of opponent that ensured that he'd be cast in the villain's role. Frank Bruno, an amiable fellow with a bodybuilder's physique and a glass jaw, had perfectly inherited the Cooper legacy, good enough to beat some decent heavyweights, but never good enough to beat the best. The English loved him, they loved his goofy sense of humour and they especially loved his humility. By contrast, Bugner got off the plane talking, boasting and ruffling feathers, and never, ever stopped. When the two stepped into a ring erected on the pitch at White Hart Lane stadium, home ground of the Tottenham Hotspur football club, there were 37,000 fans in attendance, and their loyalty was clear. "Picture this," Bugner says. "Thirty seven thousand people, and I reckon I had 36,990 people hating me. I've got to tell you it was bloody awful, mate. It was bloody awful."

The fight was awful as well, one-sided in Bruno's favour before it was stopped in the eighth round.

Bugner, not surprisingly, claims there were extenuating circumstances. "The fight was the most disgraceful affair ever in a boxing ring," he says. "I was rabbit-punched eight or ten times in the back of the head. Even in the eighth round when I was on the ropes he was doing it. There's no doubt in my mind that the whole affair was rigged. It was a set-up. They only wanted one winner and that was Frank Bruno." It wasn't all bad for Bugner, though: He walked away from the fight and back into retirement with a purse of close to a million pounds.

As it turned out, that wasn't nearly enough. "I should never be let near money again," Bugner would later admit. A series of bad investments bankrupted him. The most disastrous, a winery that Joe and Marlene bought in Australia's famous Hunter Valley, went bust during the recession of 1989, costing them two million dollars. Naturally, the idea of a comeback again crossed his mind, especially since Foreman had managed to miraculously win back the heavyweight championship in 1994, and former champion Larry Holmes was still plugging away. In 1995, eight years after he'd last stepped into the ring, Bugner returned, in front of a cheering, supportive crowd on Australia's Gold Coast, to win a twelve-round decision over an unremarkable though obviously much younger fighter named Vince Cervi and claim the Australian heavyweight championship. Bugner showed decent hand speed, though not much power, and afterwards clamoured for a geezers' showdown with Foreman. "I'm broke," he acknowledged, "and I would like just one big fight to win a million so that Marlene and I can live the lifestyle to which we had become accustomed." He proposed that he and Foreman ought to meet in a battle of ancients, to be staged in the shadow of Ayers Rock in Australia's Northern Territory. "The oldest rock in the world. What better place could there be? Don't worry about a crowd. All you need is a couple of television cameras and a pay TV channel and you've got an audience of a hundred million."

That big score never came close to materializing. Instead, in 1996 Bugner found himself far from home in Europe, meeting an English fighter named Scott Welch for the Commonwealth Championship, and taking a nasty beating. He suffered a broken rib in the second round, and was down and nearly out when the fight was stopped, twelve seconds before the end of the sixth round—his thirteenth loss in eighty-three fights. "I really truly don't like this business," Bugner said after the fight. "I can tell you that now because it's over. I guarantee my name will never be associated with boxing again. I've hated it since I was seventeen. I don't like associating with boxing people. They're crude. Very ruthless. They're only interested in one thing: big bucks. . . . It's back to a civilized life for me. Boxing is a joke these days. I'd like to think the general public cannot be fooled by the imbeciles who surround the fighters. I have achieved a lot. Okay, I failed to fight for the world title at the age of forty-six. Big deal. But I can walk away and not look back."

He looked at Marlene. "I swear it darling," he said.

"At last," she answered.

Well, not quite. In 1998, he was back, against former heavyweight champ James "Bonecrusher" Smith, who at age forty-five was three years younger than Bugner. Smith hurt him with a right hand in the first round, but Bugner managed to hold on. Smith then conveniently quit after the first three minutes, claiming that he'd dislocated his shoulder. In June of 1999, just a little more than a year before the Sydney Olympics, Bugner took on journeyman Levi Billups and gained the victory when Billups was disqualified in the ninth round for throwing low blows.

Surely that really was it. Before rushing back to ringside to resume his Olympic television duties—a performance that was panned by the Australian sports press—Bugner claimed that he wouldn't fight again, or at least that he wouldn't unless someone offered him very serious money. "I refuse to live on my laurels," he says. "I think boxing was one part of my life, and now I've gone on to another." He and Marlene live comfortably in a place called Paradise. He was just about to start filming a television series, called the *Lost World,* and had just wrapped up a movie with a well-known action-film star, who will, for obvious, legal reasons, remain nameless here. "I worked with that little turd," Bugner says with characteristic diplomacy. "Geez, what a turkey that was. He had more dust up his nose than I have up my. . . ."

Maybe he'd take a shot at politics one of these days, Bugner suggests. And there is also the meat pie. Ubiquitous in Australia, unpalatable to outsiders, a version of the favourite national snack food has just come onto the market, dubbed the Aussie Joe Heavyweight Meat Pie.

"And do you know the greatest thing about it? If something should happen to me, my name will live on. It's a bit like Colonel Sanders and Kentucky Fried Chicken. What a bloody great thing that is."

KEN NORTON

Canastota, New York

HE CLIMBS THE STAIRS slowly, an old man's struggle, as though every step conquered represents a small victory, and then carefully, gingerly takes a seat. For the fans hoping to grab an autograph at the International Boxing Hall of Fame, recognition takes a second. Still, beneath a baseball cap, Ken Norton's strong, handsome features become familiar, and despite the stiff, awkward movements, there are hints of that once near-perfect physique. He was such a specimen that after boxing, it looked for a while as though he might have a career in the movies, or in broadcasting. (He made a handful of films, most notably the campy plantation potboiler *Mandingo*.) Norton still talks about getting back into that line of work, though it's hard to imagine, since his voice is slow and tentative and raspy, each word, each thought, emerging as though it were the product of careful deliberation.

Those who don't know better tend to assume he must be simply another casualty of a savage sport, the embodiment of one more cautionary tale. It is no small irony that boxing had nothing to do with it, that Norton surfaced after more than a decade spent among the top contenders in the heavyweight division—and briefly, as a world champion, though with an asterisk appended—sound of mind and body. A final, devastating knockout loss to Gerry Cooney in 1981 told him it was time to quit, and unlike many of his peers, he resisted the siren song of a late-life, greed-driven comeback.

But while driving alone on the night of February 23, 1986, in Los Angeles, Norton was involved in a single-car accident that will forever remain mysterious, since only he witnessed what happened and those memories were immediately stripped away. He was left with a broken leg and jaw, a fractured skull and serious brain injuries. "I was paralyzed for a year and a half on my right side," Norton says. "My speech . . . I knew what I was saying but no one else did. It was quite awhile before it became audible again. Now it's not perfect, but it's better. I have to concentrate now and talk slower and try to articulate more. It doesn't matter what I do now, I can't forget the accident. Because there's something in my body—my voice, my walk—that lets me know that God gave me another chance.

"Since my car accident I've forgotten a lot of things," he says. Three years of memories before the accident and the first three years of his recovery were all but erased. "So now I figure I'm going to live for six years longer," he jokes. "I'm going to hang around for a long time." To a degree, over time, through the process of writing his autobiography, *Going the Distance,* studying his own life as though it were someone else's, Norton regained the ability to tell his story. The most remarkable part of it is that he is alive and functioning and coherent, when for so long it seemed he would never again be more than a shell of a man.

The fight fans wait patiently as he slowly signs autographs and then ask him, always, about one man.

Norton is as inextricably linked to Muhammad Ali as Joe Frazier is, the fighter who once employed Norton as a sparring partner. Their roles were vastly different though: While Frazier was The Other, the great contrast against whom Ali was so clearly measured and defined, Norton was the nemesis, the riddle never quite fully solved. Other opponents hit Ali harder, had greater boxing skills, were more aggressive—and Ali picked apart their styles and exploited their weaknesses, at least until he himself became too old, too limited, to do so. By any objective measure, Ken Norton was a very good—but not great—heavyweight, a decent boxer, a respectable puncher without overwhelming power and a fighter who had trouble with knockout artists like George Foreman and Earnie Shavers. Take away Ali, and his greatest moment came when he lost a very close match against Larry Holmes, who would go on to become the best heavyweight of his era.

With Ali, though, Norton was something else again: dogged, frustrating, dangerous, incapable of looking bad. It seemed like a fluke the first time, the memorable afternoon in San Diego when he broke Ali's jaw and registered one of the sport's greatest upsets in front of a disbelieving Howard Cosell and a nation of doubters. By the time they concluded their third and final fight, the last great bout ever staged at Yankee Stadium, it was clear that Norton's success was well-earned, and far less clear which one of them was the better man.

NORTON'S LIFE HISTORY IS atypical in a sport that draws so much of its talent from among the desperate. He grew up not in poverty, not in an inner-city ghetto, but with two loving parents in comfortable middle-class surroundings in the Midwestern town of Jacksonville, Illinois. His athletic abilities were obvious early, and he says that the acclaim he received from sport shielded him in large part from the pain of racism. In high school, guided by the coach who would become his mentor, Norton excelled in track and field, and football. He was offered scholarships to more than ninety colleges and universities, finally choosing to stay close to home, at Northeast Missouri State. Norton spent two years there and failed to live up to expectations, academically and athletically. He came home and joined the United States Marine Corps.

It was only in the service that he took up boxing, a late start by any standard. But he immediately showed a knack for the sport. By the time he left the Marines, Norton had been married and divorced, and had fathered a son—Ken Norton Jr., who would go on to become a great linebacker in the National Football League—of whom he was the single custodial parent and sole financial supporter. Though he intended to become a policeman, Norton was instead convinced to turn professional by a group of San Diego businessmen, who offered him the princely sum of $100, guaranteed, a week.

During the day, Norton worked on the assembly line at a Ford plant. At night he trained in the gym, eventually coming under the guidance of Eddie Futch, a trainer who had begun as a friend and sometime sparring partner of Joe Louis, and who would be closely associated with Frazier, among others. "His greatest strength was that he followed instructions," Futch told me when I spoke with him a few weeks before his death, in the fall of 2001. "He did what I told him to do." With Futch, Norton developed his distinctive style, using a cross-armed defence reminiscent of Archie Moore, and won his first sixteen fights before being knocked out by the Venezuelan Jose Luis Garcia. The truth is, there was very little in his early career to suggest that big things were on the horizon, and he was better known as Frazier's sparring partner than as a contender in his own right. "I used to have to bring Joe Frazier from Philadelphia to publicize Ken Norton's fights," Futch said. "If I tried to get ink with Ken Norton, no chance. I'd bring Joe and say, 'Just give us a hand here; talk up the Norton fight.'"

It was during those years of obscurity that Norton first encountered the man who would define his boxing career and change his life. One day while Norton was training, Muhammad Ali dropped in at what was then his home base, the Hoover Gym in Los Angeles. "Ali came by—being big, brave Ali—and challenged everybody in the gym," Norton remembers. "And some of the trainers said, 'Ken Norton's here. He's a heavyweight.' So he challenged me. At first, Eddie wasn't going to let me do it, because Ali wanted to make a fight out of it. Then he said, 'What the heck,' and let me box with him; I think it was two rounds. And it was kind of even. That, in my mind, lifted me up quite a bit. I became a better fighter from that point on."

Futch told Norton after the sparring session that he had exactly the style to beat Ali. Gradually, he began to work on the tactics that would give him that chance. "I said, 'Now, when he jabs, you jab with him,'" Futch said. "His right hand is out of position and yours is where it should be. You will catch his jab and he will catch your jab on the face. I said, 'Now, he's done that all his life, and so he'll continue to do it.' That's a habit that he had gotten away with. He thought there was no reason to change it boxing Ken Norton. But I saw that if he couldn't change it, he was going to get hit. When that happens—you're two heavyweights and you start in the centre of the ring. When you hit him with your jab because his right is out of position, he's going to step back and jab again, and you're going to do it again. That was three jabs, he's against the ropes. Now when he hits the ropes, don't do what the other fighters do. Instead of going for his head—because what he'll do is lean back and make you miss—I want you to go to the body with hard body shots with both hands until he brings his hands down to protect himself against your body attack. And then you'll go to the head."

Ali and Norton were eventually matched on March 31, 1973, the fight staged in Norton's adopted home town of San Diego. Not that the boxing public was exactly demanding the bout. Ali had been spinning his wheels since his 1971 loss to Frazier in their first fight and was immediately coming off a boring, twelve-round win over passive Joe Bugner in Las Vegas. Meanwhile, Frazier, who was on the verge of signing for a rematch with Ali, had just been destroyed by George Foreman in Jamaica, and it seemed clear the torch had been passed to a new, huge, dominant young heavyweight champion.

Norton had beaten a collection of the usual opponents, his biggest wins coming over a couple of California rivals, Henry Clark and Jack O'Halloran. His role was to provide Ali with a tune-up, to keep him busy and keep him interested until something more important came along. For the first time in six years, an Ali fight would be shown not on closed circuit, but on network television, with Cosell calling the bout live for ABC. Desperate for an angle to sell tickets, the promoters decided to try and turn the fight into a battle between Ali the draft evader and Norton the ex-Marine. Though Ali had long since won his fight in the Supreme Court and his stand was widely supported, the times hadn't really changed much: The war in Vietnam continued, and Richard Nixon had just been re-elected in a landslide victory over the Democrats' anti-war candidate, George McGovern.

The former serviceman, though, was reluctant to play the part he was assigned, preferring to remain above the fray, and privately respecting Ali for the choice he'd made. "It took a heck of a man to want to give his career up for his beliefs," Norton says. "He wasn't going to go into the army. He was going to go to jail instead to prove his point, because he believed that much in it. That takes a lot for a man to give up that much for what you believe in. Ali, as people found out later, was validated in not going. For me at that time, I didn't go in pro or con. It was a man's business. I didn't say anything. So I didn't bite on that. I didn't get behind that and try and use that as motivation in the first fight. I just forgot it."

The time he'd spent around Frazier had taught Norton about more than simply what needed to be done in the ring. He'd watched Ali's pre-fight act, listened to the boasts, the insults, the nicknames, and saw how it ate away at Frazier. He wouldn't let that happen. "I think the main thing is that I didn't fall for all his talk," he says. "With Frazier and with Foreman, he beat them mentally a lot. When Foreman couldn't stop him with all of those big shots in the early rounds, and Ali was talking to him, it took his edge away. With Joe, he had Joe so mad, Joe was trying to kill him and loading up on everything. You do that and you miss. It takes twice as much out of you. And Ali is just a genius at manipulating people. Ali took advantage of Joe's lack of education. He took advantage of his knowledge of certain things. He took advantage of Joe period. Ali was a quick man. He knew what bothered Joe. What made him angry. So he picked at that and picked at that until Joe was just so furious that, by the time the fight came, he just wanted to kill Ali—and it worked in Ali's favour. And so Ali used it for all three fights. Ali, to me, was not a vindictive man. He was not a man who would say those things and then harp on them and keep doing them. After the fight was over, he forgot the whole thing and moved on. Joe, in his head, it just stuck, all of the things that Ali said. If Ali had not said them at that time, the gate would not have been that big. They would not have made as much money.

"Me, I didn't fall for the okey-doke. Because I knew what he was trying to do, and I was so into myself at that time, at being the best I could be for that fight, I didn't listen to anything except Eddie Futch."

The fact is, there was nothing much Ali could say or do that would build public interest for the fight. It was universally perceived as a gross mismatch. "No one thought that he had a possible chance," Futch said. "Howard Cosell went on the air from San Diego the night before the fight. He didn't know me either. He said, 'Whoever that man is who put that boy in with Muhammad Ali ought to have his licence picked up.'"

And then the bell rang.

LATER, IN LIGHT OF THE evidence accumulated over thirty-nine rounds of boxing, it would come to seem like a moot point, though at the time, the debate raged on and on: When had Muhammad Ali's jaw been broken? Was it a single, lucky punch that had allowed Ken Norton to beat him? Did the injury explain the ex-champion's strangely lethargic performance? Was he simply washed up at age thirty-one, or had he, in fact, demonstrated his own greatness, his own courage, by fighting most of a long, tough bout with a condition that would have forced most mere mortals to quit? In the confusion following Norton's unanimous-decision victory, in the desperate attempts to explain away the second loss of Ali's professional career, the more palatable explanation certainly seemed to be that the break had occurred early. Ali, and those who worked his corner, would forever claim that a right hand in the second round has shattered his jaw, and that against everyone's better judgment, he fought on.

In the Norton camp, they felt differently, and perhaps a bit defensive, having their great victory diminished by the suggestion that it couldn't possibly have been what it seemed.

"Ali says it happened in the first or second round," Norton says today. "I say it was in the last round. Because when you have an inch-and-a-half break in the jaw and someone is popping you upside the jaw as much as I hit Ali, with that pain, the mind would take over and shut down, I think."

"It happened in the seventh round," Futch says. "Ali got hit by so many right hands, if his jaw had been broken earlier than that, he would have been spitting out splinters of bone. But people believe what they want to believe."

Lost in the confusion was the fact that Norton entered the ring with a kind of serene confidence that was almost unimaginable, given the challenge he was facing, given his own lack of big-fight experience. "That night I could have beaten Godzilla," he says. "I was that sure of myself. And in that kind of shape, I could have fought for fifty rounds, easy. I was just so cocky at that point. I knew before the bell rang, in my head and in my camp, that I was going to win the fight. There was no negativity. There was nobody in my camp who said *maybe*. There were no maybes. It was *you will win*."

Futch's analysis of the two fighters' styles proved to be prescient. Whenever the break occurred, the fact was that Ali had trouble hitting Norton, that he couldn't back him up, that Norton was free to walk in, jab and follow with the right hand. The young Ali, with his blinding hand and foot speed, might have had an easier night. But this Ali, who couldn't dance for twelve or fifteen rounds, was more vulnerable than most had imagined—not just against a great fighter like Frazier, but against a strong, awkward and, to some degree, limited foe. "During the reading of the scorecards, I had a little doubt," Norton admits. "I wasn't thinking, well I lost. But I was on edge. When they mentioned that I won the last card, I was elated. I was like a newborn baby. I didn't sleep for two days.

"After the decision was announced, I went right to Howard Cosell and said, 'What do you say now, Howard?' I made a point to walk directly to him and say that. And still, Howard and I became very good friends. Howard, myself and his wife became very good friends."

Norton's life changed in that instant. For his last fight before Ali, his purse had been $300. But "the bank doors opened," he explains. "The bank doors opened when I became known around the world as one of the men to defeat Ali. Ali was the best-known figure in the world at that time. You defeated him, and your name rang throughout the world. Mentally it kept me up high and floating. If you're high mentally, you go in the gym, you work hard and you do things that you wouldn't ordinarily do. It kept me in a high place for quite a while."

The day after the fight, there was a press conference in San Diego for the new heavyweight contender. "All of San Diego was excited now," Futch remembered, "all of the sportswriters who didn't give Norton a chance. So all these people who didn't believe in Norton, who wouldn't give him a chance, they were there. A number of them were on the dais to speak. I wanted to be last. I said, 'Make me last.' And when my turn came to get up and make my speech, I looked into a lot of faces around that table. And when I opened my mouth to speak, I said, 'Oh ye of little faith.' And that's all I said. That was it. I got a lot of good feeling from that. I didn't have to go on and on. Because everybody knew what I was talking about."

OF COURSE THERE HAD TO be a rematch, and for Ali the sooner or better, since he desperately needed to convince the public that what they'd witnessed was merely an aberration, that he still had enough left to challenge Frazier again, and perhaps even to take on Foreman. From Norton's point of view, a second date with Ali would represent by far his largest payday, and brimming with confidence, he had little to lose when they met again, six months later, this time in Los Angeles. "I prepared the same way," he says. "The only difference was that for the first fight I weighed about 210. I thought that if I went down in weight, I'd be quicker. I went down to about 201 pounds. And I was weaker. The last part of the fight, I tired out." In fact, the fight was dead even going into the last round, which Ali pulled out to claim a unanimous decision. But if, in the public mind, the second fight served as Ali's redemption, proof that he wasn't quite done yet, it equally confirmed the value of Norton's performance the first time around. While Ali would move on to his second fight with Frazier, Norton was now firmly ensconced among the ranks of top heavyweights, in line for a shot at Foreman's title.

"I know that conditioning was probably the difference in the [second fight]," Norton says. "But then again, I think that the fight could have gone either way. All three fights could have. . . ." Then he stops to correct himself. "No, the first two could have. The last fight, I know I won."

Many, many miles would be travelled, though, between the second Ali–Norton fight in September 1973 and the third, in September 1976. Norton went straight into a title matchup against Foreman in Caracas, Venezuela, which proved something else about his awkward style: He couldn't do anything against a big puncher strong enough to make him move backwards (a point that would later be reinforced by Earnie Shavers and Gerry Cooney, both of whom scored devastating early knockouts over Norton). Foreman literally shoved Norton off balance and then let his heaviest shots fly, knocking him out in the second round. It was that result that convinced the world that Ali, who had struggled so desperately against Norton, had no chance against Foreman.

Ali bounced back to beat Frazier in their rather dull second fight and then miraculously out-thought and, in the end, out-fought Foreman in Zaire. In 1975, he mixed the sublime and the ridiculous, bracketing the Thrilla in Manila with stinkers against Chuck Wepner, Jean-Pierre Coopman and, most embarrassingly, the Japanese wrestler Antonio Inoki. Most telling, though, was that in the fights following his third bout with Frazier, Ali's skills seemed to have diminished alarmingly. Meanwhile Norton, who had lost trainer Eddie Futch along the way due to a dispute with his manager, had bounced back with seven knockout wins in a row, including victories over Jerry Quarry and the fighter who had beaten him years before, Jose Luis Garcia. Norton, by virtue of his relatively late start in boxing, seemed a young thirty-one in 1976, while Ali seemed an old, tired thirty-four. Though Ali was installed as a betting favourite for their title fight at Yankee Stadium, many in the boxing world felt sure Norton would have the upper hand.

He did, decisively, during the early rounds of the fight, pushing Ali, landing better, cleaner punches, making Ali cover, and catching little in return. Ali rallied late, and Norton seemed, especially in the last round, to be convinced that he had the decision in the bag. At the time, many agreed with him, and watching the fight now, it's still hard to find enough rounds that justify giving the decision to Ali. To this day, Norton tries to understand what happened, to find an explanation for his loss. "I was crushed," he says. "It was the only time that I've cried since I've been over about eight years old. It was just crushing to me. I knew I had won the fight. He knew I won the fight. The judges knew I won the fight. But yet, they gave it to him.

"Boxing in those days went as Ali went. If Ali had lost that fight, boxing would have took a big turn. And they knew. Boxing *was* Ali then, so he won. And you notice that he came back and we were supposed to fight again. And he came back and lost to Leon Spinks on purpose, then came back and beat Spinks. So boxing stayed there."

"He won the third fight," Futch says. "But being where he was, and not having somebody to make it understood . . . I wouldn't have gone to New York, because the people that controlled boxing, they were in charge that night too."

AFTER LOSING HIS THIRD fight against Muhammad Ali, Norton kept on fighting, but he acknowledges that he didn't really try as hard again. In terms of human nature, it shouldn't come as any surprise, but given the way athletes talk about themselves, it's a startling admission. "I never did train the same," he says. "I never trained the same, I never fought the same, I never sacrificed any more. I did whatever I wanted to do. When I wanted to go out and party, I'd party. When I wanted to drink, I'd drink. When I wanted to stay up late in camp, I stayed up late. When I wanted to go party in Palm Springs during camp, I'd party and then come back. And you can't burn both ends of the candle. I just fell apart."

That said, most fight fans still remember Norton's 1978 fight against Larry Holmes as the most thrilling performance of his career, and as one of the most exciting heavyweight fights of the era. Despite his decreased intensity, Norton had bounced back from his loss to Ali by winning three fights in a row, including a first-round knockout of the rising prospect Duane Bobick and a fifteen-round decision win over tough Jimmy Young. That last fight would give Norton a world championship, at least on paper; as the number-one contender, he was awarded the World Boxing Council title when Leon Spinks chose an immediate rematch with Ali over a mandatory defence against Norton. The belt would immediately be put on the line against Holmes, Ali's long-time sparring partner, who was undefeated though also underrated, a great boxer who relied on a quick left jab and a deceptively powerful right hand.

"I could have been a little better against Holmes," Norton says. "I did not train for him the same as I trained for Ali. I didn't sacrifice. I went to Palm Springs and partied. Mentally, I wasn't into it as much. Number one, I didn't have the respect for Larry that I had for Ali at the time. But I still think, without Don King, I won that fight. Don King won the fight for Holmes. They said Larry won by one point. You don't beat a champion by one point. You beat him decisively, or you don't get it."

For Norton, the Holmes fight was the real end of the line. He was crushed in one round by Shavers, held to a draw by journeyman Scott LeDoux and, finally, was kayoed by rising star Gerry Cooney and decided to call it a career.

"I was going to go into movies," Norton says, "or maybe commentating for boxing. I thought that I carried myself in such a way that other doors would open, that I would take advantage of it. I believe that during my career, I never downplayed anyone. And if you treat people correctly, they'll come back."

THE YEARS IMMEDIATELY before and after the accident remain a blur, fragments of memory that don't necessarily connect, weeks and months compressed into a few flickering images. "I can't say a lot because I don't remember anything for four or five years," Norton says. "But I know that I was told that when I was in my house, I had the nurse's aide put me by my steps so that I could stare at the steps. The only reason I can think of why I would have her do that is because I was saying to myself that someday I would walk up those steps. I started walking and getting about a lot sooner than what they thought. One day I left the house, when I first started walking, and I walked about six miles from the house and got lost. I was gone all afternoon, and finally I came back. I didn't tell them where I'd been because I had no memory. At that time in my life I had no memory.

"I don't—I can't—really put the pieces back together. There are some things I remember from the hospital that come in and out, when I'm laying there thinking at night. But as far as remembering those years that have passed, I don't. I think that about four or five years afterwards, I started to remember things, and I would do things to make my memory better. I'd hide something then write it down, and then put the paper up in the drawer. About an hour later, I'd try to think where I put it. At first I couldn't find them. I had to look in the drawer with the paper. But eventually I started finding the articles. It was just a thing of retraining myself and my memory."

One vague memory that did return was of a man, standing by his bedside in hospital in the early days of his recuperation, smiling, saying nothing, performing a series of simple magic tricks. Muhammad Ali had come to visit.

Today, Norton is involved in promoting his autobiography, and in the formation of an automobile-racing team that will carry his name. He hopes, still, to get back on television, and into the movies, when his voice improves sufficiently, when his memory allows him to remember lines.

"The doctors said that I wouldn't walk again, I wouldn't talk audibly again. My memory was gone. But it's a thing where I was blessed. God never gave me the memory back, but then again, he gave me the tools to work on getting that memory back and make it stay there."

GEORGE FOREMAN

Houston, Texas

EVERYONE WHO KNOWS even the bare-bones story of Muhammad Ali's life and career also knows those moments when a twist of fate might have changed it all. What if Cassius Clay's glove hadn't split after Henry Cooper landed the perfect left hook that knocked him down in their first fight? (For that matter, what if Angelo Dundee hadn't helped the tear along between rounds, delaying matters long enough for Clay to clear his head?) What if, when blinded by something on Sonny Liston's gloves during their first go round in Miami, Clay hadn't recovered his sight in time to avoid a knockout punch? What if he had convinced Dundee to let him quit? What if Liston hadn't taken that apparent dive in their second fight in Lewiston?

What if Ali had never been reclassified for the draft, and Vietnam had never become an issue? What if he'd lost his court battle and gone to jail, never returning to the ring? What if, after the fourteenth round of the Thrilla in Manila, Joe Frazier had been allowed to come out of his corner? Would Ali have had the strength and fortitude left to come out of his?

Each of those moments was essential to the legend, turning a very good prize fighter into something greater, something iconic.

There's one question that rarely gets asked, though, because the events as they transpired are now so deeply embedded in the most widely understood version of the Ali myth: What if George Foreman had beaten him in Zaire? Watch the Oscar-winning documentary *When We Were Kings,* or Michael Mann's film *Ali,* and you may very well be left with the impression that it was inevitable that Ali would outsmart him, out-psych him and turn Foreman's own strength against him. The cleverest fighter alive against that big, slow, expressionless punching robot: It was a mismatch from the start.

Except that at the time, Foreman could have won and, had straight logic prevailed, should have won. He was the young Sonny Liston, and Ali was past it, his legs and his speed nearly gone. With Ali lying on the ropes—crazily daring Foreman to throw the kind of shot that had launched Joe Frazier into midair, that had beaten Ken Norton senseless, that had landed on every other professional opponent who had stepped in front of him—one clean punch would have done it. Ali crumpled to the canvas, Foreman raising his arms in triumph, the African crowd stunned silent: That night, before the bell rang, it was the finish that nearly everyone imagined.

How do both men's stories unfold then?

Sitting in a back office at the George Foreman Community Center in Houston, the man with his name written above the door reacts to the question as though he's never considered it before. This place—the weight rooms, the boxing gym, the basketball courts, all just down the street from the tiny church where he preaches twice a week—is the product of Foreman's second career, the apparently quixotic ten-year return to the ring that eventually brought him all the way back to the heavyweight championship of the world. The image of big, fat, smiling George, the boxing senior citizen, had all but erased the memory of his first incarnation, at least until the movies came along.

But think about it. Foreman certainly seemed unbeatable then, too big, too strong, too powerful for the best heavyweights of his day. What if he'd stood back, taken a deep breath, understood Ali's rope-a-dope game, conserved his energy, measured his attack and made his own mark in history?

"When I look back on it, devastated at that time as I was from losing the fight, I'm just happy that I didn't win it," Foreman says. He is smiling that big, open pitchman's smile that makes you want to believe him. "Just happy that I didn't land that big shot and knock him out. Boy, am I happy about that. Because you could have changed everything then. The second chances. Even now, with Muhammad Ali being proclaimed The Greatest. Everything could have been messed up."

He laughs a big belly laugh.

"One shot could have changed all of that, and I'm so happy I didn't throw that shot."

But why, I ask him, since he would have been the beneficiary?

"It could have changed everything," he says once again. "It's harmony to me when I hear people say Muhammad Ali is the greatest. When they call him the greatest and he walks around and people give him standing ovations. And I'm thinking, he deserves it. He *deserves* it. Life is a rough journey with a lot of problems. A lot of things happen to you. If a person can leave with some applause, amen to them.

"I think of the Sonny Liston fight, maybe the Joe Frazier Thrilla in Manila, and the George Foreman fight—you take any pieces of that puzzle away and you don't crown him that.

"Then I get a second chance to come back because of the devastation with that fight. It forced me to just turn over every stone. What's wrong? I'm not supposed to lose. Something is wrong here. I couldn't figure that out. And eventually having a fight with Jimmy Young, trying to become the number-one contender, pushing myself to my limits just to go twelve rounds made me fall into the hands of God.

And if any one of those little things . . . it was that fragile, that one little thing could have messed the whole thing up. And my world could have been totally different. Muhammad Ali's world, Joe Frazier's. All of us. The world could have been different for us."

But if he'd beaten The Greatest, if he'd landed that one punch, couldn't George Foreman have been The Greatest?

"That's true," he says "I don't think the result was predestined. Muhammad Ali whipped me. He whipped me because he landed the right hand. He beat me because he was able to throw that right hand and clocked me."

Foreman pounds his own, huge right fist into the palm of his left hand, and the *smack* echoes across the room.

"That's why he won. But if I could take anything away and change anything . . . to hear someone say George Foreman is the greatest of all time would scare me to the point where I'm not interested in that. And I'm sure there is someone who would love to have that. I think Muhammad loves it. Because of the trials that he's going through, he should have that. I wouldn't want anyone else to be that, especially myself.

"The other day, I was watching the ESPN Classic Network. They were trying to put together who was the greatest puncher of all time. Can you believe they had Archie Moore, Joe Louis and myself? I'm not supposed to be in there tampering with anything like that. I got upset. When they proclaimed Joe Louis the best, I was happy about that. Joe Louis was the greatest fighter of all time, the greatest puncher of all time. You see how close you can come to messing things up? I liked winning and I liked what I accomplished, but to put my name in there, to mess with Joe Louis and Muhammad and Archie Moore and all these guys, I don't want anything to do with that."

Foreman had to lose so that others could win, and so that many years down the road he could win and be redeemed. Not a fighter's words, those. A preacher's words.

THE FIRST TIME MOST people noticed George Foreman was in Mexico City in 1968, as he was sending a message apparently at odds with the times. It was the year Robert Kennedy and Martin Luther King Jr. died, the year of the Chicago riots, of Richard Nixon's election. Ali was in exile for opposing the draft. And when they played "The Star-Spangled Banner" at the Olympic Games that summer, some black American athletes chose to stand on the medal podium with heads bowed, fists in the air, sporting a black glove. But after Foreman won the heavyweight gold in boxing, he pulled out a tiny American flag and walked around the ring waving it. He explained later that he wasn't trying to be the anti-Ali, or the anti-John Carlos—the American sprinter who was one of the protesters at those same Olympics—that he was simply acting as a proud citizen who had grown up desperately poor, who had found his way thanks to the government's Job Corps program, who was living the American dream. Most didn't see it that way, though. Those who had taken to the streets hated him for it. And for those who felt threatened by the anger and unrest around them, who never wanted a heavyweight champion who would refuse to serve his country, Foreman's gesture was profoundly comforting.

He turned professional and began pounding his way through the usual collection of opponents, his tremendous power obvious; but it was also obvious that he was raw and a bit awkward, that he could seem ponderous and slow. The knockouts kept coming, but the jury was out on whether or not Foreman was the next champion in waiting.

"I remember meeting Muhammad Ali after I won the gold medal in '68," he says. "Muhammad wasn't even boxing. I met him on a couple of occasions and I was really excited about it. The first time, though, I admit I expected more. I really did."

Ali walked into a gym where Foreman was training in Florida. "Hey man," he said, greeting the young fighter.

"I was happy to meet him," Foreman remembers. "He went downstairs and said, 'Wait here, I've got something to show you. I'm going to show you something that when you get to be champ you're going to have.' I thought, wow. He came back in with a briefcase. I thought, this guy's going to show me maybe a hundred thousand dollars in cash. And he opened the briefcase and there was a telephone in it. 'See, it's a briefcase telephone,' he said. It wasn't working. It wasn't hooked up. But the point of it is, he was like a kid. And that's what I can remember about him. I expected more of him.

"Later on, I was occupying a nice spot when Muhammad Ali made his re-entry into the sport [in 1970]. Came back with the Jerry Quarry fight in Atlanta. Boy, was he popular. And the crowds that would follow him. People would come out and they would dress up for the Atlanta fight. There were movie stars there. They were hugging him. They were happy. You get just incredible jealousy. Do you understand? You really are jealous, even when you become heavyweight champ of the world. I liked being heavyweight champion of the world. I was really something. And everybody was really on me with the money coming and everything. But that was still . . . they're not coming to you like Ali had been treated. So you think you hate the guy. But you're really extremely jealous of this guy. And I think that jealousy turns into a rage. An awful rage. You want to beat him. And you don't want to beat him because he's done something to you and you don't like him. You just want to beat him because you're jealous of him. If you really mash him down into the ground then they'll say, 'Uh-huh, that's my man. George is my man.' That was the thing with Ali and myself."

Of course, no one was thinking much about Foreman at that point. They were thinking about Ali finally stepping in against Joe Frazier. And once Frazier triumphed in their first fight in 1971, he was the one acknowledged as the best of the moment, as the true champion. Whether or not they loved Frazier, the fact was that many of the same people who had cheered Foreman's flag-waving still hated Ali and were thrilled to see him put in his place.

"I remember people walking up to me and talking about 'that no good Ali,'" Foreman says. "The police stopped me one time in Oakland, California, around the time Muhammad Ali was coming back. I really felt bad because the officer stopped me, but he didn't give me a ticket. He just said, 'George Foreman, what do you think of Ali coming back?' I said, 'Well, he should have got a lighter fight to start back with. Jerry Quarry is a good fighter.' The officer said, 'I hope [Quarry] kicks his *da da da da da.*' He went off into the cuss words. And other times I would go out to a place and they'd say, 'We're glad to have you here, George, but we wouldn't have that such-and-such Ali here.' I would feel bad because of the words they'd say about him—that he was a dog for what he did, that he didn't love the country. There were people who would say some terrible things about him. He would incite hate. And they'd go out to see his fights and scream, 'Get him, get him.' They were upset when he won. I remember that. Nobody was cheering him in Las Vegas, Nevada, when he beat Ron Lyle or when he beat Jerry Quarry again."

JOE FRAZIER SURE DIDN'T see Foreman coming. After beating Ali, he took a couple of easy fights, quick paydays, the kind of free ride to which every champion feels he is entitled. And then he decided, with a big-money rematch against Ali surely in the cards, to give a shot to the new kid, the one who'd won an Olympic gold medal just as he had. Foreman was big and slow, and Frazier must have figured he'd slip past that heavy Sonny Liston jab and crack him with a left hook, easy. "You've got to create that disbelief in order to get a title shot," Foreman says. "I got a title fight with Joe Frazier because he figured, 'He can't do it. You're just giving him a break.' Joe Frazier thought he was just doing me a favour. He really did." Styles make fights, they say, and as it turned out, Joe Frazier could fight George Foreman a hundred times, and a hundred times he'd get bounced off the canvas like a basketball, a victim of those long, powerful punches. "Down goes Frazier!" Howard Cosell hollered. "Down goes Frazier." Joe might feel these days like he didn't get his due for beating Ali, and he's right. But in part, the reason is that following the Fight of the Century, his title reign consisted of wins over non-entities Ron Stander and Terry Daniels, followed by an ignominious defeat.

All at once everyone looked to the expressionless, merciless giant who now held the title and figured this was the prototype of the perfect modern heavyweight. Foreman's two-round destruction of Norton in Caracas, Venezuela—the same Norton who had given Ali fits—was proof positive of the new order.

Foreman versus Ali? On the face of it, it seemed like a dangerous nostalgia exercise. Even if Ali ran, even if he danced, this wasn't 1966. He'd slow down eventually; he'd run, but he couldn't hide. Even Cosell, Ali's greatest booster, couldn't disguise his own dread. His pre-fight commentary carried the tone of a eulogy.

What happened in Zaire has been very well-documented, though it can't ever be fully explained. Foreman initially claimed after the strange knockout that he'd been poisoned, that they'd slipped something into his water, that it couldn't have been how it appeared. No one was listening much though. The result confirmed Ali's magic powers. The other guy, the "dope" in rope-a-dope, was hardly given a second thought.

When Foreman returned to boxing, for the memorable, multiple-knockdown war against Ron Lyle, for the less memorable night when he fought five stiffs, back to back, at Toronto's Maple Leaf Gardens, there was a slightly pathetic Primo Carnera air about him. And when he lost again, to the slick-boxing, light-punching Jimmy Young in San Juan, Puerto Rico, on March 17, 1977, it was the final evidence that you didn't need to out-punch him, but simply to outsmart him.

In the dressing room that night after the fight, Foreman had a vision. Heat prostration, his handlers figured. No, it was God speaking to him directly, Foreman said. He walked away from boxing without a second thought. He disappeared. He had seen the light.

DURING THE TEN YEARS that George Foreman was away from the sport, a story would surface now and then. The former heavyweight champion, nearly unrecognizable since he'd gained a massive amount of weight, was discovered preaching in tiny churches in Texas, or delivering impromptu sermons on the street. At first, he tried not to let on who he was, or at least who he had been. "I was preaching on street corners, and people didn't pay any attention," he says. "I shaved my face. No one knew me any more, this big guy. Finally, I started saying, 'Yes, I am George Foreman. I fought Muhammad Ali and Joe Frazier.' They said, 'What, you fought Ali?' The next thing I know I had crowds around me. And whenever they would leave I'd bring it up again. I found out that this was the best thing that ever happened to me. In my newfound faith and my evangelism, bringing up that name can wake up a sleeping guy. You know how people are when they hear a preacher. But if you say, 'Yeah, I fought Ali,' they'll stand up and I get their attention. I would get people to stop on a street corner. That's the most difficult thing in the world, when someone is heading somewhere. No one is on the street just to hear someone. They're on their way, or they're getting ready for a bus. I could make them stop and wait for another bus with my preaching.

"There's a front door to the world and a back door to the world. The front door had been heavyweight champ of the world. The back door is that preacher, that evangelist. During the ten years that I was away from boxing, I'd be invited to places like Africa—Zaire. I went back there, to Kinshasa, to preach. And that arena was filled with people, more people than with the boxing match. And they heard me preach and give my testimony. None of the boxing people even knew I was there."

It was one thing to admit that he'd fought Ali, though, and another to acknowledge what had really happened that night. For years, Foreman clung to his conspiracy theories. Then, around the time Ali was meeting Leon Spinks in their rematch in New Orleans, a sportswriter made the short trek to Marshall, Texas, where Foreman was living, planning to write another one of those whatever-became-of stories.

"He did an interview," Foreman remembers. "And he asked me, 'What happened in that fight in Zaire?' I said, 'You know what, I lost. I got beat fair and square. Muhammad Ali knocked me out.' Then I went on to tell him what I was doing. He was looking for that old story that I got cheated. I said, 'I really lost. I lost the fight.' For the first time, I said it. I said, 'I lost. He beat me fair and square. The guy could fight. He could punch.' When it comes out of your mouth like that, it was a little relief for me."

IT SEEMS LIKE ALL FIGHTERS come back eventually. Just take a gander at the record books. Even the greatest champions of all time tend to have one thing in common: They're losers in the end because they couldn't walk away, because they couldn't resist the allure of one more payday, because they deluded themselves—or were deluded by others—into believing that the old magic might return. Unlike other professional athletes, who have whole seasons to assess their diminishing skills, for boxers it's always make or break. They never see the end coming—which is why so many fighters wind up broke, which is why they need to fight on. That it invariably ends badly for nearly everyone else still isn't enough to discourage the next guy.

When George Foreman announced that he was returning to boxing at age thirty-eight, after ten years of retirement, the universal reaction was that this was some kind of terrible joke. Then came the pathos, the assumption that the former heavyweight champion of the world must be so sad, so desperate, so hard up for cash that he'd risk his health and reputation for a few measly paydays. No one was buying his answer: that he was coming back to raise two million dollars to build his youth centre in Houston, and that boxing seemed like the quickest way to the money.

The new, old Foreman first appeared in the ring in Sacramento on March 9, 1987, to meet a journeyman by the name of Steve Zouski, and the fight played out like a cartoon. His head shaved, his body very round and very middle-aged, his movement slow as molasses, Foreman looked nothing like his former self. The calls came immediately to take away his licence, to ban him from boxing, to protect him from himself. "You've got to endure the humiliation," Foreman remembers. "I'd do these talk shows with guys and they'd say, 'George, a lot of people are thinking you'll get hurt.' You've got to make jokes and keep talking. Because you know what you're going to do. You *hope* you know what you're going to do. Nobody knows the future for sure."

Foreman, indeed, had a plan: to start slowly, like a young fighter, to build his confidence and his record against a series of unthreatening opponents; to gradually make believers out of the promoters and the fans; to take work anywhere, to fight in small towns for small purses if necessary; and especially, to keep on smiling. If this was all a big joke, Foreman always seemed to be in on it. The great, glowering menace of his early years was replaced by a jolly fat man who didn't take himself all that seriously.

The fact is that, away from the spotlight, Foreman wasn't always like that; the pleasant public persona could disappear, and someone considerably less cheery would turn up in his place. But people liked the new George, the happy George, who was always willing to throw out a line about how many cheeseburgers he could eat at one sitting. They watched his fights and noticed that even if he was old and fat, he could still knock people out. Slowly, they began to buy in.

"I remember after one fight, I told my wife what I really wanted was to go to the International House of Pancakes and eat something," Foreman says. "We went out way on the other side of West Houston. And I ordered everything I wanted. I was sitting there eating and a guy came up and said, 'Hey George, George Foreman. Man, I need you to sign this for me. Please, I just want your autograph.' I said, 'Wait until I finish eating.' My wife said, 'Listen, you go all around the country promoting that you are this nice guy. You'd better make up your mind if you're going to be that. If you're going to be that, be that. If not, don't play that game any more.' I said, 'I'm not playing.' And so I said to the guy, 'Hey come back,' and I signed his autograph. That's how much I've been sold on this."

Foreman acknowledges that a few times, early on, when it seemed the comeback was heading nowhere, he was ready to pack it in. He remembers one particular night in Springfield, Missouri, fighting a palooka named Bobby Crabtree in front of twelve hundred people, for a purse of, maybe, $25,000. "The guy starts boxing me. He didn't come forward at all. He started moving good and he was jabbing. Then about the fourth round I heard his corner start screaming, 'His old legs are tired. Get him. His old legs are tired.' I'm thinking, what am I doing here? This guy's hitting me a few times, getting a little swelling on my head. Why am I doing this? You go back to your corner and say, I quit. What the heck am I doing? I'm a preacher. I don't really need this in my life. A few times I tried to talk myself out of boxing. But that night, for some reason I went back out and tricked him and knocked the guy out."

Eventually though, he says, "the athlete came alive again." He started feeling like a fighter. And the two-million-dollar comeback turned into a legitimate quest to regain the heavyweight championship of the world. The opponents started getting a little better: former light heavyweight champ Dwight Qawi, Bert Cooper, Gerry Cooney ("the Geezers at Caesars," they dubbed that promotion). The knockouts kept piling up.

In April 1991, having just won the heavyweight championship from Buster Douglas, Evander Holyfield chose Foreman for his first title defence: a classic big-payday, low-risk option. Foreman had a ball during the buildup. He revelled in the attention, even hanging out in the press room the night before the fight, of his own accord, just in case anyone might want to talk to him. And though battered and bruised, he survived all twelve rounds while losing a unanimous decision, occasionally giving Holyfield something to think about, but never really threatening him.

It could have ended right there, a moral victory, confirmation that it was no joke, that at age forty-two he could acquit himself well against the best heavyweight in the world. But Foreman chose to go on. "I just kept the pressure on, kept the pressure on." In fact, he lost a decision to Tommy Morrison, a one-dimensional White Hope heavyweight who made Foreman look terrible, boxing circles around him. "Then when Holyfield lost to Michael Moorer, it was like a gift. Because Michael Moorer needed a bum of the month. He needed a bum. Every fighter, when they get to be champion, they think, now I'm going to get the easy one. The easy one. There I am. I had become easy in his sight. They don't watch anything. They just listen to people talk."

The fight was billed as a last hurrah. Moorer wasn't anything special—he had been a great light heavyweight who moved up and won the heavyweight title on a night when Holyfield seemed set to expire from some kind of heart trouble. But he was young, he was a southpaw, he was undefeated as a pro and Foreman was now nearly forty-six years old and significantly slower even than when he'd begun his comeback.

Still, Foreman had a plan.

"It had taken me years to develop this heavy jab. It just knocks you back out of the way. Then I tried to get a right hand in. And I'd beaten Holyfield good with that jab, but I'd get ready to throw a right hand and the jab would knock him far away. I couldn't connect. So I went into training this time and I slapped with my left jab. Slap. And I nearly cried, because you can't do this. You know how many years it took me to develop that jab? I didn't even tell my trainer about it.

"So there I am in the fight. I have to alter my stiff jab. Tap with it and then boom with the right. And I got it. I got him the first time and he didn't even move. I didn't drop him. So I just brought it down a little bit. That was it. Something I'd been practising every night in my gym. And I'm thinking, you know what? It worked. A miracle. It worked. . . . I jabbed him and stayed my distance and was going under to the body. Nobody was paying any attention to that. Right in the side. Keeping in my position. Don't drop my head so he can't get in any good shots. He started thinking too. He'd forgotten that this is a guy who had beaten Joe Frazier and all these guys. He started standing around right in front of me looking for a good shot. *Smack.*"

There's that sound again.

"Pie in the sky. He wasn't getting up. I waited for the count and then got down on my knees and thanked God."

For anyone who was there that night at the arena in the MGM Grand Casino in Las Vegas, the moment when Foreman connected remains vividly etched in memory. Moorer had been completely in control of the fight until the tenth round. He'd boxed, thrown combinations, and found Foreman hard to miss. And all Foreman could answer with was that slapping jab. The right that ended the fight travelled all of six inches. Moorer lay flat on his back, staring up into the arena rafters, as he was counted out. Foreman kneeled and prayed in his corner. And the crowd erupted as though watching a World Series winning home run—except there, you would have at least known the pitch was on its way.

Afterwards, at the press conference, Foreman was asked a question about how it all felt. He answered by quoting a familiar line of lyrics from "Somewhere over the Rainbow," a nod to the casino's old movie motif.

BEING A FIGHTER, FOREMAN couldn't just call it quits on that high note. "You open up the book and you become an athlete, you become a boxer," he says. "Probably the only wise cat that we can consider in this sport was Rocky Marciano. Just walked away. That was the last of them.

"When you open up the book to be the boxer, it's not like you can take on a fraction of it. You take on the foolishness too. A guy overstays his welcome. I mean, I was in there. I really came back to being a boxer. Part of it is not knowing when to stop, or picking the wrong fight. I admit to that. I really came back into it. The other fights, I said I'm going to make these millions of dollars. I'd set these programs up and scholarships. I'm going to get these millions of dollars. How am I going to get them? I'm going to go on boxing. I'm not going to ask anyone for anything. And of course like any other boxer, I took stupid fights. You find yourself asking, 'Why is he doing this one?' Ten million dollars, that's why. It's not like, he's won it, now get out of there. Boxers don't think like that."

And so came a series of pointless fights, a disputed decision win over a mediocre German heavyweight named Axel Schulz, two more decision victories over second-rate opponents and then, finally, in November 1997, a loss to Shannon Briggs, who in historical terms became, for a brief moment (until he was knocked out by Lennox Lewis), the linear heavyweight champion of the world. That was Foreman's last fight to date, though he has never officially retired. "I never did say it," he says. "Because there's been some talk of me coming back at fifty-five if I still have my legs. By then I'm certain Lennox Lewis will be off the book, Tyson will be out of it. There will be a whole new group. And what's very important in boxing more than any other sport is the changing of the guard in the reporters. I've got to wait even for the people at HBO to get out. Everybody has got to get out so there's a young guy sitting there saying, 'Wow, can we bring him back?' The past has nothing to do with them. They're only interested in the future."

Who would his ideal opponent be?

"Someone who can't fight," he says, laughing.

In the meantime, there will be no tag days for Foreman. His community centre is finished, he has his house and his ranch, and these days the bills are paid not by boxing, but by television. Foreman works regularly for HBO as a commentator, but his real second career is selling mufflers and hamburger grills in television commercials. He learned to make a pitch, he says, while working as a street-corner preacher.

"I knew that I could sell. All I needed was something I believed in to sell. So I wasn't surprised that the thing came about. Everybody loves a little honest advertisement.

"The old saying is that the meek shall inherit the earth. It's like when I was boxing. I'd be at home and these other boxers had these agents. They'd say, 'We can get Tim Witherspoon'—he was the heavyweight champion of the world—and Witherspoon says, 'Sure—$250,000.' Then they'd call me and say, 'George, we want you to fight on this card for $7,000.' I said, 'Sure.' 'Will you come to Florida? George, we can't get Witherspoon, we can't get Holmes. They want $100,000.' 'How much have you got?' They'd say ten thousand, and I'd say okay.

"[You do it the same way] with commercials. And before you know it, it's not like you're the best name going, but you're the only one that's willing to do it. All you've got to do is be accessible and don't make people spend their last dime on you. And if you believe in a product, you can sell it. Then it starts coming to you. Don't mess with people. If people have something for you, just say, 'Yes, I'll do it.'"

He has succeeded to the point that now, when walking through an airport, he'll hear someone shout, "George Foreman. Hey, George Foreman . . ."

"And then they say, 'I love your grill.' I want to scream to them, 'I used to be a boxer, you know. I used to be heavyweight champion of the world.'"

It's not quite Ali, but it's pretty darn close.

I ASK FOREMAN ONE last time about the man who he says changed his life for the better by knocking him out.

"Ali really kind of elevated himself for me when he did the torch thing at the Olympics in Atlanta. Just think. Most people in this country get a little sickness, especially if they've been noticed or are celebrities, and they hide. They won't come out. Someone has something like Parkinson's, they'll just stay in the house and hide. They'll say, 'I don't want them to see me like this.' This guy came up with that torch shaking and lighting that thing like that—I felt so proud of him. Muhammad Ali did a lot for the world when he did that. You'll never know how much he did for people who generally hide themselves. That man did a lot. To see him do it and not be ashamed. To say, 'I am the greatest and still alive.' He deserves the feeling that people have for him. I wouldn't have said so much about his boxing days, but after he did that, he deserved everything.

"One of my boys came home the other day and he had a shirt that he had bought from the store and it had Ali on it. I said, 'Man, where did you get that?' He kind of meekly said such and such. I said, 'Boy, that's nice.' He said, 'Everybody said you'd better not wear that around George.' I said, 'What? Would you get me one?' And he couldn't find that one because it wasn't big enough, so he got me a red one with a great big picture of Ali. Some designer is selling them. And I wore it. I wore it everywhere. Everybody wondered what I was doing. But can you imagine that someone would think that I lost to Muhammad Ali—

we fought in 1974, it's almost thirty years later—and that they would think that that fight continues to this day. I was ashamed, the idea that a fight happened almost thirty years ago and you are still messed up about it. Thirty years later? I don't want anyone to think that that is still in existence.

"Joe Frazier, he may have got stuck in this time warp and hasn't gotten himself out. It takes real good guidance and council and a love of mankind to throw those things away. You just throw that away. I like Ali. I admire him. And when I saw that film *When We Were Kings*—they sent me a copy of it—my kids were laughing. He was talking about the shuffle and what he'll do—they were laughing and carrying on, with no regard for me. Then I realized it wasn't about me. They were just enjoying this fellow that I used to enjoy as a boy, too. He would tell a joke and do a poem and I was so happy. And I recaptured that when I saw that film. I recaptured everything. And now I just love everything."

CHUCK WEPNER

Bayonne, New Jersey

THE LIVING ROOM OF the condominium Chuck and Linda Wepner share is neat as a pin. Through the window, the view extends past a small park to one of the waterways that snake around the various islands and peninsulas that make up the geography of greater New York City. This isn't the glamorous East Side, or the West Side, but Bayonne, New Jersey, for all sixty-three years of his life the home of the man known as the Bayonne Bleeder. Its streets are the streets of working-class America. Maybe because it's within spitting distance of lower Manhattan, maybe because the events of September 11, 2001, are still fresh in memory, there are flags hanging above nearly every doorstep. And joining all of those stars and stripes, more than a few Irish tricolours: It's St. Patrick's Day, and Wepner, a local legend, will be prominently featured in the parade.

Right now, though, Chuck is talking and Linda is listening while puttering away in the background, occasionally feeling moved to interject. Anyone who is or has been married understands the familiar rhythms of the continuing discourse between man and wife. The subject is one of intense interest to both of them: Sylvester Stallone has acknowledged that Wepner, specifically his 1975 fight with Muhammad Ali, was the model for Rocky, the movie character that made the actor famous, that won him an Oscar, that made him enormously wealthy through a series of lucrative sequels. Other fighters have occasionally claimed that they were Stallone's inspiration, including Joe Frazier—who, like Rocky, came from Philadelphia, ran up the Art Museum stairs during his training and worked in a slaughterhouse. Wepner, though, dismisses those notions out of hand. ("It was a white guy against a black champ. Joe is black. Maybe he doesn't know that. Look in the mirror, Joe.") He's the real Rocky and, in his mind, that's been a blessing, only slightly mixed.

"Stallone's been good to me in a lot of ways," he says. "Unfortunately, I'm a little disappointed in him because he promised me some things that he never came through with. He promised me a part in a couple of his movies. He gave me a part in *Rocky II*—Ching Webber. I had thirty-two lines. I read for the part in Philadelphia. They cut me out. I wasn't an actor. I barely studied for the part. I didn't do real well. But then he promised me a lot of other things. I thought possibly down the road somewhere I'd reap some kind of financial benefits from *Rocky*. The guy's made nine hundred million, almost a billion, dollars from it so far. It's the greatest grossing movie of all time, except for one or two. But we've remained friends over the years. I was so embarrassed about the fact that I never got any money for the movie that I told people he offered me one per cent against $70,000 and I took the $70,000. I made up that story. I never received a penny from *Rocky*. As a matter of fact I never received anything. He gave me a try for a part in the movie and then rejected it, and that's about it. He never offered me anything. He never offered me another part in a movie or any kind of money or anything like that. It doesn't bother me nearly as much as it bothers my wife and a lot of my friends. A lot of my friends have wanted me to get lawyers and I don't want to do that. That's sour grapes. I don't want to do that. I like Stallone."

Hearing those last words, Linda Wepner can barely contain herself.

"He would do it to you, Chuck," she says, in a thick Jersey accent that echoes her husband's.

Chuck pauses only long enough to acknowledge that he isn't ignoring her completely and then continues.

"In the meantime, I liked him," he says. "Sylvester Stallone is a terrific guy. I've had lawyers say, 'Why don't you sue him, just for nuisance sake.' I'm sure he's covered by insurance. The way I look at it is he's done a lot for me with the movie *Rocky* and everything else. Everybody knows I'm the real Rocky. What am I going to do? To me it would just be sour grapes and I don't really want to go into it."

Now Linda can't take it any more. She steps, literally, physically, into the middle of the conversation. "Can I talk?" she asks. "Is it okay if I talk?"

Chuck says, "Go ahead," with the resignation of someone who just perhaps has had this chat a couple of times before.

"You've gotta be kidding me," Linda says. "Sour grapes? This guy's got millions. God bless him. But that's not the point. It's unjust, Chuck. They treated you like you were a jerk. I just found out two years ago. You don't know how this aggravates me. I don't even watch *Rocky*. This man is the real deal. Not some actor that you see outside of Planet Hollywood. People saying, 'Oh, I want to take a picture with Stallone.' I've got nothing against the man. It's just that if you want to take a picture with Rocky, he's here. It's the principle. You make a jerk out of somebody. And they say fight promoters—in plain English—screw the fighters? The producers and directors of *Rocky*—he got screwed, number-one highway robbery."

At this point, Chuck yawns audibly.

"How many millions of dollars?" Linda continues. "They're still getting money. DVDs, CVDs, whatever the heck they are. They're getting money hand over fist and you got nothing."

"Okay, you said your piece, honey," Chuck says. "Thank you."

"Do I get the part?" Linda says, knowing just when to lighten the mood.

"Yeah," says Chuck. "You get the part."

IN ONE CORNER OF Wepner's parlour, there's a bronze statue, life-sized, that he bought for twenty-four hundred bucks. It's of a kid wearing adult-sized boxing regalia; oversized trunks, enormous gloves, shoes several sizes too big. "I bought it because that was me," he says. "That's exactly what I looked like." As a boy, he fought in "smokers" at the Police Athletic League gym in Bayonne, two kids flailing away with big pillow gloves for the entertainment of adults. Boxing-wise, that's where the real Rocky got his start.

But then he took a detour into basketball, the sport in which Chuck Wepner still holds the Bayonne church-league record for points scored in a single three-man game: 101. "I was pretty good," he says. "I was big under the boards and I shot a lot. I threw in thirty or thirty-five points a game. They used to call me a chucker. That's what they called me in them days."

When he was old enough, Wepner joined the Marines. At his final stop in the service, Cherry Point, North Carolina, the boxing instructor asked him if he'd like to try out for the team. He picked up where he'd left off as a kid, winning seven fights in a row. "Those were great fights because the referee let you do anything," Wepner says. "And I could use my three best punches: the rabbit punch, the low blow and the choke hold."

In 1960, he was discharged from the Marines and came back to Bayonne, where he worked as a security guard at General Motors, then as a liquor salesman for Majestic Wine and Spirits. In 1964, while dropping in on a "go-go place on Seventeenth Street," he ran into a local boxing coach who, knowing something of Wepner's history in the Marines, suggested he take a crack at the Golden Gloves. He won, and won the AAUs [the Amateur Athletic Union title] as well, and immediately decided to turn pro. "I said, why the hell should I fight amateur? I'm twenty-five years old now. I might as well try to make some money. I was a white guy and at that time there wasn't too many good white fighters around in any division. Most of the really good fighters were either black or Hispanic."

It was true in less enlightened times, and it's probably just as true now: a universally recognized, white heavyweight champion (there hasn't been one in more than forty years) would be a licence to print money. Whether Wepner ever really looked the part was beside the point: He was tough as nails and, because he was more than willing to scrap, consistently entertaining. He won his first eleven professional fights in a row before running into Sonny Liston in 1969. Liston was of indeterminate age, his glory years long past, playing out the string. But he could still punch like hell, and Wepner provided a willing target. Before the fight was stopped in the tenth round, he broke Wepner's nose and his cheekbone, and tore his face to pieces, opening wounds that required seventy-two stitches to close. "I was pretty busted up," Wepner says, betraying a talent for understatement. "A magazine rated it one of the ten bloodiest fights of all time. I'm real honoured about that. That was the night [sportswriter] Rosie Rosenberg from the *Bayonne Times* coined the name the Bayonne Bleeder. He was sitting in the second row and he got splattered with blood a couple of times from the punches."

The fight also spawned another famous line. When he was asked afterwards if Wepner was the bravest man he'd ever met, Liston, famously frugal with words, said, "No. His manager is."

It was Liston's last fight. Not long afterwards, they found him dead in Las Vegas, apparently of an overdose, the true circumstances mysterious to this day.

LOOKING AROUND BAYONNE, seeing all of those flags waving, knowing that Chuck Wepner was a proud Marine, it's not hard to surmise how he might have felt when Cassius Clay beat Liston, became Muhammad Ali and set off the culture-shaking events that began with that transformation. "To tell you the truth, in the beginning, because I didn't know Muhammad Ali real good, I thought he was a draft dodger," Wepner says. "But now, knowing Ali, all these years have passed, and knowing what a great guy he really is, I really believe they bamboozled him into becoming a Muslim and saying, 'Hey, Muslims don't go to war.' He thought he was doing the right thing for his people. Early on, I thought he was a draft dodger. But after a while, when you get to know this guy, you know that the guy gave up four years of his life, maybe the four best years of his life."

Whatever Wepner's political leanings, Ali the fighter wasn't really in his sights, since he came of age as a pro during the champion's period in exile. As a professional, Wepner found himself under the management of Al Braverman, one of the true characters of the sport and a man who, early on, forged a strong relationship with an ex-con-turned-promoter from Cleveland, Ohio, named Don King. Braverman moved Wepner skilfully before and after the loss to Liston: Though no one seriously thought of Wepner as championship material, for forty-two straight months, he was rated among the top ten heavyweights in the world.

Braverman also faced the challenge of dealing with Wepner's extreme fondness for women, which occasionally distracted him from the task at hand. At least during his younger, less married days, Wepner was open about his many friends and acquaintances. He'd entertain visitors to his home by bringing out a shoebox filled with small, plastic slide viewers of the kind that they used to sell in such tourist traps as Niagara Falls. Instead of natural wonders, though, each one contained the image of a comely young woman—or more often, of comely young women in intimate situations with Chuck Wepner, including at least one former Miss New Jersey. Braverman used to tell a story of working Wepner's corner during a fight. His fighter was losing, and during the minute between rounds, Braverman was trying desperately to get that message across. But while he screamed and gestured, he noticed Wepner's gaze wandering: It was following the scantily clad woman who carried the card announcing what round was coming up. Braverman slugged Wepner hard across the chops—one of the better shots landed that night by all accounts—and Wepner went on to win the fight.

He was that kind of guy, but remained committed enough to his craft that when the reigning heavyweight champion George Foreman was scheduled to face Muhammad Ali in Zaire in the fall of 1974, Wepner was positioned to face the winner. That would be Foreman, of course—at least that's what Wepner assumed.

To qualify for a title-shot fight, he'd ventured to Salt Lake City and beaten a guy named Terry Hinke, "The Stormin' Mormon," who was cast as Foreman's policeman, the fighter you had to get by to get a date with the champ. "Bob Hope was the MC of the show that night," Wepner remembers. "It was to raise money for famine relief in Biafra. Two dollars from every ticket went to the Biafra cause. It went eleven rounds; I had him down seven times and knocked him out in the eleventh round. Bob Hope came into the dressing room after that. I was lying down as they were stitching me up. Bob said to me, 'Chuck, I just want to congratulate you and tell you that was the greatest heavyweight fight I ever saw.'

"So now I'm waiting for Foreman to knock out Ali. To be honest, I didn't think he could go six rounds against George."

That was the consensus. When Ali shocked Foreman, and shocked the world, Wepner figured his big chance was gone. King assured him that Ali would fight him eventually. "I never believed it," Chuck said.

"Three months and a day to my fight against Hinke in Salt Lake City, Utah, I was home watching 'Kojak,'" he remembers. "Telly Savalas was a good friend of mine; actually, at that time he was just an acquaintance. And I always watched the program. The phone rings and my mother was on the other end of the line." The conversation that followed went something like this.

"Chuck! Chuck!"

"She was all excited. 'Mom, what is it? I told you, never call me during "Kojak." Don't interrupt.'"

"Did you see the paper? Did you see the news?"

"No, I didn't, Mom. What's in it?"

"Go out and get it."

"Mom, tell me what's in it. I'm not just going to run out."

"On the back page, the whole back page, it says, 'Ali to defend against Wepner in Cleveland March 24.'"

"So I put my clothes on and ran up to the Embassy Theater at Forty-seventh and Broadway. The kid had four papers left. They sold them in front of theatres in them days. I said, 'Give me those four papers.' I turned the paper over and sure enough. . . ."

It was not unlike Rocky getting the call from Apollo Creed, and with some of the same rationale. Ali was coming off the ordeal of Africa. He was looking for an easy night's work. Wepner was at least rated in the top ten. And maybe there was a promotional story there, the kind of story that would make a decent movie—a working-class hero getting his one big shot.

CHUCK WEPNER HAD NEVER had the luxury of training full-time for a fight before. "I was never subsidized," he says, "so I used to wake up in the morning at, like, 6:15, go down to the park and do my roadwork, come back and work all day and then go to the gym at night. It was real tough. A lot of times when I went to the gym at night after working all day I didn't feel like doing nothing."

This time it would be different. This time it would be first class all the way, starting with a real training camp in the Catskills, where the great champions of history used to prepare. "I got myself into great shape. I went up there for seven weeks of training. That was maybe the greatest seven weeks of my life—the most exciting, anyway."

At this point Linda, who's still tuned in, gives him a look.

"Except for the day I got married to my wife, Linda," he continues. "It was great. I had never experienced anything like that. I had the run of the whole hotel. Every day they had national media there. I had my own private dining room, where I would eat with my sparring partners. I could order anything I wanted. Every night, we'd take a car and go to other hotels, see shows. Of course, there was no drinking, no fooling around. I didn't do anything for seven weeks except train, and train hard. I got myself in terrific shape."

The promotion of the fight didn't go quite so smoothly. Despite his world ranking, Wepner was all but unknown outside of New Jersey. And those who had seen him fight, and understood his limitations, figured it would be relaxing night for the champion. Wepner was established as a huge betting underdog, and that perception didn't shift at all as the fight neared, despite Ali's best efforts to beat the drums. "He never gave me a nickname," Wepner remembers. "As a matter of fact, I had buttons that said 'Give the White Guy a Break.' I was the White Guy. That was my name.

"I remember we had to do a couple of TV things. We were on 'The Mike Douglas Show.' When we took a break, Ali leans over to me and says, 'Hey Chuck. Do me a favour. When they come back onstage, call me an *effing* nigger.' And I said to him, 'Champ, I can't do that. I have a lot of black friends. A couple of my sparring partners are black. I don't even like to use that word.' He said, 'No, no, no, we'll make it look like a grudge match and sell tickets.' I said, 'I'm not doing that.'"

When the host returned to the set, Ali immediately started shouting, "Do you know what he called me? Do you know what he called me?" Wepner had to clamp his hand over his mouth to prevent him from dropping that particular bomb.

"Ali was a promoter," Wepner says. "He was a great promoter and they were trying to hype up the fight. Because even though I was ranked sixth or seventh in the world, I wasn't the biggest name. He used to get into [his opponents'] minds. He used to get into their head. But Ali never got into my head. Ali used to write a lot of poems in them days about guys. He didn't write any poems about me, but I wrote two about him: 'Goodbye Ali, Hello Chuck' and 'What's in a Name.' As a matter of fact, they were both published. One of the lines from it was, 'And by March twenty-fourth there'll be a new king and his name will be Big Chuck.' That was the last line in 'Goodbye Ali, Hello Chuck. . . .'

"By the time we left for Cleveland, I'll tell you, I felt like I could run through walls. I'd never felt like that before. I felt like a million bucks. I was ready. And I thought Muhammad Ali would look past me, overlook me, he would run out of gas and I would probably beat him. I was a twenty-to-one underdog. The over/under was three or four rounds. Ali predicted he'd knock me out in three rounds."

It was around that time that Wepner says he was lying in bed with his then wife, Phyllis, and said something along the lines of, "Even if I don't win, I just want to prove I belong there."

"That's the line Stallone says laying in bed with Adrian the night before the fight," he says. "That was my line. I gave that to Stallone."

He was feeling so confident that the day before the match, he took some time out on the afternoon of fight day to go shopping, looking for a special gift for Phyllis. "I bought a powder-blue negligee and I gave it to her. And I said to her, 'Tonight I want you to wear this negligee to bed, because tonight you're going to be sleeping with the heavyweight champion of the world.'"

Phyllis was waiting in bed, wearing the negligee, when Wepner returned to his hotel after the fight.

"Do I go to Ali's room," she asked him. "Or does he come to mine?"

OF COURSE HE LOST. Anyone who's seen *Rocky* knows that. And it wasn't pretty, or Hollywood dramatic, or even particularly close. "The first seven or eight rounds he was moving and I was pressing him, getting him against the ropes and nailing him," Wepner says, perhaps being slightly overgenerous to himself. "I think one judge gave me three rounds. I mean, if you look at that fight, he didn't throw any punches the first four or five rounds. I was the aggressor. You've got to give me those early rounds. He popped me a couple of times, but I threw three or four times as many punches as him. But I knew that I had to knock out Muhammad Ali to win. I knew I wasn't going to get a decision. I'd seen other fights where he was involved, and it looked to me like he lost the fight, but they gave him the decision. He's Muhammad Ali."

Still, there was that brief shining moment, the one that put Wepner in the history books, the instant when it seemed anything was possible. It was merely a trip, Ali claimed afterwards (and to a degree, the film record supports him). He got tangled up with Wepner, he had his foot stepped on, he was pushed; he certainly wasn't hurt. The referee should never have ruled it a knockdown.

For Wepner, who had the image printed on his business cards, who commissioned a painting immortalizing the great event, it was something else again. There may well be people who remember that Ali stopped Wepner in the eleventh round, that the referee stepped in to save him from further punishment. But there are a heck of a lot more who carry the image of an ordinary, working fighter standing over the most famous man in the world.

"When I dropped Ali in the ninth round of the fight, I was excited," Wepner says, "because when I hit him, he almost fell through the ropes. A couple of guys at ringside went like this [caught Ali's fall with their outstretched hands] and held him up. With a fluke of luck, if somebody don't hold him up and maybe he falls out of the ring, I win the title. When Ali was down, I remember saying to Al Braverman, 'Start the car, we're going to the bank, we're millionaires.' And Al said, 'You'd better turn around. Because he's getting up and he looks pissed off.' And he was. He was more embarrassed than anything else. It wasn't a great punch. He was pulling away from a jab and I threw a right hand and caught him right under the heart. And he went down. He was off balance. When he got up, boy, we really went to war. He backed me into a corner and we started trading punches. That's the first time we really opened up."

It's a short list: Sonny Banks (and there are some who say Ali slipped on water spilled in a corner that night), Henry Cooper, Joe Frazier, Chuck Wepner. The only men to knock down Muhammad Ali as a professional.

"But I was the only guy to have him down as champion of the world," Wepner says. "As a matter of fact that was just on a trivia question on 'Hollywood Squares.' They didn't guess it."

FOUR DAYS AFTER THE fight, this Stallone guy calls and says he's writing a script based on Wepner's life and the Ali bout. "I had no idea who he was. Then he told me he had been in a movie called *Lords of Flatbush,* and I remembered him because I saw the movie. It's a good movie. I was actually very excited and thrilled about it. But I had been in a couple of movies before, and I figured, here's another movie, it's going to be poorly done, it's not going to be anything exceptional. And so it didn't really excite me until I was on the set a couple of times and I saw different things done. Then we went to the premiere of *Rocky* and it was a complete blockbuster. People were coming up to me and hugging me and saying, 'Chuck, congratulations, it's a great movie, blah blah blah.' Then I realized what a terrific movie it really was and what a great job he had done. And I give him credit because he stuck to his guns. They wanted other people to play the part—Jon Voigt and some other people—and he refused. He said, 'No, I wrote the movie and I'm going to play the part.' This is why he's a megastar now, because of his stick-to-it-ness."

WEPNER WAS PAID $125,000 for the Ali fight. By the time everyone got their piece of the pie, he was left with less than $60,000. "It was decent money. But the kids now, they have one fight for the title, they get two or three million dollars. I missed the big money by probably five years." He stayed in boxing for a while and then did his best to spin a few dollars out of his celebrity. "I've capitalized. I've marketed myself very well, I think." Wepner and Ali continued to be linked occasionally. They starred together in an educational film in which Chuck played Mr. Tooth Decay. "I'd knock him down and they'd come in and brush his teeth and he'd jump up. I'd knock him down and he'd jump up." And they were co-featured in one of the more bizarre nights in the history of the sport: Before Ali's bout with the Japanese professional wrestler Antonio Inoki (which ended in a draw, after Inoki spent the whole fight in a crab position, kicking at Ali's legs), Wepner appeared on the undercard, taking on wrestler Andre the Giant at Shea Stadium. (Think of Rocky, in one of those interminable sequels, meeting the wrestler Thunderlips: The parallels continue.)

The script called for Andre to finally subdue Wepner with a body slam. "I was going to go for that," he says. "They paid me very well for that fight. Then we weighed in on a meat scale. I got on, and I was 220 pounds. He gets on—515. I said, 'You know what, the body slam is out. I'm not doing that. We've got to think of something else.'"

It was decided instead that Andre would hurl Chuck out of the ring, onto the baseball infield, where in theory he could land without damaging himself too badly. But at the moment of truth, Andre lifted Wepner above his head and turned towards the side of the ring where the press were seated at a table. "No, no, not there," Wepner hollered at him from high. "That's going to hurt. Take me over to the other side."

"So he threw me out of the ring. Gorilla Monsoon was his manager. And when I landed, I was going to try to land on my feet, but I landed on my side. It knocked the wind out of me temporarily. Gorilla came over and put his hand out to help me up and kneeled on my chest. He was 419 pounds then. I didn't make it back into the ring by ten. I got disqualified."

Wepner followed up that glorious night by twice getting into the ring with a wrestling bear named Victor. For the record, both times he was disqualified for running away.

All the while, Wepner kept up his day job selling liquor. He stayed in Bayonne. And he started to live rather large. "I was doing a lot of partying. This is before I married Linda. I was divorced then. I had a completely different lifestyle at the time. You know, in them days it was the early eighties, the middle eighties, and everyone was doing cocaine and partying and everything else." Women, drugs. Drugs, women. Those were the recurring themes. And then, in 1985, it caught up with him.

"Between you and I, it was a sting operation," Wepner says. "A guy called me up, said, 'Do me a favour.' I picked something up. Then they stopped me with it. They set me up. That's the way they get a lot of things. They're doing their job." Wepner was arrested with four ounces of cocaine in his possession. Three years later, following a plea bargain, he was sentenced to ten years in prison and wound up serving two.

"I always tell people that probably saved my life," he says. "I did my time. I kept my mouth shut. I didn't involve nobody else. I did the crime, I did the time. And I came home and I changed my lifestyle. I've got sixteen going on seventeen years clean now. That was the only time I've ever been arrested in my life. And it's over. It will never happen again."

He first met Linda, who is his third wife, a couple of months after the Ali fight. They didn't see each other again for sixteen years, until they crossed paths in the bar where she worked. Eight years ago, they were married.

"I was twelve at the time," Linda chimes in.

"Linda's terrific," Wepner continues. "She doesn't drink, she stopped smoking. She doesn't do anything. She never did drugs in her life. We're a good match. She loves boxing. She loves sports. And she lets me control the TV clicker. That's very important.

"One time, after we got married, I remember I was sitting in the living room and I hear her shouting from the bedroom, 'Get him. Kill him. Punch him.' She was watching a tape of the Ali fight. There's a wife that supports you. Then I hear her yell, 'Hit him, Ali. Kill him. Smash him.' Hit him, *Ali?* Hit him, *Ali?* I went in and I said, 'What's with this Muhammad Ali stuff?' She said, 'I love Muhammad Ali.' 'But that's your husband fighting. Are you out of your mind?' She said, 'Oh, I just lost my head. I meant to say, 'Hit him, Chuck.'"

Wepner remains connected to boxing now through the FIST organization, the Fighters' Institute for Support and Training, which helps ex-fighters who are down on their luck. He remains friendly with many of his contemporaries, including Larry Holmes and Frazier. (Though he's frustrated with Frazier's ongoing hostility towards Ali. Wepner's attempt to stage a public reconciliation between the two at Madison Square Garden fell apart when Frazier refused to go through with it. "Do you know how much money these two guys could make together?" Wepner says, exasperated.)

Occasionally, he still crosses paths with Ali at autograph signings and the like. "He was such a fun guy and so exciting and everything," Wepner says. "Now I do some appearances with him and it just breaks my heart to see the shape he's in. I read a piece in the *New York Post* that I think really explains it. It said Muhammad Ali is a prisoner in his own body. He knows what he wants to do. His mind is still all right but he can't do it. His body motor is just completely gone. Unfortunately, I think he's getting worse, as I see him.

"The last time we were together, he had on these big, wide shoes. Ali used to be a sharp dresser. When he got up, I said, 'Champ, what's with the shoes?' He said, 'They help my balance.' He's gotta wear these shoes to help his balance."

How would it have been, I ask Wepner, if he and Ali had never come together? What would his life have been like without the fight, without the knockdown, without the Rocky story?

Linda pauses to listen in.

"It would have been a lot different," he says. "I would have just been Chuck Wepner, local celebrity or personality, because I played basketball and I was the Golden Gloves champ and the New Jersey champ. Stuff like that. I'm doing better now than I've ever done in my whole life. I've got a good job with a great company. I've got a lot of friends. I've got a great wife. And I've been very lucky because, physically, I'm okay. I'm not hurt."

RON LYLE

Canastota, New York

THEY ARE REMARKABLE EYES, jet black, their gaze imploring, demanding. When Ron Lyle locks in, now over a small table, outdoors, on a pleasant summer afternoon, it seems unwise to turn away, even to blink, lest an innocent gesture be taken the wrong way. "I don't know if I'm making sense," he says. "I don't know if I'm getting to you, to where you understand where I'm coming from." He is smiling, but it is not a reassuring smile. Lyle didn't volunteer for the conversation. He doesn't seek out contact. Other old fighters at the International Boxing Hall of Fame's induction weekend seem thrilled to be recognized, being treated for a moment like the stars they once were (including those who, like Lyle, aren't yet enshrined in the Hall). Right beside us, Earnie Shavers—whom Lyle knocked out more than twenty-five years ago—gathers a crowd like an evangelist. But for most of the day, Lyle has strolled the grounds, nearly anonymous, a tractor hat pulled low over his eyes, and had at first seemed as though he'd be quite happy not to have to engage with anyone at all. Though the place is, quite naturally, populated with tough guys, his reputation is daunting, even in this context: not only, since retiring from the sport, has he been described in stories as a kind of angry loner; twice in his life, once as a kid and once much later, he was in close proximity when another human being died under violent circumstances.

But now that he's been persuaded to talk, it seems that he savours the chance to tell his story, that he wants desperately to communicate. "Do you understand?" he asks again. "I want you to understand."

THERE WERE NINETEEN children in the Lyle family, growing up in Denver, Colorado. His father was a preacher, his mother a missionary who found God when she was eight years old and whose core values were such that she never once entered a movie theatre in her life. Lyle was the third oldest and the only one of their offspring to go to jail. "I'm a good person," he says, as if to counter what's to come. Lyle was also big, and tough, and rebelled against his strict religious upbringing. He dropped out of high school at fourteen, joined a street gang and was eventually drawn into the incident that shaped his life. At nineteen, he was arrested and charged with shooting and killing a rival gang member. Lyle argued at the time in court that he'd acted in self-defence, that he was being attacked with a lead pipe when he fired the shot. Now, he says that he didn't do it at all. "Unfortunately, I was the only one caught, so that meant I couldn't tell who did it. And so I had to take the fall." Nonetheless, he was convicted of second-degree murder and sentenced to fifteen to twenty-five years in prison. This was hard time, real time, and Lyle would serve seven and a half years of his sentence before finally being paroled. At least once, he was stabbed while in prison, and nearly died. "In the meantime, I learned to box," he says. "I learned the art of self-defence. They had a program, but you had to do everything on your own. No one was going to take you by the arm and lead you. You had to do everything yourself. I went to the gym and I was playing basketball, baseball and football. I excelled in all those sports. I was a pretty good athlete. I learned boxing. And from there I had a second chance in life."

Lyle, a natural heavyweight, demonstrated knockout power from the start. Though it was possible that he wouldn't be released from prison until long after he might have reasonably expected to begin a professional career, he began to dream of becoming the champion of the world and, by doing so, of redeeming himself in the eyes of his broken-hearted mother. "Having the misfortune to be incarcerated, it taught me patience," he says. "But it also taught me how to look ahead, to plan ahead and to be able to see the dream when it appears. If I don't pursue it, I miss the boat. That's the way I approached it."

Would he ever have had that dream if his life had taken a different turn? I ask him. "Had I not went to jail? Had I not been incarcerated, could I? I don't think so. I think that's the route that God intended me to travel. He's the one that gave me the dream, so obviously that was the route. I had to follow the route. And I did."

Others began to buy into Lyle's dream. "My learning experience was very limited within walls," he says. "So what the coach there did, the athletic director, was bring people in from the outside. Fighters from the Fort Carson army base. And I fought some good fighters." A wealthy Colorado businessman named Bill Daniels heard the story of the prison heavyweight who was knocking out all comers. The cable-television magnate who had already put his money into automobile racing and professional basketball began to think of himself as Lyle's angel, and future professional backer. He exerted his considerable political influence in the state in the hopes of winning Lyle parole.

"I went to the parole board, and they sent me back for a year, two years," Lyle says. "They said [boxing's] not a parole plan. You can't fight your way out of a wet bag. You'll never make it. I told them that this is what I'm going to do when I get out. They said, 'Prove it to us. You've got two more years.' And I proved it to them. . . . The same guy [from the parole board] that sent me back came to see me later when I had a gym in Colorado. He came in that gym one day and he shook my hand. His name was Ralph. He told me, 'Congratulations. You made it.' And I said, 'Thank you.'"

Lyle was released from prison on November 29, 1969. He had entered jail as a teenager. He emerged as a twenty-seven-year-old, without a single official fight on his record. If his dream was going to come true, it was going to have to come true in a hurry.

WHEN RON LYLE WENT TO prison, Sonny Liston, who, like him, had served time, was the heavyweight champion of the world, and Cassius Clay was the raw, untested light-heavyweight gold medallist from the Rome Olympics. By the time he was released, Liston was dead, the first phase of Muhammad Ali's career was over and he was in exile from the sport because of his refusal to enter the draft. Lyle says that he and his fellow inmates were very aware of what was happening in the boxing world. "You get to watch fights," he says. "I wrote [to Ali's trainer] Angelo Dundee when I was in there and he wrote me back. That's why when I see Mr. Dundee I always speak to him. Because he's the guy that really held the door open for me in the professional end. He's a very special person. I love him. He's a good man."

As an amateur, Lyle immediately made an impact—in some ways he was a man fighting boys—winning the national AAU title in the United States. "I won the

North American championships. I toured Europe. I represented America on TV. I'm the first American heavyweight ever to knock a Russian out right at Caesars Palace. They introduced me to Joe Louis there. Joe Louis thought that I would be able to make it as a pro. He endorsed me." In January 1971, in the trials for the Pan American Games, Lyle knocked out the other top American amateur heavyweight of the time, Duane Bobick. The Olympics were still a year away, though, and Lyle felt that he couldn't afford to wait that long. Instead, he turned professional. (Bobick went to Munich as the U.S. representative, where he was knocked out by Cuba's Teofilo Stevenson.)

"I felt that I was at my peak as an athlete," Lyle says. "An athlete knows when he's at his peak. He knows when he's gone as far as he can go at the level that he's at. I felt like I had gone as far as I could go as an amateur. And to wait around another year or two years, that's not a guarantee. Because as an amateur, you don't know who you fight. As a pro, you know who you fight, how to prepare for him, what he can do and what he can't do." With Daniels' backing, he mapped out a plan for his professional career.

At the time, Ali and Joe Frazier were in the final stages of preparation for their first fight. The U.S. television program "60 Minutes" had picked up on Lyle's story and, as part of a feature on his journey from prison, brought him to both fighters' camps. "First they took me down to Miami to see if I was for real. And I sparred with Ali in the gym there. He didn't try to take advantage of me. He worked with me. He gave me three or four rounds.

"Then I went to Frazier's camp. [Frazier's trainer] Yancey Durham welcomed me. I talked with Yancey for about an hour. I was very impressed with him. Very impressed. He said, 'I can't let you spar with Frazier right now because he'll hurt you. But I'll let you spar with Ken Norton. That's his ace sparring partner.' And I stood up [to Norton]. Yancey was impressed. I knew then that this is where I belonged. I could handle these guys. But that was just one of the tests that I passed."

This becomes the recurring theme of the conversation: tests in boxing, tests in life, how sometimes what seems like failure can really be success. "Do you understand what I'm saying?" Lyle asks again and again. "Do you really understand?"

LYLE TURNED PRO IN 1971, and by 1973 was rated number three in the world. He won his first nineteen fights, seventeen of them by knockout, and seemed destined for a quick title shot. Then in February 1973, at New York's Madison Square Garden, Lyle lost a decision to the vastly more experienced Jerry Quarry, and understood that he had much to learn. "Eventually I caught up to the pack," he says. "But in the meantime I had a lot of tests to take. And I had to pass the tests. Some of them I passed. Some of them, I just missed some of the answers. I mean, I lost fights. The losses are a bitter pill to swallow, but when you swallow that pill, that's what makes you better."

Lyle followed the loss to Quarry with a string of significant wins over the likes of Jose Luis Garcia,

Jurgen Blin and Oscar Bonavena. In July of 1974, he was matched against the former world champion Jimmy Ellis. "And Jimmy Ellis was [Ali's] dog. That was his little pit bull. And he was tough. Going into the fight with Ellis, I knew that Ellis was his chief sparring partner. Now I'm thinking as a fighter myself. I'm thinking that what I want to do is satisfy my own insecurities as to how I would do. Instead of trying to knock this guy out, I'm going to try and out-think him and outbox him. Things went my way this time. I got the decision."

That win helped position him for a shot at the title, though perhaps not as much as his loss did, in February 1975, to the slick-boxing Jimmy Young. It's reasonable to surmise that Ali and his handlers, watching that fight, figured that the aging champion still had enough guile and experience to get past a relatively raw opponent. The title bout was scheduled for May 16, 1975, to be shown in the United States on network television. Because Ali's skills were clearly fading, this was one of those matches in which dread was very much a part of the storyline: The anticipation was not so much that Lyle would win, but rather that Ali would finally lose.

For his part, Lyle understood well that he was a bit player, stepping into the ring against an icon. "At a time when America—when black America—was in the revolution of equal rights, Ali was at the forefront. Not only am I fighting a fighter, I'm fighting against a guy that represents freedom for black people in America. Now, was I aware of this? Absolutely. I've always been aware. I've always been politically aware. I never said nothing, because no one's ever asked me. No one ever asked me my opinion about it until now. Yes, I knew. I understood. Was it hard? Yeah, it was hard. Was I trying to win? Absolutely.

"Ali was a guy that I admired, that I have always admired from a distance. Because he represents a lot of things to a lot of people. But I had to fight this guy. I think getting to that point was tough because [of] the people we live around and the emotional feelings about this same guy. It was like you against the world. He was the world's symbol. Did I make the best of it? I think I did. Did I win? In my own mind, in my own self-satisfaction and well-being, I thought I upheld my ability as well as any man could against the obstacles that was ahead of me."

For his part, Ali didn't try to mess with Lyle, didn't taunt him, didn't tag him with a nickname, didn't try to get inside his head. Lyle thinks that was because Ali, without saying it, understood where he'd come from. "He was sharp enough to see that I had that same mentality. And I think that's why he has always given me my respect. I think it was the people that he was surrounded with, people like Herbert Muhammad, Angelo Dundee. People that understood my struggle, and they gave me that opportunity."

ALI WAS THERE TO BE beaten that night. From the moment the fight began, he seemed to have little to offer beside taunts. "Show me something," he barked at Lyle. "You ain't got nothing." Lyle boxed cleverly, picked his shots and landed them with power, with precision, and there was nothing this suddenly very old, tentative Ali could do about it. Through ten rounds of a scheduled fifteen, Lyle led on two of the three judges' scorecards. He was cruising to victory. He was going to be the heavyweight champion of the world, the dream come true.

Then, in the eleventh, Ali landed a left hook, and Lyle suddenly seemed frozen in his tracks. A right hand followed, and Lyle wobbled. On a desperate night when he had very little left, Ali understood that this was his chance. He let his hands fly, throwing what seemed like a single extended combination, landing, by one count, thirty-seven unanswered punches. Lyle might not have been seriously hurt. He might not have been on the verge of being knocked out. He might have weathered the storm, watched Ali expend his energy and then come back to score a knockout himself.

But for the referee, Ferd Hernandez, those were the kind of assumptions he couldn't afford to make. It sure looked like a one-sided beating. And this, after all, was Ali the Great, a fact judges and referees had always taken into account, whether or not they'd admit to it. With the crowd screaming, with the old champion once again digging deep to pull one out of the fire, it must have seemed the only right decision to step in and stop the fight.

"Was I bitter?" Lyle asks the question of himself, without prompting. "No. I was glad for the opportunity. Was I disappointed in the judges', or the powers that be, decision to stop the fight? No, because, like I said, it wasn't my time."

LYLE CONTINUED HIS QUEST, but that's as close as he would ever come to the championship. Still, fight fans remember a couple of memorable bouts. Against Shavers, one of the hardest punchers of his generation, Lyle was dropped before coming back to win. "The first time in my life I'd ever been knocked off my feet. When I was in jail, I said if I ever get knocked down, I'm going to get up. That's what I said then. But I have never in my life been hit that hard. That was a whole new ball game. But I passed that test because I got up and went on to fight back. Regardless of the outcome, the thing is I passed the test by standing up. That assured that I could make it, that I could stand up with the world's greatest heavyweights. There's certain tests that fighters have, and if a fighter don't pass his own tests, he can't make it."

The other Lyle classic was his slugfest with George Foreman, by then the ex-champion. Both fighters went down, both fighters threw caution to the wind and pounded away. On any list of the most exciting fights of the last quarter century, Foreman–Lyle ranks high, but in the end, it was Foreman who was left standing. Lyle sued Daniels after that fight, ending their long partnership. In 1977, he recorded two significant wins, beating Stan Ward and Joe Bugner, putting himself into position for a potentially career-boosting shot at Larry Holmes.

On New Year's Eve of that year, Lyle called one of his neighbours, a policeman. "Come to my house," he said. "I have something important to tell you." The cop found the body of Vernon Clark, a former boxing trainer, who had been shot dead. There were no witnesses. Fingerprints were wiped off the murder weapon by mistake. Lyle, charged with second-degree murder, said that Clark had reached for the gun, and that during a struggle had accidentally shot himself in the head.

In December 1978, Lyle was acquitted, but by then the opportunity to fight Holmes was gone.

Lyle's career went into decline, the capper being a one-round knockout loss to up-and-coming Gerry Cooney in October 1980.

In retirement, those who managed to track down Lyle found an unhappy, bitter man. That has changed now, he says. "I realize how much a part of history I am. And it took me—I'm fifty-nine, I retired when I was forty-one, forty-two—until I was in my fifties to say, hold it, wait a minute. Just stop looking around and smell the roses. People are telling you that you stood up. Accept that and keep on going. If I had my life to live over again, would I change it? No. Because I know and God knows. When I was in prison, God showed me the dream. When I fought Ali, that was the dream, and I never knew how the dream ended. And that was it. I have always been comfortable with the decisions that were made in the fight, because God showed me the dream.

"I retired when I was forty-two. I stepped out. I never officially announced my retirement; I just backed away. And that's when I really got a chance to see the people and to hear the people. I've learned one thing since I retired from boxing: Sincerity is something that can't be hidden and can't be faked."

(It is telling that Lyle chooses not to mention an abortive four-fight comeback in 1995, carried out exclusively in states without a legitimate boxing commission, Kentucky and Colorado, and inspired, as were several old fighters, by the financial success of George Foreman's second career. In Lyle's case, as in all of the others, the comeback didn't go anywhere.)

These days, he lives in Las Vegas, where he was, for a time, a security guard at a casino hotel and where he's now working with a couple of fighters. The trip to the Hall of Fame has given Lyle a rare opportunity, to mingle with boxing fans and to acknowledge his career though, unlike some of the other old fighters, he certainly doesn't seem inclined to milk that semi-celebrity.

The organizers have to track him down and ask him to speak. He is called to the microphone to say a few words to the crowd and does so reluctantly, shyly. One on one, he is passionate about making his point. Now, though, the ferocity disappears and Lyle seems vulnerable, his words poignant.

"Thank you for inviting me to your community," he begins.

"You have to be a champion to get into the Boxing Hall of Fame. I was never a champion. But if I get in before I die, if I can ever see my name in the Boxing Hall of Fame then I can say that it's been worthwhile."

The ovation that follows is loud and warm and genuine.

ROUND THIRTEEN

JEAN-PIERRE COOPMAN

Ghent, Belgium

HIS MUSE, FOR MYSTERIOUS reasons, has departed. His inspiration has vanished. "Mentally," Jean-Pierre Coopman says, through his friend Alain Van Driessche, who translates his words into English from Flemish Dutch, "I am in a bit of a dip. Normally I used to paint every day, between training sessions. But right now, no." He is sitting, sipping strong black coffee and soda water in a bar in the ancient grey-brown cathedral town of Ghent, where he now makes his home. Across the street is the boxing gym where Coopman still trains each day. Inside the eating and drinking establishment, the walls are decorated with badly rendered caricatures of American icons, from Marilyn Monroe to Leonardo DiCaprio. (That might be James Dean, but then again. . . .) Pop songs from the 1950s and '60s blare over the loudspeakers. It is mid-afternoon, and we're the only ones here.

Coopman was instructed from childhood as a sculptor, an artisan, someone who could repair the medieval stone in the great churches when it fell into disrepair. He became, of course, a boxer, and he fought for the heavyweight championship of the world, the only Belgian to do so. But his finest work, Coopman believes, is a painting, a portrait of Muhammad Ali after a famous photograph by Neil Leifer. In it, beads of sweat pour down Ali's face, lit like tiny diamonds. In years past, they'd show his work, especially in the summer towns along the Belgian coast. "That painting doesn't see Ali just as a fighter. But always as a human being," says Van Driessche. "He's much greater as a human being than as a fighter. In that painting he had the combination of the fighter and the human being. Everyone who sees it is fascinated. It really was his masterpiece."

"I wanted to write to Ali and send him the portrait afterwards," Coopman says. "I wrote but I never got an answer, so I never sent it anywhere.

"Ali changed my life," he continues. "The Ali fight was the defining moment of my career. Everybody forgets I was the European heavyweight champion. Nobody talks about that. But everybody asks me questions about the Ali fight, wherever I go in Belgium. Ali is part of my life forever. That fight changed my life. It was the defining moment not only of my career, but of my life."

AMONG THE STORIES OF THOSE who stepped into the ring against Muhammad Ali are some extremely unlikely tales, longshots, no-hopers, fighters lifted out of obscurity for their date with the most famous man on earth. The wildest, the weirdest, the least likely belongs to Jean-Pierre Coopman, dubbed on a publicist's whim the Lion of Flanders, the man many in boxing believe is the least talented fighter ever to challenge for the heavyweight championship of the world.

That's a debating point, of course. There are certainly other candidates. But in the long history of boxing, it's tough to find anyone quite so obscure, quite so unqualified, who was given a title shot—and given it precisely because he was so obscure, so unqualified. Still, if he became a joke to those who remember him only for that hopeless loss to Ali in 1976, at home he was something else, a national hero, then a national embarrassment, then a hero once more. And those who really know him also understood that Coopman has a bit of the poet in his soul.

He was born in the small Flemish village of Ingelmunster in 1946. His father died when he was a boy and his mother later married a man who was in the business of restoring historic buildings. Coopman had shown a gift for drawing and painting, so his stepfather brought him into the trade, teaching him how to sculpt, how to work as men had worked centuries before. Together they helped restore the medieval church of St. Nicholas in Ghent. "We had to recreate things as they were in the Middle Ages," Coopman says. "We worked all day with a chisel and hammer." His arms and hands grew strong.

Belgium was not then, is not now and never really was, a boxing country. There was a minor boom in the sport during the dark years between World Wars, but even the best Belgian boxers, at most, harboured dreams of a European championship. The best of all was probably Cyrille Delannoit, who in 1948 at the Heysel Stadium in Brussels won a fifteen-round decision over the great Marcel Cerdan—though Van Driessche, in his role as Belgian boxing historian, has his doubts about the result. "He should have lost the fight, but he impressed the English referee so much that he said, 'For your effort I'll give you the victory.'" Cerdan won the rematch six weeks later, and that was that.

In 1960, Belgium sent its last full boxing team to the Olympic Games. Included was a light heavyweight who was drawn in the first round against the representative of the United States, Cassius Marcellus Clay. "The coach of the Belgian team said, 'Don't worry, you're just fighting an American. You'll win.' He [the Belgian] was knocked out in the second round," Van Driessche says. "The sixties were a real disaster for boxing."

The sport was of so little importance then that the one major indoor venue in the country, the Palais des Sports in Brussels, was torn down in 1966. But in the early seventies, there was a fighter of at least national renown, a middleweight named Gilbert Montagne, who also hailed from Ingelmunster. He and Coopman were social companions as young men, and in those days Coopman was exceptionally social. "The thing he did most was drinking and smoking," Van Driessche says. "If you ask him, he will tell you straight away, 'Before I started fighting I was a champion—at sitting in the bar and drinking and smoking. You couldn't beat me.'" Every once in a while, the two men would spar, and on one of those occasions, Montagne's manager Albert de Jager watched them, and thought he saw something in Coopman that suggested he might have potential as a fighter. "Belgium is a very small country," Van Driessche says. "The boxing world here is very, very small. Someone said to Coopman, 'Why don't you try?' That's said by every drunk sitting at the bar. Why don't you try? Coopman said, 'Well, I'll try.' He stopped smoking and drinking in one day. He never smoked or had a drink again in his life."

"I decided to change my way of life," Coopman says. "At the time, I couldn't move from here to there. I had very bad blood circulation due to constant smoking. If you saw me, you saw a cigarette in my mouth. When I decided to become a boxer, you never saw a cigarette in my mouth. It was a total change of life."

De Jager had arranged for an exhibition to benefit local orphans, but Montagne's opponent didn't show up. "It was a big disaster," Coopman says. "But de

Jager knew that I was doing things with Gilbert all the time. He said, 'You go into the ring.' The situation, with those orphans being there, I had to agree to fight. And after watching us, de Jager said to me, 'You should have a career.'" Later, they fought a second exhibition, this time with many of Belgium's boxing trainers and managers in attendance. "They said, 'You've got some talent.' I said, 'If everybody tells me I've got to fight, I've got to fight, so get me a licence.' That's where it started."

This is not to suggest that Coopman actually *could* fight. He was strong and he was willing; he would crowd his opponents and kind of suffocate them, using a cross-armed Archie Moore-style defence. But he couldn't really punch and he couldn't really box, and in Belgium it wasn't like he was going to get the chance to refine his skills. "He isn't serious but he's popular," Van Driessche says. "He's a very nice guy. Everybody can speak with him. Everybody can reach him. He's a good guy, too good to be a fighter. The real, brutal fighting heart isn't there." Coopman began as an amateur, and got as far as the 1971 European championships, where, with all of fifteen bouts under his belt, he took on the Soviet champion, who had fought 315 times. Coopman, like all of the other members of the Belgian team, was knocked out in the first round.

In 1972, at the relatively advanced age of twenty-six, Coopman turned pro, hoping to make a little extra money fighting in Belgium and dreaming that, some day, if everything went right, he might get a shot at the European title. He won his first four fights at home and then ventured to Oslo, where he was beaten by a local hero named Harald Skog. "After that," Van Driessche says, "they kept him at home."

From the day he turned professional until the day that changed his life forever, February 20, 1976, there is not a hint in Coopman's record to suggest that he was ready for bigger things. He lost to the Dutchman Rudi Lubbers, who lost to Ali by decision in 1973. He won a hugely questionable disqualification victory over Terry Daniels—one of Joe Frazier's joke opponents, and one of the five men George Foreman once fought and beat in one night. Coopman hoped that he might get a shot at the European champ Joe Bugner or the number-one contender, Richard Dunn, but those fights never came together, which may have been a blessing. "Dunn [who was knocked out by Ali in five rounds in 1975] would have knocked him out in one round," Van Driessche says. "He was a puncher." Still, Coopman was likeable and popular and he could sell a few tickets to fights in Belgium. By late 1975, he was actually able to give up his day job and concentrate on boxing full-time (the company for whom he sculpted paid him a salary to fight instead), which made him unique among his countrymen, perhaps unique in Belgian history. There was nothing in his experience, though, nothing in his training, nothing in his life, that could have prepared him for what was to come next.

MUHAMMAD ALI WAS TIRED, he was worn out and he was beaten. His third fight with Joe Frazier, the Thrilla in Manila, had been the most draining experience of his life. There was plenty of demand for him to step right back into the ring after that titanic battle, but Ali was looking for an easy night's work. The search for a suitable, soft opponent was turned over to the veteran matchmaker George Kanter, who, it happened, was Belgian by birth, and who knew the international boxing scene well. His job was to come up with a fighter who could be sold to a skeptical American public as a legitimate challenger for the title, but also someone who wouldn't cause the champion to break a sweat. Kanter immediately looked to Europe. "European heavyweights weren't much at the time, and the heavyweights in Belgium were even less," Kanter, who has since died, told author Thomas Hauser for the oral history *Muhammad Ali: His Life and Times*. "But then Ali said he was tired of fighting tough opponents, and that after Manila he was entitled to an easy bout. And Coopman was perfect. Now, generally speaking, if you're trying to sell a mediocre fighter in the United States, you're at an advantage if he's European. That's because nobody knows him. As the French say, it's easy to lie when you come from far away." Kanter contacted de Jager and says that Coopman's manager was so excited at the prospect that he offered to have his fighter meet Ali for free. "Don't tell the promoter that," Kanter told him, "because if you do, that's exactly what you'll be fighting for."

After hearing from Kanter, de Jager phoned every manager and trainer he knew in Belgium, asking them what they thought of the fight. "He's a clever guy in his own village," Van Driessche says, "but he doesn't know the world. What he does know is that

Coopman doesn't stand a chance against Ali." The question, then, wasn't of winning or losing, but simply whether Coopman would get seriously hurt. "Most of the trainers told him, 'Ali isn't a killer,'" Van Driessche says. "If he would have had an offer to fight Foreman or Frazier, he would have said no. Those guys are killers. Ali had that human side. He had a kind of humanity in fighting. The feeling was that Ali will understand."

ONE DAY, DURING A SHORT break from training, Coopman visited his doctor in Ghent. He found him standing outside of his office. "He was pale as a ghost," Coopman remembers. "He was very excited. He said, 'Jean-Pierre, your manager just called. Guess who you're going to fight?'"

"I think I'm going to fight Joe Bugner for the European title," Coopman replied.

"No, no," said the doc. "You're going to fight Muhammad Ali for the world title."

"I was knocked out," Coopman says. "I still feel that moment. It still thrills me. It was an enormous moment."

It seemed for a while, he says, like the whole world wanted to come and visit him at his little house in Ingelmunster. Television crews arrived from across Europe. Then Coopman was flown to New York for the pre-fight press conference at Mamma Leone's restaurant, where he saw Ali in the flesh for the first time. "For moments like these," he says, "there are no words."

The press conference was also the occasion at which Kanter famously came up with the nickname the Lion of Flanders, which no one had ever called Coopman before. "But don't forget," Van Driessche says, "that Jean-Pierre was born on the eleventh of July, which is the national holiday of Flanders. That day, the Flemish army beat the French army in 1302. There is a myth about that battle—the myth of the golden spurs. During that battle, there was one mysterious fighter who made a difference. And he was called the Lion of Flanders. As Jean-Pierre was born on the eleventh of July, it was as though the Lion of Flanders was fighting again."

In a desperate attempt to build up the fight, Ali had tried his best to cast the eminently likeable Coopman as a cold-hearted racist. "Ali was a bit aggressive," Van Driessche says. "They played the racist thing. He was a negro hater and so on and so on. But during question time it became clear that Jean-Pierre wasn't a racist at all." And when Ali went into his full act, talking about all of the terrible things he was going to do to Coopman in the ring, Coopman responded in a way no opponent had before. He said nothing, walked up to Ali and gave him a kiss.

The reporters asked Coopman how he thought he'd do in the fight.

"Well," he said, "I'm going to do my best." (By all accounts, a typically straightforward, honest, Flemish response.)

Afterwards, the promoters told him not to say that any more. "We can't sell a fight with a guy doing his best," they explained. "You have to say you're going to win." Coopman played along. He started to tell everyone that he was going to beat the Great Ali.

Eventually, hearing it so many times in his own voice, he even started to believe it.

THE FIRST CLUE SHOULD HAVE been training camp. A month before the fight, Coopman travelled to San Juan, Puerto Rico, where the bout would be held, to acclimatize himself and to prepare as best he could. He brought along a fellow Belgian fighter, an old friend, and when they sparred, Coopman didn't look too bad. But for the first public sparring sessions, staged at a local hotel, three American fighters stepped in, each working three rounds against the challenger. At the mention of one of them, Charlie Green, Coopman lets out a great, comic book moan: "Oooooh." After the session with Green, Coopman told de Jager, "You may be alive on the twentieth of February, but I will be long dead. If this doesn't change, I'm not going to make the fight."

It didn't change. The sparring partners nearly killed him. Coopman continued to look awful. But he was starting to get in shape, not just from the sparring sessions, but from running and chopping wood, kayaking, even playing ping-pong. His confidence actually began to build. "He saw the Frazier fight, he saw the Foreman fight. He saw those guys pushing Ali, having him on the ropes," Van Driessche says. "He thought to himself, 'That's my way of fighting. I get him on the ropes. I kill him.' He really believed he could do that."

He told his fellow Belgians that he *was* going to do that. He started talking like an American, shilling for the fight. But Belgians come from a reserved society that doesn't much like braggarts, that regards hubris with deep suspicion. So while some of his countrymen began to believe the impossible along with him, most were sitting back and waiting for Coopman to fail.

The fight wouldn't be shown live on Belgian television. No fights were; the government there was the first to ban boxing broadcasts. But there was always German TV, where Belgian fight fans had long got their fix of Ali. And three hundred fans, an enormous number given the logistics, given the size of the country, would make the trip to Puerto Rico to cheer on the Lion of Flanders. "It was the biggest event in Belgian sporting history," Van Driessche says without qualification. "A Belgian guy fighting for the world title. Unbelievable. It was history. It was everything at once."

IT WAS ALSO, IN BOXING terms, mostly a fiasco. Coopman was every bit as bad as expected. "Until the bell had sounded, I thought I could win," he says. "But two seconds after the bell, he knew that I was nothing more than a fly. I wanted to spend four or five rounds just putting on the pressure and blocking the shots. But against Ali it didn't work. It came from all sides, from all angles." In fact, Ali seemed not entirely interested. The fight was stopped in the fifth round, with Coopman battered but not desperately hurt, a fact in which he takes some pride. "George Chuvalo took a beating for fifteen rounds [against Ali]," he says. "I myself didn't take a beating that long, and it wasn't that terrible, which is why it was possible to continue afterwards."

He would, however, like to clear up one misconception. It was reported by Kanter, and others, that before the fight Coopman was drinking champagne in his dressing room, understanding his fate, thrilled by the payday (four million Belgian francs, or about $100,000), not entirely serious about the actual fighting part. Not so, he says. He only drank champagne *during* the fight. "I had heard a story that Joe Frazier used to wash his mouth between rounds with champagne. To get rid of the slime and so on and so on," Coopman says. "Frazier, he was my idol, he was my man. Frazier, he spit the champagne out. I had always tried to get pointers and tips from everywhere. So I tried it out. I found that cleaning your mouth with champagne actually worked very well. During the first four or five rounds I just spit it out. And from round five or six on, I swallowed a bit of champagne, which made me a little bit euphoric, and made me go faster and faster."

How did he feel, I ask Coopman, when they stopped the fight? "It was just in time," he says. "Just in time to get out safe. Surviving the fight was more important than the result. In the dressing room afterwards, a lot of Americans were poking around, asking questions. The general feeling was relief. It was never a question of winning or losing. Just surviving. Yes, I lost the fight. But most of them do against Ali. But surviving the fight, that was okay."

He returned home to Ingelmunster, where he initially received the kind of loser-hero's welcome that Georges Carpentier enjoyed in Paris after he was knocked out by Jack Dempsey, or that Henry Cooper still receives in England, or Karl Mildenberger in Germany, or Chuvalo in Canada after their losses to Ali. But then, opinion turned. "The press people really broke him," Van Driessche says. "They broke him for his performance. Before the fight, they actually believed along with Jean-Pierre that he had a chance. But when he lost after the fight, they destroyed him. The critics were very, very harsh. He still feels it. He came home and he's a laughingstock. They kept asking the questions: We thought you were going to beat Ali. What happened, man? To try your best is the name of the game over here. Do your best—that's all they accept. But they didn't understand the American way of selling a fight. They didn't understand what he had to say. That was a big problem. And they punished him for it."

For non-Belgians, that part may be hard to understand. But not nearly so hard as Coopman's path to redemption. On his return from Puerto Rico, he wanted to get back into the ring immediately, if for no other reason than to prove his many critics wrong. The European heavyweight title at that moment was vacant, though it was clear that Lucien Rodriguez, a Frenchman who had already beaten Coopman rather easily, was the class of the field since Joe Bugner had relinquished the crown. But Rodriguez had a small promotional problem: No one in France much cared about him (that country's most popular fighter was Jean-Claude Bouttier, the fine middleweight, and the great Argentinian champion Carlos Monzon had made Monaco his base of operations), to the point where he had trouble selling tickets even on home soil.

So how to make some money? The mandatory contender for the title was Jose Urtain, a lumbering Spanish fighter who, by that point, was absolutely shot. Next in line (remember, it was a very shallow pool) was Coopman. Thus was struck a promotional arrangement of convenience. Coopman would fight Urtain, a bout that he figured to win, and then, as the new European champion, immediately fight Rodriguez in Belgium, where everyone assumed they'd draw a crowd. And of course, Coopman would lose.

The plan worked to perfection. Coopman beat Urtain. Less than two months later, in front of a wildly partisan home crowd in Antwerp, he lost to Rodriguez.

But for that brief spell, Jean-Pierre Coopman achieved his dream. He was the European heavyweight champion. "He'd already lost it before he won it," Van Driessche says. "But when he won, people forgave him. It was front-page news all over the country. Today, they remember that he fought Ali, but they also remember him because he became the European champion afterwards."

"I proved my critics wrong. I proved that I was the best in Europe at a certain moment in time, which was actually my original goal."

Would that have been the right time to quit?

"Looking back at it, yes, that was the moment. I [proved] my critics wrong, and I'm gone."

Of course, he wasn't gone, because he's a fighter, and because at this point the strange saga of Jean-Pierre Coopman becomes a lot like other boxing stories. He held on too long. He embarrassed himself. He lost to fighters with whom he should never have been in the ring.

He tried to exploit his local fame, taking speaking engagements (at which he wasn't very good), opening a pub with his name on it, and falling out with his business partner. His wife at the time ran through most of his money. Coopman lived the high life, was usually found in the company of beautiful women. But, as Van Driessche says, "It was very sad stuff. He was going down the drain."

Art became his salvation. When a Belgian town commissioned a statue of Cyrille Delannoit, the fighter who had beaten Cerdan, Coopman was awarded the contract. The work was widely admired. And his paintings of boxing scenes seem to capture something beyond the obvious, to get at the heart of the suffering, the pain, of what it meant to win, and especially how it felt to lose.

Still, even before his artistic inspiration faded, Coopman earned most of his living as a custodian at a public building. Plus, there was one final comeback, a half-comic old-timers bout against fellow Belgian Freddy De Kerpel, which astoundingly drew four thousand people. "It's the power of *nostalgie,*" Van Driessche explains. "People want to have boxing stars again."

At the café, I ask Coopman how he feels about Ali now. He pauses for a moment. His face is unmistakably that of a fighter. There is scar tissue around both eyes. His nose is flattened and pushed to one side. When he is about to make a point, he puckers his lips, as though about to blow a kiss.

"If there is a God," he wonders aloud, "what must have been going through His mind to give a disease like Parkinson's to a man like Ali? He's such a great man."

ROUND FOURTEEN

EARNIE SHAVERS

Canastota, New York

EARNIE SHAVERS HAS A PLAN, an idea that will make him rich. As he explains it, spinning out the numbers, totalling up the millions of dollars that will surely be coming his way, his speech gets faster and faster, the words start to blur together in a unique blending of accents: middle American mixed with just a hint of Merseyside. Shavers seems shorter than in memory, though his shoulders are broad and strong, and his handshake betrays serious intent. His head is still shaved, which once upon a time inspired

Muhammad Ali to add to his list of opponents' nicknames: Shavers became the "The Acorn." At the Boxing Hall of Fame induction weekend in Canastota, New York, he draws a long line of autograph seekers. After he signs for them, they are asked to sign a piece of paper for him. It's all part of the larger scheme.

Fighters can become addicted to the idea of the big score. They train for weeks at a stretch to earn hundreds or thousands or millions for one night's work, and so naturally they don't easily adapt to the world of nine-to-five, forty-hour weeks and comfortable annual salaries. That's why, so often, they're played for patsies, why their ring earnings sometimes vanish almost immediately into a nightclub, or a restaurant, or a clothing line, or another get-rich-quick scheme foisted upon them by exploiters who smell an easy mark.

In this case, though, there's no one else pulling the strings. This invention is Shavers' own, and it isn't at all what one might suspect. "One guy sent me seven hundred fifty dollars," he says. "I've got cheques coming now. I send them back. We are not touching any cheques until January first. We're going to put all of the money away. It will be fifty million dollars. We're not going to spend one dime on anybody. We're just going to use the interest, and I'll have five million dollars a year for the rest of my life."

All of that for writing a book, the story of his life.

SHAVERS WAS BORN IN Alabama, but grew up in rural Ohio, near the town of Garland. He explains that one day his father got into a dispute about payments for a mule, pulled a gun on a white man and then was encouraged by the Ku Klux Klan to take his family north. Farm work made Shavers strong. "I grew up throwing heavy bales of hay, carrying big bags of wheat and doing a lot of chopping trees for firewood, developing my back and leg muscles. Little did I know at the time that I would be a fighter. But I had the back muscles and leg muscles, and that's where the power comes from."

He decided early on that farming would not be his chosen career. "At the age of twelve, I knew that I wanted to be a professional athlete one day," Shavers says, "but I thought it would be American football. I never got into boxing until I was twenty-two years old. And that was my last opportunity to become a professional athlete. A friend invited me to a gym in Youngstown, Ohio, where I saw the trainer. I was always a big guy. When I walked in, he took one look at me and immediately said, 'A heavyweight! Do you want to be the champ of the world some day and make a lot of money?' You never mention money to a broke man. So he put the gloves on me right away. I got in the ring. I had no boxing skills, but I could punch. The other guy came out boxing, *jab, jab*. I hit him and he went flying across the ring and the trainer went crazy, 'Oh man, oh man!'

"I went home for one week and thought about it. I went to the gym on January 3, 1967. I went home, thought about it until the tenth of January, came back and had my first fight on January 17. It was a first-round knockout. The local paper came in and did a story and it took off from there—boom. Before you knew it, two years, I was at the top of the ladder as an amateur."

It is a cliché of the sport that punchers are born, that power comes naturally, that it can't really be taught. Strength is only a part of it, which explains muscle-bound fighters who can't punch a lick, and others who look too skinny, or too fat, but who seem to have explosive fists. Landing a knockout punch involves a combination of muscle memory and hand-eye coordination, finely tuned reflexes and a certain *je ne sais quoi.* Even though he started late, even though he never had the chance to learn the fine points of the fistic arts, Earnie Shavers could bang from day one, and that, combined with his being a heavyweight, automatically made him a hot commodity. His amateur career was short: no use wasting that kind of talent on a side of the game where punching power wasn't highly valued, especially since he'd started late. Instead, in November 1969, Shavers turned pro, won his first paid fight by first-round knockout and eventually began a stretch in which he won thirty-three in a row, all but one inside the distance. "Because I could punch so hard, all the trainers wanted me to do was improve on my punching, not on my boxing skills," he says. "I never became a complete boxer, a complete fighter. I was concentrating on my power too much, and that hurt me in the long run here and there."

In fact, it became an all-or-nothing proposition when Shavers moved into the upper echelons of the heavyweight division: Either he'd score a quick knockout, or he'd run out of gas trying, and the opponent would take advantage. "I used to just burn myself out," he says. "But I finally learned to relax, and I won enough to come out ahead."

Historically, Shavers is still remembered for his right hand; he was voted the hardest puncher of the century in one not entirely scientific poll. But in truth, his most significant contribution to the world of professional sport in the twentieth century was as the first fighter handled by a former numbers runner, a convicted murderer, an ex-con from Cleveland with a flare for oratory, named Don King. After first getting involved in the game by promoting a charity fund-raiser for a local hospital featuring Ali—the beginning of a relationship that flowered with the Rumble in the Jungle—King sought first-hand experience in the business. The former major-league pitcher Dean Chance and an Ohio boxing figure called Blackie Gennaro were Shavers' co-managers. King bought out Chance and began to learn the game from scratch. "Don just started getting into the fight game before me with Ali. I was the fighter to get him into New York. He got to New York with me. Don got me a couple of fights. I fought Jerry Quarry, and I fought Jimmy Ellis—and I never got paid for it. Don and I, we had our differences. But it wasn't like everyone says. When I retired from the fight game, Don kept paying me $200,000 a year. His wife took care of me down the road. She said, 'I can't go against Don, but I'll take care of you.'"

As to the circumstances of King's departure as his manager, Shavers speaks coyly about the "Family," about how unnamed organized crime figures squeezed King out and left him to be controlled by other, even less savoury characters. It is certainly not beyond the realm of possibility.

ANOTHER LEGENDARY FIGURE was involved for a time in Shavers' career and also left a lasting impression. Archie Moore, the great light-heavyweight champion and one of the sport's true visionaries, acted as Shavers' trainer, while also explaining to him the money-making fine points of the game. Selling a fight was a skill Moore had mastered during his long career. He understood that Shavers needed a hook, an act, something to help him stand out from the crowd. "I was fighting, but I wasn't making any money," Shavers says. "There were so many black fighters around, you needed a gimmick. I knew it was security for the family. It was the only way I was going to make any money in the fight game. Archie Moore said, 'Earnie, you've got to use what talent you've got, to be what you want to be. You may not mean it, but [when you fight Jimmy Ellis] look at Jimmy as though he killed your mother.' And Jimmy was all smiles. I like the guy. But at that fight, it worked. So I started using it. I decided I would shave my head and not smile. I did it when I fought Henry Clark over in Paris, France, on March 28, '76. I shaved my head. I stared him down. He told me after the fight, 'Earnie, you scared the heck out of me.' I intimidated probably ninety-five per cent of my opponents. But Larry Holmes and Ali wouldn't buy it. I stared at them and they stared right back. It was a long night."

Moore left the picture after nine months, following Shavers' first-round knockout loss to Jerry Quarry in December 1973. "My jaw broke, they stopped the fight and they needed a fall guy. It wasn't going to be Don King and it wasn't going to be me, so Archie was the fall guy." But he'd left a lasting impression. Shavers never changed his act, especially when given the chance to work opposite the greatest performer in the history of the sport.

IT WAS NATURAL THAT he'd eventually face Muhammad Ali. Shavers had remained in the top ten for several years and had fought many of those who would be benchmarks in Ali's own career. But any match with Shavers came with considerable risk, especially for a fighter in the late stages of his career. Among those Ali faced, only Sonny Liston and George Foreman were in Shavers' class as pure punchers. And so it was a match that Ali and his management didn't necessarily relish, and didn't enter into lightly.

"Ali kept saying he would give me a fight. I fought on the Ali–Ken Norton card at Yankee Stadium. I fought Henry Clark, a second-round knockout. And my manager and my trainer said, 'Ali, when are you going to give Earnie a shot?'

"Ali had a sparring partner named Roy "Tiger" Williams. He said, 'If you beat Tiger Williams, I'll give you a shot.' I knew Tiger Williams. He was a tough, tough guy. So I made my mind up I would knock this guy out. We took the fight, I trained hard. The first eight rounds, I was ahead on points. He came back in the ninth and the beginning of the tenth, and damned near destroyed me. But I knew I had to win for the Ali fight. They gave me a standing eight count, asked me questions, asked me my name, where was I fighting, who was I fighting? I said Las Vegas, Earnie Shavers, Roy 'Tiger' Williams. So I knew then, I had to go on the chin and stop him. He came toward me and I stepped in and hit him on the chin and I hurt him. And that's when God gave me strength, and I stopped him.

"But Ali still didn't want to give me the fight. He said, 'Well, you beat him. Why don't you beat Howard Smith?' I knocked Howard out and then he finally had to give me the fight. It was a risky proposition for him. But he had made the promise. Ali had a heart as big as all outdoors. He never would have said he was afraid. Never. He would have died first. That's why I could respect all his pride. Thank God for the pride."

The fight was set for September 29, 1977, at New York's Madison Square Garden. The promotional buildup had a familiar feel, Ali doing his best to intimidate his opponent, and Shavers using his menacing glare; but the fact is, neither had much effect.

"He was a very good friend," Shavers says. "Long before I fought Ali, he had invited me to his training camp in 1973 to train for the Jimmy Ellis fight. And he told me with other guys I was fighting how to beat them. So we were good friends. I knew Ali quite well, so he couldn't psych me. I'd been in his training camp, and we'd talk like you and I.

"When the press would come in and he'd jump and start shouting, I knew this guy would try and con me. But when we fought, he couldn't con me, because I knew him. I'd give him one of these." He offers a cold stare. "I'd say, hey champ, it's going to be a long night. He'd say, 'You've got that right.'"

That's when Shavers became the "Acorn." "And when the fight was over, he told me, 'Shavers, you're a hard nut to crack.'"

While Ali's standard repertoire of intimidation tactics may not have been effective against Shavers, the fact is that the fight may have been won and lost in Shavers' head. All of those years of being a one-punch knockout artist—and all of those questions about his own stamina—left him in a tactical bind. Ali, to that point, had never been stopped and had shown an uncanny ability both for avoiding punches, and for being able to recover quickly on the rare occasions when he'd been caught. Joe Frazier, the only fighter to have beaten him, had done so by winning a fifteen-round war of attrition. So Shavers was drawn away from doing what he did best: throwing caution to the wind, punching as hard as he could, going for the kill from the opening bell.

"In my corner, my trainer had programmed me to go the distance. The fact is, I couldn't beat Ali by going the distance. In the second round I had him hurt." Shavers landed a terrific overhand right, which stunned Ali. "And if I'd followed up, I would have knocked him out. He wouldn't have got away. But I hurt him, and then I backed off. I thought he was playing possum. My mind said, 'You've got to go the distance.' It said, 'Earnie, Ali is going the distance, so you have to go the distance.' But you don't beat Ali by going the distance." Still, he came close. Ali was ahead eight rounds to four on two score cards after twelve rounds, eight rounds to three with one even on the other. (For that fight, the scoring was relayed to the television audience after each round—and to Angelo Dundee in Ali's corner, who had someone watch the broadcast for him and then signal between rounds.) But Shavers won the thirteenth, and won the fourteenth and was landing enough big shots that it still seemed possible he might knock Ali out. But though he seemed absolutely spent, nearly out on his feet, Ali found a reserve of energy and outboxed Shavers decisively through the final three minutes, at one point nearly knocking him down. Pat Putnam, the long-time boxing writer for *Sports Illustrated*, remembered that round, though part of a not particularly classic fight, as one of the greatest of Ali's career.

Even by losing, even by blowing his chance on a night when Ali was certainly beatable, Shavers had reached a higher plateau, and his career was given new momentum. He'd go on to make a memorable challenge for the title against Larry Holmes. But the Ali fight was the pinnacle. "Fighting Ali was probably the greatest thing in my whole fight career," he says. "When Ali fought, the whole world stopped and watched for an hour, and the fact that I did well opened up a lot of doors for me. Even now I get bookings in Timbuktu because of Ali. In my book, the Ali fight makes the whole book."

The book again. The surefire fifty-million-dollar best-seller. But to get to that, you first have to get Earnie Shavers from Ohio to Moreton-on-Wirral.

EARNIE SHAVERS

THERE IS A LONG STRETCH of Earnie Shavers' post-boxing life that he doesn't talk about much now: he has been married and divorced five times, for instance, and has nine offspring from those unions; he was involved in a number of business ventures in the United States, none of which quite panned out; he came back for two sad late-life fights, in the hope of somehow snagging a big money match against the sport's one successful senior citizen, George Foreman; and, like a lot of fighters, he obviously had a bit of trouble settling down, adjusting to civilian life, making his way outside the limelight. For the longest time, he just fell off the map, only to reappear as a newborn minor celebrity in England.

He's told that particular story so often now—his British press clippings are extensive—that the lines seem almost rehearsed. He received a fan letter from a young English fighter named Kenny Rainford, seeking his advice. He eventually visited Rainford, trained him a bit and, one day in December 1997, was sitting in his house when Rainford's aunt, Sue Craig, dropped by for a spot of tea. "She was like a house with every brick in the right place," Shavers says, a phrase he just might have trotted out before. Love at first sight. "Pretty soon," he told Rainford, "you'll be able to call me Uncle."

"I went home. Packed up everything in March, flew back there and stayed," Shavers says. He and Craig set up housekeeping together in the modest town not far from Liverpool, and he found work as a greeter at a wine bar—"Not a bouncer," Shavers is always careful to point out. He found that, far more than in the United States, he was remembered and embraced by the English and that he could parlay that affection into a second career. "I had two-thirds of my fans in England before I went there," he says. "I never fought there. But they love punchers. Moving over there was the best move I ever made in my adult life. It opened a whole lot for me, opened doors. I've got so much coverage there, it's unbelievable. I do after-dinner speaking. I do a lot of personal appearances. I do a lot of work in the prisons too; that's all free. I work with the youth. And I do a lot of boxing memorabilia. They take good care of me. I started out at three hundred pounds a speech. Then I started doing research. I went up to one thousand, two thousand, three thousand. I'm worth five thousand pounds now, but I won't do it any more because I'm tired. I've turned down probably ten to fifteen thousand a month average."

It should be noted that there are less glamorous, less optimistic accounts of Shavers' speaking career. A story in the British newspaper *The Observer* from 1998 relives one particularly desultory evening in Hartlepool, where Shavers appeared with another former boxer, John H. Stracey, along with a godawful comedian. The writer describes a sign advertising the event at a local club: "'Earnie Shavers Plus Four-Course Dinner' had been on sale for fifteen pounds, an offer since crossed out with a biro [marker]. The tickets, the sign now reads, are five pounds, and the four-course dinner has been reduced to 'Pie and Peas.'"

"Ali is the only guy in the world that gets more press in England than I do," Shavers says. "No one compares to me except Ali. I probably get five to ten interview calls a week. The stories—unbelievable, man. They want to know mostly about fighting Ali, about Larry Holmes, about how I learned to punch so hard. I get full pages. So it's unbelievable."

AND SO NATURALLY, IS THE book. It will be called "Earnie Shavers: Welcome to the Big Times." "God gave me the idea," he says. "God gave me the step-by-step. It come to me about a year ago. I said to myself, that won't work. But it worked." For ten years he's been concentrating on it, pulling all of the stories together. "I did the research and everything. It will be out the first of January." (In the past, he's given other publication dates, which never quite materialized, but this time, he assures me that it's for real.) The true genius, he explains, will be in the marketing. Everywhere he goes, every time he talks to somebody, every time he's interviewed, he turns it into a way to find names—names of fans, names of potential book buyers. "We have a mailing list of about seven or eight million names. It's unbelievable. It's *unbelievable.* I did something that no one's ever done before. I contacted newspapers all over the country, England, Canada and America, and I got such great response. Little stories with my name and address. One guy came in and sent me eighty-five hundred names of fight fans. Another sent me three thousand. They come in every day. They're still coming now. Every day. Newspapers. Radio. TV. Internet. We keep adding on.

"If I don't do ten million books I'll be very disappointed. Every five names that come in want three books. Because if you buy one book, you get an autographed book and an autographed picture. If you call two friends and buy three books, you get one of my videos. I'm the only guy who owns my own video rights. It's seventy-two minutes long: Ali, Larry Holmes, Ken Norton, Joe Bugner, Jimmy Ellis, Ron Lyle. On and on. If you order three books you get three signed books, three signed pictures and a video. Otherwise it costs you twenty-four dollars. Right now, every five orders that come in want three books. One lady wanted five books. I said, 'Order six books, you get two videos.' We got one guy that wants fifteen, another guy that wants twelve. Unbelievable.

"When the book comes out, I should share about fifty million dollars. The way it's going now, we share fifty million. Now Larry Holmes called me. He wants me to market his book. I said, 'Larry, I'll charge you one million, tax free. I'll guarantee you five million dollars. Everything beyond five million, I want one-third of the profits.'

"The largest book publisher in England called me and wanted to publish my book. You know what I told them? 'Put it in writing. Send me a letter.' I'll probably go with Richard Branson because he's got all of the Hilton hotels all over the world, so I'll probably go with him. But I don't really need bookstores."

At Canastota, where he is not, and likely never will be, a member of the Hall of Fame, the line for his autograph stretches far out into the parking lot. They're all on Earnie Shavers' list now. They'll all be hearing from him. "I've never in my entire life lived a better life," he says. "The peace of mind that I have. And everything is falling right into line."

LARRY HOLMES

Easton, Pennsylvania

LARRY HOLMES VOLUNTEERS A story. He is sitting in his personal office, located in one of several buildings he owns in this small city, an hour's drive west of New York. Holmes's digs are on the second floor, and his restaurant and travel agency are downstairs. It's a quiet afternoon, and the former heavyweight champion of the world has just come back from the eye doctor, with his pupils uncomfortably dilated. The light's killing him. Still, he's eager to talk, and especially to set the record straight.

"Once, I met a lady in Las Vegas," Holmes says. "She came up to me and said, 'You're Larry Holmes.'

"I said I was, and she said, 'I hate you. I can't stand you. Get away from me.'

"I said, 'Lady, I don't even know you. What the hell is your problem?' She said, 'You beat Ali.' I told her, 'It was either him or me.' But that's how some people feel. She don't know Ali, not like I know Ali. You don't know Ali like I know Ali. The press didn't know Ali like I know Ali. And if they did know Ali, they didn't say nothing about what he did and how he did it. All that people know now is that movie. Everybody says it's a great movie. Shit, the movie sucks, I think. Give it a five. One to ten, give it a five. Will Smith did a great acting job—*in spots*. I ain't here to knock Will Smith. I think he's a good actor playing what he plays on 'Diff'rent Strokes' or whatever the hell he plays on. In the movie, one to ten, I'll give it a five.

"Look, I still admire Ali. I just don't admire all of the shit he did. He ain't as great as everybody wants to say he is. He wasn't a saint. But if you tell people something like that, they kick your ass. You can't talk bad about Muhammad Ali. He was great. He was God."

At the age of fifty-two, Holmes has reached a stage in life where he's not interested in being careful any more. He's not willing to tiptoe around in the hope that people might like him better, that he might be more accepted and acknowledged by boxing fans, that he might emerge out from under the shadow of the man who employed him as a sparring partner and whom he finally had to beat in a terrible, horrifying no-win fight, only to be hated for it by some. Once upon a time, Larry Holmes said, after the first loss of his professional career, that Rocky Marciano couldn't carry his jockstrap, and the sportswriters crucified him for it. Once upon a time, he would have done just about anything to make the public understand that he was the best heavyweight of his generation and, arguably, one of the best of all time.

Now, still not officially retired, he would like to make it perfectly clear that he doesn't really give a damn.

"There are a lot of guys out here who get a little fame and a little fortune and they forget about shit," he says. "They think they're better than everybody. I want people to look up to me. But what's the difference? I'd like for people to remember me when I'm gone, but I'm not going to know anything about it. I'm not like the Jehovah's Witnesses who believe that dead people still walk around the earth and see what's happening. I believe when you're dead, you're just dead. Just like before I was born, I didn't know nothing. So I believe that you do what you can do right now when you're here. I believe you do the best that you can. And you certainly would like to leave something behind for your kids so they don't have to grow up in starvation or hunger. You don't want them to grow up like I did with poorness and ghettoness and the welfare. You want them to have something, to be able to say, 'My dad did this.' That's how I guess you live on. But still, you gonna be dead. You know what I mean? You ain't going to be here to look at it.

"I liked the fame. But now that I'm older and I understand a little bit more about what it is, I don't go through that. If people want an autograph, sign it, give it to them. Before I might have had a little problem, but now I don't have no problem."

HOLMES MOVED TO EASTON from rural Georgia as a five-year-old and says he never once wanted to leave. He has built a life in the city, he has built a substantial business empire, and it was here that he learned to fight. A local trainer named Ernie Butler got him into the sport and led him through the amateur ranks. Holmes grew into a heavyweight and developed a style of sticking and moving behind a sharp, quick left jab, while throwing his right hand with knockout power. "In the beginning, I never thought I was going to go pro," he says. "I didn't go pro until I was twenty-three to twenty-four years old. I just liked the fact that boxing gave me something to do every day. It gave me something to work for, and then it gave me a chance to make a few dollars

"I dropped out of school in the seventh grade. What could I do? I couldn't go to college. I went to the steel mills driving a truck and I didn't like that. I did that for five years. But I kept boxing and working as a sparring partner, and I was getting good at it. Working with Ali, working with Joe Frazier, working with guys like Earnie Shavers and other top heavyweights. I was getting good at it."

But in what should have been his breakthrough moment as an amateur, Holmes instead suffered a humiliating setback. In the trials to select the American team for the 1972 Olympics in Munich, he was disqualified for excessive holding in a bout with the eventual U.S. heavyweight representative at the Games, Duane Bobick. Holmes was ridiculed, labelled a coward and written off as a second-rate Ali impersonator.

"Everybody said I ran out of the ring," he says now. "Fuck, I didn't run out of the ring. I didn't want to go. I didn't want to go to the Olympics. I knew that if you clinched, they were going to disqualify you. They told me that. I said, 'I'm not letting this big guy knock me out.' I only weighed 185 pounds. I lost weight before the trials. I was going to fight Bobick, two hundred and some pounds. I don't want to go anyway. Who cares? I had this rough feeling in my gut that something bad was going to happen, so I just didn't want to go. I clinched, got disqualified and that was fine with me. I turned pro in 1973. I didn't look back until 1985. I never lost."

Of course, something bad did happen in Munich: the massacre of Israeli athletes. And Bobick was knocked out there by the great Cuban amateur Teofilo Stevenson. Still, there's a certain cachet that goes with being an American Olympic heavyweight, not to mention monetary advantages. Instead, when Holmes turned pro, his rewards were distinctly modest. "I was ready to make some money," he says. "And I made sixty-three dollars for my first fight. You know how much money that was? That was all right. I got a hundred bucks, but when they were finished I ended up with sixty-three. I was rich, man. I could buy everybody dinner. One hot dog for a dollar."

What no one realized about him then, what few were willing to acknowledge until much, much later, when he beat Ken Norton for a portion of the heavyweight title, was that Holmes was a great talent, with a tremendous work ethic. Fighters who arrive in the wake of larger-than-life champions always have a difficult time establishing themselves in the public imagination, no matter how good they are. Comparisons are always being made with the fading star. Even if the crown is passed in the ring, there's always the doubt about how the new guy would have done against the old guy in his prime.

Holmes is a classic example, made all the more dramatic because of the many years he spent within Muhammad Ali's circle, as sparring partner and protégé. He was constantly underestimated, constantly put down as a wannabe. What few could see, especially in the swirl of the Ali circus, was just how badly Holmes wanted it, how hard he worked, how diligently he went about his business, understanding that one day, his chance would come. "Why did I get up and run?" he says. "Because I thought that the other guy was running. Why did I go to the gym and train? Because I thought that the other guy was training? And that kept my mind focused on what I wanted to do."

HOLMES HAD BEEN LINKED with Ali even before the Bobick fight. "I met him earlier, in '71," Holmes remembers. "He was looking at a piece of land up in Deer Lake, Pennsylvania, for his training camp. My trainer, Ernie Butler, knew Angelo Dundee. When he went up there with Angelo Dundee, he met Ali. Ali was going to put on an exhibition in Reading, Pennsylvania. He wanted me to work with him. So I did. He gave me a black eye. I liked it. He said, 'You're pretty good. Come up and work with me.' So I did."

For most of the next four years, he would be part of the Ali roadshow, in the role of the number-one sparring partner. Holmes fought for himself, on Ali undercards and in small shows, but his primary role—as was the case for the many hangers-on who made up the entourage—was as a supporting act. At the beginning, Holmes found that subordinate status no problem. "I was thrilled. I was a little kid in a candy store, man. I was happy," he says. "I liked Ali. I still like Ali. He was a great man. I had no problems with Ali." He honed his skills, learning something new in the ring every day. "I didn't try to become Muhammad Ali, but people said I did," Holmes says. "My style was always to move, and try to keep away from the punches that would hurt me, and block and make sure that I didn't do any stupid-ass stuff, and train. My thing was to learn to become as good as Ali and learn to become better than Ali."

He also learned a different kind of lesson, from seeing some of the other, less savoury, goings-on in camp.

"I watched," Holmes says. "I took it all in. I said, 'That ain't going to happen to me. I ain't going to do it like this, I ain't going to do it like that.' And I didn't do it like that. I was careful. I watched myself. To this day, a lot of things, I say, shit, man, no way. It was money, women, everything else. You name it. The hangers-on. Letting anybody in the camp. Ali liked people. I was with him and I seen a lot of it. I seen *a lot* of it. A lot of it I didn't approve of. But who was I to say, 'Hey, don't do this?' Just shut the fuck up. Do your job, man. Don't worry about it. But to myself, I said don't do it. Don't do it. That's wrong.

"I know how he lived. I knew what he did. I seen the people come into camp and leaving camp. I know he walked around with a stiff dick every day. I knew that. He would fuck a snake if you hold its head. You don't even have to hold the motherfucker's head. Just give him the snake."

Holmes also began to understand some of the seamier aspects of the boxing business, which would become a recurring theme in his career. He says that before one of his early fights, against Jeff Merritt in Cleveland, Ohio, he asked the promoter Don King for a fifty-dollar loan. King refused. "I remember that shit," he says. "I don't forget that. It taught me that nobody wants to do nothing for you. You've got to do it on your own. I still don't need nobody. If my secretary don't want to work here, then get your ass out. If my brother don't want to work here, then get your ass out. I do it myself. I'm not handicapped."

Most boxing fans consider Holmes's victory over Ken Norton for the World Boxing Council heavyweight title his real coming of age. But Holmes himself remembers an earlier fight, when he was still in the Ali orbit. "Guys like [manager] Al Braverman told Don King that I was never going to be nothing.

Howard Cosell said that I was just a copy of Muhammad Ali. He said it on TV and in person and everything. They didn't have no problem telling me what they felt." That image began to change, Holmes says, when he fought contender Roy Williams on the undercard of Ali's title defence against Jimmy Young in Landover, Maryland. "Williams was one of the most serious contenders out there at that time. No one wanted to fight him. I didn't want to fight him either. For three thousand dollars? Why should I fight Roy Williams in a ten-round fight for three thousand dollars? A guy that would knock your head off. But it was either that or you were afraid of him, you ain't going to never be nothing. I didn't want them to say that I was afraid of him and I wanted to show people that I wanted to be something. So I fought him and broke my left hand on his elbow in the third or fourth round and still won ten rounds out of ten."

In 1975, immediately following Ali's defence against Chuck Wepner, Holmes left the camp for good. "At that point, [Ali] couldn't handle me anyway. I was too fast. I knew every move he made. Four years of boxing with him, I know him. When he spit, I knew he was getting ready to spit. I knew him. And I didn't want to go on to be labelled as just a sparring partner. I didn't want to be just a sparring partner. I wanted to be a sparring partner to learn. And I did. I learned with Joe Frazier, I learned with Earnie Shavers, I learned with a lot of heavyweight contenders. But I wanted to get on my own and make some money—not five hundred dollars a week."

Three years later, Norton was awarded the WBC title outside the ring because Leon Spinks opted for an immediate rematch with Ali, rather than a mandatory defence against Norton. The condition was that he take on the undefeated number-one challenger, Larry Holmes. Their fifteen-round fight is still counted among the classics of the era, with Holmes finally winning by a single point on the scorecards.

"Winning that fight meant that I proved every damn body wrong," he says. "They said, 'Your legs are too small, you can't punch. Ken Norton will beat the shit out of you. Ken Norton will kill you. You can't fight them guys. You ain't big enough, you ain't strong enough.'

"I proved them wrong. I beat him. I beat the shit out of him. Not by one point—that was the judges' opinion. But I was satisfied because I won it. He was a good fighter. He was strong. He punched hard. He was determined. And my left arm was shot. Six days before the fight, it was shot. I pulled a muscle. I should have called the fight off. But when the bell rang, I used that motherfucker like there was no tomorrow. That's what I had to do. I had to do it because I needed to do it, not for everyone around me, but I needed to do it for me, to prove to everybody around me that I could do it."

Larry Holmes was a heavyweight champion of the world. Ali, after beating Spinks in their second fight, claimed that he was finally retiring for good. But still, there remained unfinished business. And any student of boxing history, thinking back to Jim Jeffries against Jack Johnson, or Joe Louis against

Rocky Marciano, understood that, inevitably, the old champion would be summoned back for one more payday and that, just as inevitably, it would prove to be a terrible mistake.

ORIGINALLY, HOLMES SAYS, Ali's management had approached him about a bloodless, orderly transition. Ali would step down. Holmes would become the champion. No one would get hurt. "I was going to sign an agreement one time with [Ali's manager] Herbert Muhammad, that I would be the one to replace Ali and take his title," Holmes says. "And then Herbert Muhammad said no way afterwards. They agreed verbally, but they pulled out. They said, 'No we're not going to let Larry fight him. We don't think he's worthy of carrying Muhammad Ali's jock. Ali will never fight him. It will never happen.' But, hey, it didn't bother me, because I didn't want to fight him either. At thirty-eight years old, you're old. I would be in a no-win situation. If I win, he was too old. And if I lost, I couldn't fight; I never had it."

What changed, unfortunately, was Ali's financial position. There are plenty of places to lay the blame, but the fact is that many fighters, forced into retirement, are unable to cope with the sudden cessation of cash flow. They never anticipate the end. They always figure that what they're spending today will be paid for with the proceeds of one more big fight. When it stops all at once, with bills and taxes and retainers still to be paid (and almost always with unscrupulous managers and promoters and "friends" who've taken advantage of them), someone capable of earning millions of dollars for a single night's work can find himself broke.

Most everyone understood that Ali should never have come back. He had been life and death to split his last two fights with Leon Spinks, the next best thing to a rank amateur. Holmes was undefeated, in his prime, a great fighter in his own right. Forget any talk of the Ali magic: This was going to be a slaughter. "I knew Ali couldn't beat me in 1975," Holmes says. "So what was he going to do in 1980?"

But as the fight approached, expert opinion slowly began to shift. Physically, Ali looked better than he had in years. (As it turned out, he'd been taking drastic measures, including diuretics, to drop weight, which further weakened him in the fight.) Watching him in training, listening to his confident boasts, some who should have known better came to believe that he was capable of doing the impossible once again, just as he had in Kinshasa against George Foreman. They were thinking with their hearts.

Holmes was not one of those who was fooled. "Y'all probably didn't know it, because he tricked everybody," he says. "He looked good. But sometimes the mind makes a date the body can't keep. He burned that candle at both ends, and something gives in the middle—the wax, you know. That's what I'm trying to tell you. You don't know what went on [in his camp]. I was in the camp when he was fighting George Foreman and Joe Frazier and those people.

"Listen, man. He had something, but he didn't have discipline. He could fight. But he didn't have discipline. He had intimidation, but he didn't have discipline. He had it all, but he didn't have discipline. And you have to have discipline when you fight me. Because I'm going to be ready. I'm more disciplined. I knew what Ali had.

"When I fought Ali, I even had six stitches in my eye. I got hit in the damn gym by a head-butt. Cut me right under the eye, where you couldn't see it. Right under the eye. And the doctors were so good in Las Vegas that they opened my eye and looked, they couldn't even find the cut. They couldn't see the stitches under the eyelid. Because I opened my eye like that and did like this, and they couldn't fuckin' see it."

The point is, Holmes understood there was no risk, understood that he could go into the fight at less than 100 per cent, because there was no way he could lose. All of those years in the gym with a younger, better Ali told him that this old man posed absolutely no risk. The only question was how to end the fight humanely, how to win without appearing to torture and humiliate a revered champion. Holmes knew full well that no one was going to love him for it afterwards, but he also understood that he had no choice. There was a job to do.

"I knew one thing. He would take a punch. And I knew another thing. He would take a beating. You see, my thing is, I tried to get rid of him, but after the first four or five rounds I stopped. I just wanted the referee to stop it. What happens to fighters after four or five good rounds of *bang, bang, bang, bang* is they get hurt if they take those punches. You take punishment, something's got to give, man."

Anyone who watched those eleven terrible rounds now wishes they hadn't. The king was finally, undeniably dead. Long live the king.

After Ali, Holmes met every worthy challenger of his era and through the first forty-eight fights of his career beat them all. There were a few close calls, but overall, his reign was longer and more dominant than that of any heavyweight champion aside from Joe Louis.

The most memorable of his title defences came in 1982, when he was challenged by Gerry Cooney, a white Irish-American heavyweight attempting to become the first Caucasian to claim the heavyweight title since Ingemar Johansson. There has always been a racist tinge to boxing promotion, going back to the search for a Great White Hope to defeat the champion Jack Johnson. What was shocking, though, in the 1980s, was the fact that the emergence of an apparently legitimate white contender could stir up so many of those same, ugly undercurrents. Holmes, who would stop Cooney in the thirteenth round, was both the beneficiary (the fight produced a huge payday for him) and the victim.

"Everybody knows what happened there," he says. "They don't forget the bullshit that went on. They might want to forget the bullshit that went on, but they can't. Because they know how big of a racist fight that was. They blew my mailbox up. They wrote KKK all over my wall. They put junk in my food at Caesars Palace. I went to the other hotel then, moved out of there. The bullshit that went on, the threatening phone calls, fuck it. They threatened to kill my son. I didn't have one yet. My wife was pregnant with him. Threatened to kill my son. Shit like that.

"I walked out in Caesars Palace, man. You see white, you think they're all against you, they're going to do something to you. Because you get one or two who say Cooney is going to whip your ass, you ain't this, you ain't that. You wonder. What the fuck's wrong with this sport? They call me a racist. Yeah, I'm a racist. Half of my family is white. So it's hard to be a racist. Yeah, I don't like white people. Some of them I like, some of them I don't. That's the same for everybody. I'm not a racist. I'm just a guy that wants to pay the bills."

Today, unfortunately, it's the way Holmes's reign as heavyweight champion ended that's remembered, more than any of the fights he won. In 1985, having fought all of the worthy challengers in the division, Holmes was matched against the undefeated light-heavyweight champion Michael Spinks. The fight seemed almost an afterthought (no reigning light-heavyweight champ had ever moved up to win the heavyweight crown), the real story being that Holmes was poised to tie Rocky Marciano's record of going undefeated in forty-nine professional fights. During his opening sparring sessions, Holmes seemed almost desperate in the way he courted the fans who paid to watch him work out, wanting badly to be loved the way Ali was loved.

But instead, the Spinks fight and its aftermath would turn into the one real blemish on Holmes's career. In a temporary arena erected in the parking lot of the Riviera Casino in Las Vegas, Spinks stayed away from Holmes's power and used a clever, awkward style to score a unanimous decision victory. "It hurt," Holmes says, "because I thought it could have been a draw, if anything. But because of the situation, the games they were playing on me, I knew I wasn't going to win."

Still, the fight wasn't the worst of it. At the post-fight press conference, with Marciano's brother (who had actively been rooting for Spinks) in the audience, Holmes was asked what he thought of the late former champion. Still angry and distraught at having lost the close, controversial decision, he replied, "Rocky Marciano couldn't carry my jockstrap." It was taken as a tasteless slight, as sour grapes, and as a sure sign that Holmes didn't really belong in the pantheon, alongside Marciano, Joe Louis, Jack Dempsey and, of course, Muhammad Ali.

"When I said it, I didn't mean it in the way that they wanted me to mean it, or that they made it out for me to mean it," Holmes explains. "I meant that I'm as good as anybody. You can't carry my jock-strap. I'm as good as anybody. You can't carry my baseball bat or my lunch bucket or anything else. I'm as good as you, or better than you. And don't put me down. I didn't say anything to hurt his family or his friends or anybody else. I didn't say that to hurt nobody. It was slang. His picture's on my wall in my restaurant."

Holmes and Spinks signed for an immediate rematch: Spinks won again, this time by an even narrower margin. Most observers felt Holmes deserved the nod. "Going in, I said, man, how can I lose? And they did it to me again. It embitters you because you don't win, but it don't embitter me to the point that I still hate Spinks because he still thinks that he won.

"If someone beats me, I say, damn, it was a close fight. I could have lost. I said the same thing with the first fight with Spinks. I thought it was a draw, but I could have lost. But the second fight I won. To me there was no doubt about it. But I don't want to go and hide. I don't care if people make fun of me. I'm not going to put a gun to my head and blow my head off. If I lose, I lose. I win, I win. Period."

THE SECOND LOSS TO SPINKS effectively ended Larry Holmes's time as a top heavyweight. He retired to pursue a singing career, and then returned for an ill-advised comeback fight against the new, ferocious young champ Mike Tyson in 1988, when Tyson was at his absolute peak. Entering the ring in something less than top condition, Holmes was knocked down in the fourth round, the only time in his professional career that he was ever stopped.

Watching George Foreman's success in his second, late-life career, which included reclaiming the heavyweight title, Holmes embarked on another comeback, which still has not officially drawn to a close. The highlight was a decision win over contender Ray Mercer, in which Holmes used his consummate boxing skills to teach the younger fighter a painful lesson and earned himself one last title shot. (He went on to lose a one-sided, twelve-round decision to Evander Holyfield in 1992.) Holmes's last fight to date was a sixth-round knockout of the similarly aged Mike Weaver in November 2000.

Champions' reputations change over time. Long after they've retired, they go in and out of fashion with boxing fans and historians. Consider the ongoing Sonny Liston revival; when he quit against Ali, he was called a bum. Now some rate him among the five best heavyweights of all time. During his long time at the top, Holmes was regarded as a dominant champion during an era of middling talent, shoehorned between the Ali and Tyson eras. Slowly, though, he is receiving his due and finally moving out of those twin shadows.

"Maybe I can't be as good as Muhammad Ali, because I wasn't with Muhammad Ali that time or that day," he says. "But to me, I'm better than Ali ever was. I'm better than Joe Louis ever was. In my opinion. *My opinion.* And I have the right to say that about myself. You can't prove it, but we're all going to have our own opinions about that.

"You ask me who was the greatest, I can't say who was the greatest. You say Ali was the greatest, I say no—he was *one* of the greatest. That's the kind of argument you would get from me. Marciano was the greatest? He was *one* of the greatest. Or Joe Louis. He was *one* of the greatest. Dempsey. Any of them. I think I'm *one* of the greatest. I don't think I was better than anybody or that anybody was better than me. That's why I put that *one of.* And I'm satisfied with that. Being one of. One of many. One of a hundred million. I don't care."

MOST OF THE LARRY HOLMES business empire in Easton is for sale. He already got rid of the hotel, which turned into a bit of a financial nightmare. He got rid of a parking lot and his old training centre. Now, the five-storey office building is on the block. The only thing he plans on keeping is the low-rise, where his own office is housed. "Why? Because I don't want to do it. Fuck it. Do I need the money? No, I don't need no money. I've got a good pension. My own pension. I set my own pension up. So I'm happy with that."

That attitude, that fierce pride in his financial independence, stems, to a large extent, from the fact that Holmes feels he was exploited during his career, primarily by promoter Don King, but also by others in the boxing business. So many great fighters, including Ali, left the sport with far less money in their pockets than they ought to have had. Or they spent lavishly, only to find themselves unable to support extravagant lifestyles. Holmes never left Easton, though he could have lived anywhere. He put his money into things he could see, things that he understood. He wasn't going to have to hustle, or beg, or be trotted out to sign autographs, or be a casino greeter. They could mess with his reputation, they could steal a close decision from him, they could refuse to give him the respect he deserved, but these assets no one could take away.

"I don't got to worry about nothing the rest of my life," he says. "I ain't got to fight. Everything I own, I don't owe nobody. It's all paid off. I own my stuff. People can't say that. I was afraid because if something happened to me I couldn't pay the bills and they were going to come and take it. So when I had the money, I paid it. So I don't have that headache. I only have to hustle up the tax money every year. Everything is mine. Brick, concrete and all."

Eventually, there's going to be a grand Larry Holmes revival, a reassessment of his place in boxing history. It will be argued that he was underappreciated in his time, that his particular set of skills would have given many of the all-time greats a tough night. He'll start turning up on all-time top-ten lists, maybe all-time top five. Someone will say that Holmes in his prime would have beaten Ali in his prime.

It would have driven the young Larry Holmes crazy, waiting for that to happen. But this Larry Holmes acts as though he won't be losing sleep. The message he'd like everyone to understand is this: His life is fine, thanks, and he earned it.

"I don't got nothing else to do now," he says. "I be here during the day. I go to the gym in the evening. I play some checkers over there. I hit the bags and run, or don't hit no bags and jump rope and run. Do whatever I want to do. Go home. Be with the old lady. Watch the football games. Watch the basketball games. On the weekend I come down here and get a couple of Budweisers, hang out with the guys and talk shit, dance on the floor. It's okay. Before, I was always watching it, trying to stay in shape, not make anybody mad at me, watch what I say. I don't give a shit what I do now. But I'm not going to hurt nobody. I don't have to hurt nobody. And I'm not going to let nobody hurt me. You know what I'm saying? I'm smart enough not to get hurt. And I'm satisfied with that."

ACKNOWLEDGMENTS

AS ANY SPORTSWRITER WILL tell you, boxers provide the best interviews of any professional athletes, and it is their words and their experiences that give this book its life. All of the fighters interviewed were generous with their time and their memories. The conversations in question took place during the years 2000, 2001 and 2002, with the exception of George Chuvalo, whom the author has interviewed many times in the recent past.

For biographical details, several works were consulted, including *Muhammad Ali: His Life and Times,* the oral history compiled by Thomas Hauser; *Going the Distance* by Ken Norton with Marshall Terrill and Mike Fitzgerald; *Smokin' Joe: The Autobiography* by Joe Frazier with Phil Berger. The author also acknowledges the influence of many previous books on the subject of Muhammad Ali, specifically the recent works *The Tao of Muhammad Ali* by Davis Miller, *King of the World* by David Remnick and *Ghosts of Manila* by Mark Kram.

Fighters' records cited here come from several editions of the *Ring Record Book,* and from *The Boxing Record Book* compiled by Fight Fax Inc.

Special thanks to Pat Hunsaker, who helped her husband, Tunney, tell his story. To my great European guides and translators, Alain Van Driessche and Rinze van der Meer, who opened doors in Germany and Belgium. To Ed Brophy at the International Boxing Hall of Fame in Canastota, New York, who was of great assistance.

Thanks, also, to Elizabeth Klinck for her brilliant research skills, her crack negotiating talent, and for her boundless goodwill and charm.

This book could not have been completed without the encouragement and co-operation of my employers, *The Globe and Mail,* a newspaper with a long, proud history of fostering independent writing projects from its staff. A nod, especially, to sports editor Steve McAllister, for allowing me the flexibility needed to balance a crazy schedule, and to the folks at CHUM/ The Team in Toronto.

From the first exploratory conversation many, many months ago, this was one of those ideas that simply made sense—enough sense to persuade a reluctant author to climb back into the saddle one more time. Thanks to Diane Martin, Scott Sellers, Gloria Goodman, Matthew Sibiga, Damián Tarnopolsky and everyone else at Knopf Canada, for their inspiration, their enthusiasm, their gentle prodding and their unwavering support.

The fact is that none of the above would have mattered, and this book would have not been possible, without the steadfast support of my family through two and a half hectic years. Everything begins and ends with my wife and first editor, Jeanie MacFarlane, who ought to have her name on the cover.

PHOTO CREDITS

page 11	**Tunney Hunsaker** *© Bettmann/CORBIS/MAGMA*
page 25	**Henry Cooper** *Allsport Hulton Deutsch/Getty Images*
page 47	**George Chuvalo** *AP/Wide World Photos*
page 67	**Brian London** *© Bettmann/CORBIS/MAGMA*
page 81	**Karl Mildenberger** *© Bettmann/CORBIS/MAGMA*
page 101	**Joe Frazier** *AP/Wide World Photos*
page 129	**Jurgen Blin** *Hulton|Archive by Getty Images*
page 141	**Joe Bugner** *© Hulton-Deutsch Collection/CORBIS/MAGMA*
page 165	**Ken Norton** *© Bettmann/CORBIS/MAGMA*
page 185	**George Foreman** *© Bettmann/CORBIS/MAGMA*
page 209	**Chuck Wepner** *© Bettmann/CORBIS/MAGMA*
page 231	**Ron Lyle** *AP/Wide World Photos*
page 245	**Jean-Pierre Coopman** *Anthony Casale/New York Daily News*
page 263	**Earnie Shavers** *© Bettmann/CORBIS/MAGMA*
page 279	**Larry Holmes** *© Bettmann/CORBIS/MAGMA*

STEPHEN BRUNT is Canada's premier sportswriter and commentator. He began to write for the sports section of *The Globe and Mail* in 1985. His 1988 series on negligence and corruption in boxing won him the Michener Award for public-service journalism. In 1991, he took his children to meet Muhammad Ali at the legendary fighter's home and was nominated for the National Newspaper Award for his account of that visit. Brunt is also the author of *Mean Business: The Rise and Fall of Shawn O'Sullivan*, *Second to None: The Roberto Alomar Story* and *Diamond Dreams: 20 Years of Blue Jays Baseball*. He was born in Hamilton, Ontario, where he now lives with his family.